A MINISTRY OF RECONCILIATION

The Historical Series of the Reformed Church in America
no. 90

A Ministry of Reconciliation:
Essays in Honor of Gregg Mast

Allan J. Janssen, Editor

31 March 1948 - 3 April 2020

William B. Eerdmans Publishing Company
Grand Rapids, Michigan / Cambridge, UK

© 2017 Reformed Church Press
All rights reserved

Wm. B. Eerdmans Publishing Co.
2140 Oak Industrial Drive SE, Grand Rapids, Michigan 49505

Cambridge CB3 9PU UK
www.eerdmans.com

Printed in the United States of America

Library of Congress Cataloging-in-Publication Data

Names: Mast, Gregg, 1952- honouree. | Janssen, Al, editor.
Title: A ministry of reconciliation : essays in honor of Gregg Mast / Allan
  J. Janssen, editor.
Description: Grand Rapids : Eerdmans Publishing Co., 2017. | Series: The
  historical series of the Reformed Church in America ; no. 90 | Includes
  bibliographical references and index.
Identifiers: LCCN 2017017711 | ISBN 9780802875983 (pbk. : alk. paper)
Subjects: LCSH: Mast, Gregg, 1952- | Reformed Church in America--Biography. |
  Reformed Church in America--History. | Reformed Church in
  America--Doctrines. | New Brunswick Theological Seminary.
Classification: LCC BX9509 .M56 2017 | DDC 285.7/32--dc23 LC record
available at https://lccn.loc.gov/2017017711

The Rev. Dr. Gregg A. Mast

7 February 1952 – 27 April 2020

The Historical Series of the Reformed Church in America

The series was inaugurated in 1968 by the General Synod of the Reformed Church in America acting through the Commission on History to communicate the church's heritage and collective memory and to reflect on our identity and mission, encouraging historical scholarship which informs both church and academy.

www.rca.org/series

General Editor
    Rev. Donald J. Bruggink, PhD, DD
    Western Theological Seminary
    Van Raalte Institute, Hope College

Associate Editor
    James Hart Brumm, MDiv
    Rensselaer, New York
    New Brunswick Theological Seminary

Copy Editor
    JoHannah Smith
    Holland, Michigan

Production Editor
    Russell L. Gasero
    Archives, Reformed Church in America

Commission on History
    James Hart Brumm, MDiv, Rensselaer, New York
    Lynn Japinga, PhD, Hope College
    David M. Tripold, PhD, Monmouth University
    Douglas Van Aartsen, MDiv, Ireton, IA
    Matthew Van Maastricht, MDiv, Milwaukee, Wisconsin
    Linda Walvoord, PhD, University of Cincinnati

Contents

	Donors	ix
	Acknowledgments	xiii
	Preface	xv
	Notes on Contributors	xvii
1.	A Ministry of Reconciliation: An Appreciation Allan J. Janssen	1
2.	The Educational Endeavors of the Reformed Dutch Church 1628–1866 Elton J. Bruins	9
3.	Emotional Intelligence as It Impacts Pastoral Leadership Cornelis G. Kors	31
4.	Natural Theology, Historical Data, and Sexual Ethics: Controversy in the Interpretation of Romans 1 James Brownson	53
5.	Bodies of Joy: German Gospel Choirs and the Church Fritz West	65
6.	Ecumenical Liturgical Influences and the Reformed Church in America 1987–2004 Carol Myers	83
7.	The Ministry of Word and Sacrament: Two Sermons Renee House	93

8.	"Worship as a Way of Seeing" Carol Bechtel	105
9.	Navigating the Changing Landscape of World Christianity Wesley Granberg-Michaelson	121
10.	Reformed Christians in Challenging Times: A Reflection from an African Perspective Setri Nyomi	137
11.	Considering the Relationship between the Concept of Gospel and Law in Reformed Theological Discourse Rodney S. Tshaka	145
12.	The Black Churches as the "Good Enough Mother": An Analysis of African American Churches from a Winnicottian Perspective Raynard Daniel Smith	157
13.	"We Have Not This Subject Among Us": Slavery, the Reformed Dutch Church, and New Brunswick Seminary John W. Coakley	179
14.	Urban Ministry in the Twenty-First Century: A Postmodern Womanist Reimagining Lorena Parrish	197
15.	Ancient Hebrew Nouns and the Questions of Today: A Modern-Day Lesson from Qoheleth Beth Tanner	215
	Index	227
	Historical Series Books in Print	235

Donors

Norm & Diane Aardema
Bob & Carolyn Akland
Dr. Virginia O. Allen
June & Karen Angelo
Delores Marcia Barrett (Rev.)
Rev. & Mrs. Robert W. Barrowclough
Frederick J. & Evelyn M. Berenbroick
Mr. Robert & Mrs. Kathleen Berenbroick
Tim & Carolyn Boersma
Rev. Dr. Donald A. Boulton
Rev. Dr. David M. Brechter
The Rev. Shari K. Brink
Dr. Gennifer Brooks
George & Willa
Western Theological Seminary
Rev. Dr. Jonathan C. Brownson
The Rev. James V. Brownson
The Rev. Dr. Donald & Mrs. Erma Bruggink
The Rev. James Hart Brumm
The Rev. Kathleen Hart Brumm
Mr. Leighton R. Burns
Nathan & Kara Busker
Rev. Neal & Carolyn Busker
The Rev. Robert E. Butcher, '66
Rev. Louis & Joyce Buytendorp
Sally Ann Castle
Reverend Karen M. Chavis
Mrs. Ting F. Chen
Dianne & Brian Clark
The Wyckoff Reformed Church
John & Margaret Coakley
Joyce & David de Velder
Rev. Robert & Carol De Young
Roger De Young
Barbara & Fred Diekman
The Rev. Philip and Rev. Stephanie Doeschot
The Rev. James P. Ebbers & Marlyn Rietveld-Ebbers
Rev. Stephen Eckert
The late Clifford R. Feakes & Barbara Feakes
Barbara A. Felker, MDiv, MS
Joanne C. Fernandez-McDermott
Lynn P. Fetherstone
First Reformed Church of Bethlehem
The Rev. Mary & Judge John Fitzgerald
Carl J. Folkert
Dr. Davis and Mrs. Eunice Folkerts
Peggy Funderburke
Mr. and Mrs. Russell L. Gasero
David F. Geddes
The Rev. Dr. & Mrs. Stephen T. Giordano
Rich & Mary Glendening
Anna L. Gonzales
Adrian & Blanche Gray
Jaco J. Hamman
Jon F. Hanson
Karen Hoffman Hanson
Adrienne & Roger Hausch
Rev. Kathryn & Mr. Peter Henry
I. John Hesselink
Arthur & Helen Hessinger
Hillsborough Reformed Church at Millstone
Lucille & Robert Hoeksema

ix

Rev. Robert G. Hoffman
Ronald L. Hoffman, '74 MDiv.
Steven Hoffman
The Revs. Craig & Jan Hoffman
Rev. Dr. Danielle L. Hunter
The Rev. Tracey Hunter Hayes
    and Kathleen Butler Hayes
Rev. Christopher L. Jacobsen
Earl & Norma James
The Rev. Debra L. Jameson
Allan Janssen
The Rev. Dr. Jeffrey S. Japinga
Carolyn Jones-Assini, MD & John
    Assini, MD
Franco Juricic
The Rev. Lewis E. Kain &
    Christine C. Kain
The Rev. Dr. and Mrs. Leonard V.
    Kalkwarf
Norm & Mary Kansfield
Mr. & Mrs. Thomas P. Kelly
The Rev. & Mrs. Norman L.
    Kolenbrander
Clifford & Jane Konitz
Cornelis & Jane Kors
Frederick "Fritz" Kruithof
John R. Kuester
Hon. John S. Kuhlthau, JSC(ret.)
    & Dr. Carol Kuhlthau
Robert & Ramona Larsen
The Rev. & Mrs. Bruce G.
    Laverman
Rev. Harold "Hank" Lay
Mr. Alexander R. Lehmann
Evangelist Lillie J. Leon
Hank & Norma Leonhard
Claire H. Leonhardt
Rev. Carolyn W. Lewis
Mary F. Linge
Mrs. Rita Yvonne Lipford

Rev. Edwin H. Lloyd
Ronald & Karen Lokhorst
The Rev. and Mrs. John L.
    Magee, Jr.
Anita D. Manuele
Rev. Dr. Luciano Márquez Jr.
Joan Marshall
The Mast Family
The Revs. Sophie & Stephen
    Mathonnet-Vanderwell
The Rev. & Mrs. Rufus
    McClendon, Jr.
Rev. Dr. Richard O. McEachern
Rev. Ellen R. Canty McEachern
Rev. Kent A. McHeard
Robert Mettler
Rev. Nickolas & Rev. Linda Miles
Rabbi Bennett F. Miller
Dr. Bonard Moise
Joline H. Mondore
Charles & Deborah Morris
Mrs. Gay Kersey Morris
Fred Mueller
The Rev. Dr. & Mrs. J. David
    Muykens
Jim & Barbara Neevel
Milton & Marilee Nieuwsma
Harvey W. Noordsy
The Rev. and Mrs. Jon N. Norton
Rev. Amy Nyland
The Rev. Nolan & the Rev. Phyllis
    Palsma
Peter & Elizabeth Paulsen
The Rev. Dr. Rand & Sally
    Peabody
John Pearson
The Rev. and Mrs. Bruce E. Penn
Tammy Peoples, NBTS '14
Annie Lee Phillips
Alvin J. Poppen

Mr. & Mrs. Harvey Prins
Cathy Proctor
Harlan & Ellen Ratmeyer
The Revs. Florence & Elmer Ridley
Anne & Walt Robb
Betty A. Rucker
Arlyn & Claire Rus
Kevin Salminen
Darell J. Schregardus, Ph.D.
Andy Shin, 2016
Rev. Dr. Laura B. Sinclair
Deacon Dennis E. Slavin, M.A.
Rev. Dr. Felecia M. Smith
The Rev. Dr. Evans L. & Dianne Spagner
The Rev. Cora W. Taitt
The Rev. & Mrs. David M. Taylor
Nancy & Norman Tellier
Patty & Ken Termott
Rev. Liz Testa & Mr. Nick Lacata
Rev. Dr. Regena L. Thomas
Diane & Victor Tice
David & Mary Timmer
Sandra E. Timmons
Mr. & Mrs. John P. Tysse
The Rev. & Mrs. Glenn Van Oort
Rev. Ronald E. Vande Bunte
Marlin & Judith VanderWilt
Jim & Wanda Veld
The Rev. and Mrs. Gerald L. Vermilyea
Frank J. Villerius
Ruth E. Waller
Paul & Debby Walther
Ross Westhuis
Robert & JoAnne White
H. Robert & Joan Williams
Maudelin Willock
Rev. Rett Zabriskie

Acknowledgments

Books are collaborative endeavors. The editor acknowledges not only the erudition and willingness of the authors of the essays in this volume and the donors who made publication financially viable but also the contributions of James Brumm, acting on behalf of the Historical Series of the Reformed Church in America; JoHannah Smith, who copy edited the variety of essays coming in all their shapes and sizes from a broad range of contributors; and Russell Gasero, the archivist of the Reformed Church in America, who typeset the volume for production.

Ramona Larson, from the Development Office of New Brunswick Theological Seminary coordinated raising funds for publication.

Finally, the editor acknowledges the signal accomplishment of the Historical Series of the Reformed Church in America with all the incarnations of the Commission on History. The series has developed an impressive library, to which the one we honor in this book has contributed significantly.

Preface

Upon arriving at NBTS for the first time, I was met by the Holy Spirit who welcomed me in as a seminarian and let me know this was where I needed to be. Here I found a community of intelligent people, mature in their faith, and eager to gain knowledge and apply it in the urban centers, suburbs, and cities. This was a community that enjoyed a great diversity of races and ethnicities, faith traditions, political persuasions, professions, and ages. We were not separate silos under one roof. We were one community—the Church. I knew from experience that a community like NBTS does not just happen. It takes vision, work, intentionality, and commitment.

Gregg also understood this. In fact, his experiences, relationships, and education helped to shape him into a person that celebrates that diversity, strives for unity, and is committed to the hard work needed to be the Church, particularly in the United States of America. The essays in this book are offered in celebration of Gregg, his commitment, and his life's work. They stem from the areas that he has worked to impact: the Reformed Church in America, the ecumenical dimension of the Church, worship and its liturgical expression, and racial justice. This book is an amazing testament to a man that has given so much.

Today, twenty-six years later, I celebrate the result of Gregg's tenure at NBTS. As the moderator of our board of trustees, I see the new building, the replenished endowment, and a strategic plan that seeks to live out a new mission. All of this came to fruition under Gregg's leadership, and we praise God for him. With all that is new and different, however, there is one thing that continues to be the same. We remain a community striving to live out our diversity as one body, and we have Gregg to thank for that. I wish you well in your retirement Gregg. Your work here is done, but you have left a legacy for that work to continue in the lives of men and women for many years to come.

The Reverand Anna Melissa Jackson

Notes on Contributors

Carol M. Bechtel is Professor of Old Testament at Western Theological Seminary in Holland, Michigan, and is a Professor of the General Synod (RCA).

James Brownson is the James and Jean Cook Professor of New Testament at Western Theological Seminary in Holland, Michigan, and (along with Dr. Gregg Mast) occupies the ecclesiastical office of General Synod Professor of Theology in the Reformed Church in America.

Elton J. Bruins is the Evert J. and Hattie E. Blekkink Professor of Religion Emeritus at Hope College and the Philip Phelps Jr. Research Professor at the Van Raalte Institute of Hope College.

John W. Coakley is Feakes Professor of Church History Emeritus at New Brunswick Theological Seminary and a Professor Emeritus of the General Synod (RCA).

Wesley Granberg-Michaelson served as General Secretary of the Reformed Church in America from 1994 to 2011. He continues to be active in ecumenical work, including the Global Christian Forum. His most recent book is *From Times Square to Timbuktu: The Post-Christian West Meets the Non-Western Church.*

Renee S. House is the Minister of the Old Dutch Church in Kingston, New York. Prior to accepting this call, she served for twenty-five years on the faculty of New Brunswick Theological Seminary and is a Professor of the General Synod (RCA).

Allan Janssen is a retired minister of the Reformed Church in America. He is an Affiliate Associate Professor of Theological Studies at New Brunswick Theological Seminary and a Professor of the General Synod (RCA).

Cornelis G. Kors has served as the Executive Director of the Ministerial Formation Certification Agency (MFCA) of the Reformed Church in America and Ecclesiastical Assistant Professor at Fuller Theological Seminary since 1991. He is also a Professor of the General Synod (RCA).

Carol Myers has served as senior elder and vice president of consistory at Hope Church (RCA) in Holland, Michigan, and as president of Holland Classis. She has also been moderator of the RCA commissions on worship and church order, consultant to the worship commission, and served on RCA tithing, consistories, and disciplinary procedures task forces. She is currently a member of Grace Episcopal Church in Holland, Michigan.

Setri Nyomi was General Secretary of the World Communion of Reformed Churches (WCRC) from April 2000 to August 2014. He is currently a Senior Lecturer at Trinity Theological Seminary, Legon, Ghana, and Senior Pastor of the Evangelical Presbyterian Church in Adenta, Ghana.

Lorena M. Parrish is the Dirk Romeyn Professor of Metro-Urban Ministry at New Brunswick Theological Seminary. She is an ordained minister in American Baptist Churches USA (ABCUSA) and has pastored urban congregations of ABCUSA, United Church of Christ, and the Reformed Church in America

Raynard D. Smith is an ordained minister in the Church of God in Christ. His academic training is in psychology and religion. He is the Associate Professor of Pastoral Care/Pastoral Theology at New Brunswick Theological Seminary.

Beth Tanner is an ordained minister in the Presbyterian Church (USA). She is the Norman and Mary Kansfield Professor of Old Testament at New Brunswick Theological Seminary.

Rothney S. Tshaka is formerly Global Scholar and Professor of Community and Ethics at New Brunswick Theological Seminary. He is an ordained minister of Word and Sacrament in the Uniting Reformed Church in Southern Africa and is currently Professor and Director of the School of Humanities at the University of South Africa

Fritz West is a retired minister in the United Church of Christ and independent liturgical scholar. For the past ten years, he has organized gospel choir exchanges between Germany and Wisconsin.

CHAPTER 1

A Ministry of Reconciliation: An Appreciation

Allan J. Janssen

God was in Christ reconciling the world to himself, not counting their trespasses against them, and entrusting to us the message of reconciliation. (2 Cor. 2:18)

In 2010 the Reformed Church in America adopted the Belhar Confession as one of its confessional bases. Reconciliation, God's reconciliation of the world to God's self, stands at the heart of that confession; it is its central paragraph. Furthermore, "God has entrusted the church with the message of reconciliation."

The ministry of Gregg A. Mast not only embodies the ministry of reconciliation, but it does so in ways that profoundly reflect the deepest intentions of the Belhar. Mast has enjoyed a widely varied ministry located in the *church*, in that small corner of the church catholic that is the Reformed Church in America. At the same time, his ministry has had a broad reach, one that extends to the church around the world. The trajectory of his ministry includes parish ministry, teaching, denominational staff, and seminary presidency.

The first significant engagement that I enjoyed with Mast came when he was appointed Minister of Social Witness and Worship for the

Reformed Church, and I was moderating the Commission on Christian Action of that denomination's General Synod. We worked together as we assisted the synod in its deliberation on matters of justice and peace. But what, I wondered, was this combination of "social witness and worship"? I knew social activists. For many of them, the point of the faith was not in the sanctuary, but what liturgy was to be a "liturgy of the streets"? On the other hand, liturgical enthusiasts were, in my experience, not terribly interested in social action. A good part of Mast's ministry was not only the reconciliation of persons but also to see in worship and witness not juxtaposition but a coherent core of the church's expression of the gospel.

Gregg's journey in ministry began in West Michigan where as a child he was formed within the core of the Reformed Church. He was nurtured in the warm piety common in more evangelically conservative sections of the church. His family, for example, practiced Sunday observance as was usual in such areas. Following the pattern of many from that part of the church, Mast attended Hope College, the Reformed Church's college in Holland, Michigan.

That trajectory would shift with the life-altering experience of a semester spent in a Lutheran congregation in the college's Philadelphia Urban Program. There Mast was immersed in an African American community and congregation. For the first time, he was confronted by the issues of poverty and racial injustice. He also came under the tutelage of the church's pastor, Rev. John Cochran, whose high church Lutheranism contrasted with the liturgical life Mast had known in the Reformed Church. Eucharist formed the core of ministry in that liturgical posture, but it was combined with a deep commitment to community. A perspective that theologically saw liturgy and God's concern for social justice as a coherent expression of the gospel would influence both the trajectory of Mast's ministry and his deepest personal commitments, as we shall see.

The Philadelphia experience altered Mast's path, and he did not continue the expected move from Hope College to Western Theological Seminary; his path led to New Brunswick Theological Seminary, just a few miles distant from Philadelphia. There he would meet a second person who would have a deep impact on his life and ministry, Rev. Dr. Howard G. Hageman, then president of New Brunswick. Hageman himself had come from the parish—as pastor of North Reformed Church in Newark—and had contributed significantly to the study of Reformed Church liturgy, particularly with his Stone Lectures given at

Princeton Theological Seminary, later to be published as an influential book, *Pulpit and Table* (1962). It was through Hageman's encouragement that Mast, now married to Vicki, would spend a year in South Africa as an assistant minister of the Andrew Murray congregation in Johannesburg. There he was again to be confronted with the issues of poverty and racial injustice, this time in the context of the country of South Africa. Moreover, in Mast's understanding, it was there that he learned the need to speak the gospel in the context of apartheid, not as judgment on the congregation, but as an invitation to dialogue. This was to reconcile the pastoral and the prophetic, a theme that was to follow Mast throughout his ministry. This was also to be an initiation into the international context of not only the global church but also of ministry in the context of economic and racial injustice.

If we see Mast's commitment to social and racial justice growing in the years of his theological maturation, then the liturgical side of his ministry was also encouraged not only by Cochran but also, not surprisingly, by Hageman. On his return to the United States, Mast enrolled in a PhD program in liturgical studies at Drew University. He would complete that degree in 1985 with his dissertation, *The Eucharistic Service of the Catholic Apostolic Church and Its Influence on Reformed Liturgical Renewals of the Nineteenth Century*.

In the meantime, Mast began parish ministry in the Reformed Church, accepting a call to the Second Reformed Church of Irvington, New Jersey, in 1978. The Irvington church was situated in a changing neighborhood just outside Newark, New Jersey. The congregation found itself in a neighborhood that was becoming racially mixed. Mast's ministry was to assist the church to reflect the racially diverse nature of its neighborhood. How would a predominantly white congregation welcome nonwhite parishioners? Remembering lessons learned in South Africa, Mast did not confront the issue head on but maintained a firm commitment to the essence of the gospel that would later be articulated in the Belhar Confession. The church first worked to open its Sunday school to children from the neighborhood. Families of Sunday school scholars soon followed their children as the church became truly racially diverse.

Mast's pastoral ministry would shift to become the senior pastor at First [Reformed] Church in Albany, New York, in 1988. First Church is an urban church set in the New York state capital and had engaged in a ministry to a community not only racially diverse but also diverse in economics and class. While there, Mast worked very hard to help a congregation work together when the various classes and races within the church had varying understandings of how the church was to move forward. Mast's pastoral style and steady focus enabled the church to flourish as an urban, multiracial congregation. He also encouraged it to deepen its commitment to the local community (the church sits on the border between the city's downtown "theater district" and one of the poorest districts in the city) as, for example, he hired the church's first social worker whose primary ministry is with and to the community. Nor was First Church's ministry solely local under Mast's leadership. The church became an active partner of a Cuban church, engaging in mutual prayer, service, and visitation.

It was while serving First Church that Mast was elected as president of the General Synod of the Reformed Church. His presidential address, given in 2000 at the synod's gathering at Hofstra University, illustrates the commitments in his ministry.[1] The synod met during Pentecost of that year, and the title of Mast's address was, appropriately, "Teach Us to Pray." His year as president was spent in careful listening, both to churches in all corners of the Reformed Church and to the global church as well. He visited churches in Rwanda, India, Oman, Nicaragua, and Cuba. He listened as they prayed for the soul of the church in North America. So he continued, "Teach us," Lord how much we have to learn "from our family abroad." In a reference to Peter's citation of Joel in that first Pentecost sermon, Mast claimed that, to be teachable, we need to learn from those on the margins. This would be an early echo of what the church would confess ten years later in the Belhar Confession.

The main emphasis of Mast's address, however, was on the offices of the church: elder, deacon, minister of Word and Sacrament, and the General Synod professor. He noted the "spiritual hunger in an age of plenty" that he had heard in his presidential travels. He went on to call for the renewal of the office of elder: "Quite remarkably, in a culture that wants to learn more about prayer and spirituality, we have for more than four hundred years called and ordained people to an office committed to prayer, spiritually, and pastoral care."

The office of deacon likewise came into view when Mast spoke of prayer. "Without prayer, we wither and die. Without prayer, our life is empty and without passion." But he then went on to speak of the deacon: "The office of deacon has assumed an increasing role in translating our prayers into action. Prayers for mercy, compassion, and

---

[1] *The Acts and Proceedings of the 194th Regular Session of the General Synod* (2000), 33-41.

justice are given feet that walk into the world in mission." This was to receive liturgical shape as Mast recommended that the synod encourage local congregations to have deacons offer prayers of intercession in Sunday worship.

Mast's ministry, however, was not only to parishes but also to the broader church. He would, for example, contribute to the life of the church through a number of occasional writings, including a revision of his mentor, Howard Hageman's, popular booklet, *Our Reformed Church*, as well as a number of smaller publications, written not for the academy but for the church at large. Perhaps just as influential was his monthly column in the *Church Herald*, "Questions of Faith," in which he functioned as, in his words, the denomination's "Ann Landers." He would be acknowledged in his role as churchman who could address the entire church with his election as president of General Synod in 1999.

Mast's ministry to the broader church was also manifest when he accepted positions in the denominational staff. He did so for the first time between his stints as pastor in Irvington and pastor in Albany when he became Minister of Social Witness and Worship. Later he was to return to "475" (then the Reformed Church's central office) following his time in Albany, now in "ministry services," a position that oversaw such matters as the placement of ministers, care for retired pastors, oversight of interim ministers, and the like. Of greatest impact, however, is likely his emphasis on the offices of the church (reflecting the emphasis of his presidential address of 2000). He did this in two ways. Already as president of the General Synod, he had begun to emphasize the place and role of what was then known as the "professor of theology." He would continue that emphasis by calling the professors to meet together to assist the church in its ministry. This move was to find its goal when the church established the professorate as an official body in 2011. Mast's second initiative was to nurture the ministry of the consistory—of the elder and the deacon.

Mast's ministry to the whole church was to culminate when he was appointed president of New Brunswick Theological Seminary in 2006. His ministry had come full circle; he had returned to the seminary that he had left forty years earlier. But it was a very different seminary. It had become diverse in both race and gender. While the average student in 1976 was a white male just out of college, most likely from the Reformed Church, in 2006 the average student was most likely an African American woman of early middle age and not Reformed. At

New Brunswick, a number of threads that we have followed throughout the appreciation penned above come together. Under Mast's leadership, the staff, the faculty, and the board of trustees would begin to reflect the demographic of the student body. The faculty, for example, is majority nonwhite, and although women remain in the minority, it is a shrinking minority. The institution of the Anti-Racism Renewal Team (ARRT) has engaged the institution in a multiyear conversion to make the seminary not only racially inclusive but also sensitive to power dynamics inherent in white privilege, an initiative that includes students and faculty, as well as staff and trustees. At the same time, Mast oversaw the faculty's adoption of a curriculum sensitive and appropriate to its ecumenical and racially diverse student body and the churches that the seminary serves.

Mast's global interests also found expression in the life of the seminary. Rev. Horace Underwood, one of the first Protestant missionaries to Korea, is an alumnus of the seminary, and as a result, the seminary has been the destination of a number of Korean students. In honor of Underwood, the seminary instituted the annual Underwood Seminar, held not in North America, but in Korea. Moreover, the seminary has begun a drive to fund an Underwood chair in missiology. More recently, under Mast's encouragement, the seminary has begun the Center for Global Studies, with study programs in South Africa, Israel, and the Netherlands.

Mast, however, faced challenges not only of a racially diverse community, but he also inherited a seminary facing serious fiscal difficulties. (Faculty meetings, for example, would often focus on fiscal restraints on the program, and Mast would have to deliver the unwelcome news of a temporary pay cut in order for the seminary to continue.) The seminary, however, sat on a large plot of land situated in the middle of Rutgers University's central campus. The land included ten buildings in various conditions of decay. Together with the board of trustees, Mast negotiated the sale of two-thirds of the land, the construction of a new seminary building, and the restoration of Sage Library (the jewel of the campus). The seminary obtained a new building, and it was able not only to restore its depleted endowment but also to establish a significant financial reserve.

I noted above that Mast's ministry to the church culminated with his presidency at New Brunswick. It is also the case that his reconciling *style* of ministry can be summarized by his ministry at the seminary. Wallace Alston, then minister at the Nassau Presbyterian Church in

Princeton, once remarked to a gathering of parish pastors that the pastor has to have something of the ward heeler about him or herself. He or she is to function as a bit of a politician. Gregg is one of the best church politicians I know. I use that not as a term of abuse but of appreciation. This is not the politics of arm twisting and horse trading but of the considered involvement of the *polis*, of the people, in decisions. I am aware of few people who can calmly get to the nub of an issue facing the church or the academy and then work for a shared solution, all without giving an inch on the core commitments of the gospel. I have never seen him intentionally embarrass another publically for the sake of personal gain, but I am well aware that he would engage those with whom personal disagreements were deep privately and respectfully.

I also noted that in returning to New Brunswick, Mast has come full circle. But of course, we never really "go home." The home has changed. But so have we. Mast began in Philadelphia and Johannesburg. The concerns that touched his soul there have deepened, even as he comes to his final days at New Brunswick. I recently asked Gregg about the future of New Brunswick's seminary and of theological education. These are difficult times for theological institutions. And indeed New Brunswick is asking questions of its future, even as its relation to the Reformed Church is changing as fewer students from Reformed churches attend the seminary in preparation for ministry. Gregg's response summarizes his ministry. He is convinced that the future is in global education. It is the global church, he maintains, that "will confront the arrogance of the Western mind and soul." These words were written in Advent 2016; few words sound more prophetic.

The contributors to this volume reflect the reconciling nature of Mast's ministry. They come from the church and the academy, from the Reformed Church that he has served and from the ecumenical church, and from women and men, from the United States and beyond.

Elton Bruins, one of Mast's professors at Hope College, along with Cor Kors and James Brownson, colleagues of Mast, offer essays that reflect on matters particular to the Reformed Church. Bruins traces the relationship of the Reformed Church to education, including the establishment of Queens College (now Rutgers University). Kors, who plays a central role in the education of ministers in the Reformed Church, details the importance of emotional intelligence in the education of ministers. Brownson, in an exegetical essay, engages the mooted topic of same-sex relationships, a matter that has embroiled the Reformed Church in vigorous, sometimes acrimonious, debate.

A number of essays focus on liturgical themes. Fritz West offers a surprising look at the influence of gospel music and the rise of gospel choirs in Germany. Carol Myers, who served alongside Mast in the development of the liturgy of the Reformed Church, reflects not only on liturgical development but also on the introduction and use of a common lectionary in the Reformed Church. Renee House, who served as dean of New Brunswick during Mast's tenure as president, contributes two sermons on the sacraments. Carol Bechtel, an Old Testament scholar from Western Theological Seminary, exegetes two Psalms that center on worship.

The international nature of the church is represented by significant contributions from figures in the world church. Wesley Granberg-Michaelson, who served as general secretary of the Reformed Church, writes on the global nature of Christianity, as its center of gravity shifts from its European-North American focus. Setri Nyomi, former general secretary of the World Alliance of Reformed Churches (later the World Communion of Reformed Churches), and Rothney Tshaka, who taught at New Brunswick (now a professor at UNISA), weigh in from Africa.

Finally, a number of essays emerge from New Brunswick Seminary's commitment to racial justice. Raynard Smith, professor of pastoral care at New Brunswick, focuses on the African American church. John Coakley, recently retired as professor of church history at New Brunswick, contributes an account of how both the seminary and the Reformed Church were implicated in the institution of slavery. Lorena Parrish, newly appointed professor of urban ministry at New Brunswick, graces this volume with an essay on womanist theology and the ministry of the church. And Beth Tanner, professor of Old Testament at New Brunswick, does an intriguing word study that focuses on Ecclesiastes, which results in surprising implications for New Brunswick's antiracism initiative.

Seen both as a whole and running through the essays, one can discern the thread of a remarkable ministry, one that has indeed been characterized by the biblical injunction to be an ambassador of reconciliation. It is with gratitude and appreciation that the authors and those whom they represent offer this volume on the occasion of Dr. Mast's—Gregg to many of us—retirement.

CHAPTER 2

The Educational Endeavors of the Reformed Dutch Church 1628-1866

Elton J. Bruins

The Reformed tradition was virtually synonymous with education after John Calvin founded the Academy in Geneva, Switzerland, in 1559.[1] After Calvin, Reformed Church polity in regard to education was more firmly established by the Synod of Dort in 1618-19.[2] The Synod resolved that every Reformed congregation would found a school, with the consistory of the local church being responsible for appointing and supervising a schoolmaster who was to be a Christian. This policy, in place for only ten years when the first

---

[1] F. L. Cross, ed., *The Oxford Dictionary of the Christian Church* (London: Oxford University Press, 1958), s.v. "Calvin, John."

[2] The Synod of Dort, held in the city of Dordrecht, the Netherlands, was "an international church assembly called by the States General of the Netherlands to settle certain ecclesiastical and doctrinal matters that had been troubling the Reformed Church of the Netherlands. It consisted of thirty-five pastors and a number of elders from the Dutch churches, five theological professors from the Netherlands, eighteen deputies from the States General, and twenty-seven foreign delegates" (M. Eugene Osterhaven, "Synod of Dort," in *Evangelical Dictionary of Theology*, ed. Walter A. Elwell [Grand Rapids: Baker Book House, 1984], 331-32).

Reformed congregation was organized on Manhattan Island in 1628, had a major effect on the Reformed Dutch Church in America.[3]

This essay will trace the efforts of the Reformed Dutch Church in America as it attempted to follow the polity of Dort in reference to education. The beginning date of such efforts is 1628, the year the first Reformed Dutch congregation was organized in America. The end date of 1866 is somewhat more arbitrary, but it was chosen as a terminus for this paper, since it was the year Hope College graduated its first students.[4]

All levels of education sponsored by the Reformed Dutch Church (RDC) will be examined in this essay. During the period from 1628 to 1866, the RDC organized grade schools, academies, and colleges, all of which contributed a great deal to the educational programs of the church. Unfortunately, much of this history has been forgotten. Many academies founded by the RDC, from Erasmus Hall in Brooklyn, New York, to Pleasant Prairie Academy in German Valley, Illinois, have ceased to exist.[5] Three colleges closely related to the RDC in their early history—Rutgers University (now the State University of Jersey), Union College in Schenectady, and New York University in New York City—exist but no longer have any relationship with the church. As it failed to retain already established educational institutions and gave up establishing new Christian grade schools and academies, the founding and growth of the present three RCA colleges (Central, Hope, and Northwestern) became even more precious and significant to the denomination. In spite of the failures, it is worth noting the great effort, time, and money that the denomination expended on its many educational endeavors between 1628 and 1866. That discussion, which follows, is divided into four periods: the Dortian Foundation, 1628-1792; the Decline of the Dortian Model, 1792-1866; the Founding of Colleges; and Dort Revisited.

---

[3] The Dutch Reformed Church in America had various titles in its early history. The Reformed Dutch Church was the one most commonly used until the denomination in 1867 adopted the title of the Reformed Church in America. See Edward Tanjore Corwin, *A Digest of Constitutional and Synodical Legislation of the Reformed Church in America* (New York: Board of Publication of the Reformed Church in America, 1906), s.v. "Title, or Name, of the Reformed Church in America," for a full discussion of the various titles.

[4] By this time Central College was already in existence and had been for over ten years (it was founded in 1853), but it did not come under the auspices of the Reformed Church in America until 1916.

[5] Erasmus Hall did not become defunct in the same way as many of the other academies did. It became part of the New York City educational system.

I. The Dortian Foundation of the Educational Endeavors of the Reformed Dutch Church in America, 1628-1792.

The delegates of the Synod of Dort began to discuss the issue of church education at its seventeenth session on 30 November 1618. The introductory paragraph of the minutes of this Synod meeting is significant: "In order that the Christian youth may be diligently instructed in the principles of religion and be trained in piety, three modes of catechising should be employed: (1) in the house, by parents; (2) in the schools, by schoolmasters; and (3) in the churches, by ministers, elders, and catechists especially appointed for the purpose. That these may diligently employ their trust, the Christian magistrates shall be requested to promote, by their authority, so sacred and necessary a work; and all who have the oversight of churches and schools shall be required to pay special attention to this matter."[6]

In mode two, "in the schools by schoolmasters," the most noteworthy part dealt with the qualifications of those who were appointed to the position of schoolmaster. The polity of Dort decreed that they must be members of the Reformed Church and appropriately pious as Christians. Just as ministers, elders, and deacons were to profess the Reformed faith according to the standards of the church, so were schoolmasters to be committed to follow Reformed doctrine as reflected in the Heidelberg Catechism. Schoolmasters were to see that the Heidelberg Catechism was committed to memory by all students, and they were to be sufficiently knowledgeable of the meaning of the points of doctrine in the Catechism in order to teach its meaning to their students.

The Articles of Dort has four articles that spell out the role of the church and the consistory in providing education for the children of the congregation. Article 21 reads as follows: "The Consistories in every congregation shall be careful to provide good Schoolmasters, who are able, not only to instruct children in reading, writing, grammar, and the liberal sciences but also to teach them the catechism and the first principles of religion." The role of the Classis was mentioned in Article

---

[6] Thomas De Witt, "A Historical Sketch of the Parochial School System in Holland Subsequent to the Reformation," in *History of the School of the Reformed Protestant Dutch Church in the City of New-York, from 1633 to the Present Time*, by Henry Webb Dunshee (New York: John Gray, 1853), 3. Later editions of the history of the Collegiate School adopted 1638 as the date of the founding of the school. The second edition was issued in 1883. A more recent history is Jean Parker Waterbury's *A History of Collegiate School 1638-1963* (New York: Clarkson N. Potter, 1965).

41: "The Praeses [president] shall moreover enquire of the Members respectively, whether they observe their Consistorial Meetings; whether the Discipline be exercised; whether the Poor, and the Schools are properly taken care of." Article 44 required that classical visitors to congregations shall also inquire if the schoolmasters "faithfully discharge their offices." Article 54 called for the schoolmaster to subscribe to the confessions of the faith of the Netherlands church.[7]

Putting this polity into practice in the New World took some time. It was ten years after its founding before the Reformed Dutch Church in Manhattan was able to establish a school, thereby putting Dortian rules into practice, but the school it founded in 1638, the Collegiate School, is the second oldest Latin school still in existence in the United States. Only the Boston Latin School predates it.[8] The Collegiate School did not, however, become a Latin school until 1658.[9] Just getting a school underway by 1638 was enough of a challenge without also establishing classical education, which included the teaching of Latin and Greek. The first schoolmaster of the Collegiate School was Adam Roelandsen.[10] As Dutch settlers in New Netherland founded other towns, other schools were established. The church in Albany, New York, founded a school in 1650.[11] The Harlem congregation in the northern part of Manhattan Island founded its school in 1663.[12]

A significant change in how Reformed Dutch Church congregations founded and supported schools came in 1664 when the Netherlands lost New Netherland to Great Britain. After this date, the local government, or "magistrate," changed and no longer ordered church congregations to found and maintain schools, as was

---

[7] The Articles of Dort can be found in Corwin's *A Digest of Synodical Legislation* as part of the introductory material in which the successive Constitutions (Polities) of the church are reprinted in their entirety. The 1619 Rules of Church Government, the 1792 Explanatory Articles, the 1833 Constitution of the Reformed Dutch Church, and the 1874 Constitution of the Reformed Church in America are reprinted in parallel fashion. References for the articles mentioned here are: Article 21 on p. xxviii, 41 on p. xlviii, 44 on p. lii, and 54 on p. lxiv.

[8] The purpose of the Boston Latin School was to prepare students for admission to Harvard College. For a history of the Latin School movement in the United States, see Harry G. Good and James D. Teller, *A History of American Education* (New York: Macmillan Company, 1973), 45-55.

[9] Waterbury, 31.

[10] Dunshee, 29.

[11] Robert S. Alexander, *Albany's First Church and Its Role in the Growth of the City, 1642-1942* (Delmar, NY: Newsgraphic Printers, 1988), 146-47.

[12] Edgar Tilton Jr., *The Reformed Low Dutch Church of Harlem organized 1660 Historical Sketch* (New York, 1910), 26-29.

the case when the Dutch controlled Manhattan. Yet the momentum for churches to found schools was sufficiently strong by the time that congregations continued to do so. By 1686 Hackensack, New Jersey, had a *voorleser*, or schoolmaster.[13] Brooklyn had a school by 1711,[14] and the upstate village of Kinderhook (later home to President Martin Van Buren) had one by 1712.[15] Bergen, New Jersey,[16] and Kingston, New York,[17] also founded schools in the eighteenth century.

The period beginning in 1664 and ending in 1792 was marked by the growing independence of the American Reformed Dutch Church from its mother church in the Netherlands. John H. Livingston, professor of theology, and other Reformed Dutch Church leaders wrote the "Explanatory Articles" to clarify and adapt the polity of Dort to the American scene. They understood that the schooling done by the church needed to be in accord with life in America. The RDC was no longer under the aegis of Great Britain but part of a new nation that affirmed the separation of church and state. The Explanatory Articles, which became part of the constitution in 1792 of the newly independent Reformed Dutch Church, added many new sections supplementing Dort church order to make Dort polity workable in America.[18] Article 56 of the newly written articles made this statement about church school education in America: "The zeal of the Reformed Church for initiating children early in the truth [expressed, Art. 54th of the Church Orders, where care is taken that Schoolmasters shall be of the reformed religion][19] cannot be evidenced in the same manner in America, where many denominations of Christians and some who do not even profess the Christian religion inhabit promiscuously; and where Schoolmasters can seldom be found who are members of the church. In such a situation, it is recommended

---

[13] *"The Old Church on the Green": The History and Traditions of the First Reformed Church, Hackensack, NJ, Founded 1686* (Privately printed, 1964), 15.

[14] Henry R. Stiles, *A History of the City of Brooklyn* (Brooklyn, NY, 1867), 181.

[15] *The Two Hundred Fiftieth Anniversary of the Kinderhook Reformed Church Kinderhook, New York 1712-1962*, 29.

[16] Benjamin C. Taylor, *Annals of the Classis of Bergen, of the Reformed Dutch, and of the Churches under Its Care: including the Civil History of the Ancient Township of Bergen, in New Jersey* (New York, 1857), 99-103.

[17] The Kingston Academy was founded in 1774. Martha B. Partlan and Dorothy A. DuMond, *The Reformed Protestant Dutch Church of Kingston, New York. Three Hundred and Twenty-Fifth Anniversary 1659-1984*, 82. The author's note that the congregation built a house in 1671 for the use of the schoolmaster indicates that a school may have been established very early in the congregation's existence.

[18] *The Constitution of the Reformed Dutch Church in the United States of America* (New York, 1793). The Explanatory Articles are at the end of the Constitution on pp. 303-54.

[19] Brackets and bracketed material in the original.

to parents to be peculiarly attentive to the religious education of their children, not only by instructing them and daily praying with them at home but also by never employing Schoolmasters whose characters are unascertained or suspicious, and especially none who scoff at the holy scriptures or whose conduct is immoral."[20]

The article continues: "It is also further recommended, that parents endeavour to prevail upon Schoolmasters to make the children belonging to the Dutch church, commit to memory, and publicly repeat in the school, one section of the Heidelbergh [sic] Catechism at least once every week." This long Explanatory Article indicated that the denomination was determined to continue church education but was facing new obstacles, such as finding worthy teachers and, above all, instilling congregations with the intention and will to maintain church-connected schools. Education in the public sphere was generally of poor quality in the seventeenth and eighteenth centuries. The movement for better public education, led by people such as Horace Mann[21] in the nineteenth century, had a profound effect upon church education and virtually wiped out education sponsored and promoted by RDC congregations. Another reason for the loss of church-related education was that public education in the nineteenth century was basically Protestant in orientation.

II. The Decline of the Dortian Model, 1792-1866.

The determination of the Reformed Dutch Church to establish church schools continued well into the nineteenth century in spite of the rise of public education. Since public education made grade school education available to all children, and high schools developed somewhat later in the nineteenth century, the emphasis of the church was placed upon education at the high school level. The academies that the RDC founded often developed into college preparatory schools. A primary example of this is Erasmus Hall, which was founded in 1787.[22] It was located just across the street from the Flatbush Reformed Dutch Church, which was founded in 1654.[23] Erasmus Hall may have been the outgrowth of a grade school that was founded very early in this

---

[20] *Constitution*, 342.
[21] For Horace Mann's key role in the development of public education in the United States, see Good, *A History of American Education*, 148-57.
[22] Willis Boughton, *Chronicles of Erasmus Hall Academy* (New York, 1906), 17-18.
[23] Edward Tanjore Corwin, *A Manual of the Reformed Church in America, 1628-1902*, 4th ed. (New York, 1902), 1007.

congregation's history. Dr. John H. Livingston, in addition to his duties as pastor of a New York City church and as the professor of sacred theology for America, served as the principal of Erasmus Hall from its conception until 1792. Erasmus Hall served as a private school until it became part of the New York City system in 1896.[24]

In the course of their development, most of the RDC academies either separated from the church or at least no longer had a close relationship with it. The Collegiate School in New York City was unusual in that it continued to be a part of the collegiate church system. This was perhaps even more unusual as it became an elite academy for the preparation of students for college during the latter part of the nineteenth century. First Church in Albany, New York, opened its academy in 1787,[25] the school where Philip Phelps Jr., first president of Hope College, had received his education in preparation for attending Union College. The founding of the academy in Schenectady came shortly before Union College was chartered in 1795.[26] The academy in New Brunswick, New Jersey, which later became Rutgers Preparatory School, had its origin in the Reformed Dutch Church, although the six persons who organized its beginnings were from other denominations as well.[27] The Columbia Academy in Bergen County, New Jersey, also had its origin in the RDC. It was considered as a possible location for the theological seminary before theological education joined Queens College in 1810.[28] It seems, although it cannot be precisely determined, that those academies that became successful educational institutions in their respective communities either gradually became independent or a part of the public school system. The move of some academies into public schools was not necessarily the result of the secularization of society. The public school system began with a strong Protestant inclination,[29] much to the chagrin of the Roman Catholic Church, which caused it to set up its own parochial school system in the early part of the nineteenth century.

---

[24] Boughton, 17-37.
[25] Alexander, *Albany's First Church*, 18.
[26] Wayne Somers, ed., *Encyclopedia of Union College History* (Schenectady: Union College Press, 2003), s.v. "Schenectady Academy."
[27] J. David Muyskens, *"The Town Clock Church": History of the First Reformed Church, New Brunswick, N.J.* (published by the consistory, 1991), 14.
[28] *Annals of the Classis of Bergen*, 106-7.
[29] James Reed and Ronnie Prevost, *A History of Christian Education* (Nashville: Broadman and Holman, 1993), 303.

There is plenty of evidence that the Reformed Dutch Church did not give up on the academy system as part of its Christian education program. In 1851 Albertus C. Van Raalte set up Pioneer School in the colony in Holland, Michigan, which became Holland Academy in 1857.[30] He recruited John Van Vleck to serve as the principal. Van Raalte and his fellow immigrants had hoped to build a Christian school system for all ages of children but were not financially able to do so, but the local public school was virtually a Christian school in its early days. An academy was founded very early in its history in Pella by Hendrik P. Scholte.[31] The German Reformed immigrants founded Pleasant Prairie Academy in German Valley, Illinois, in 1894, for the purpose of preparing pastors for German-speaking congregations in the RDC.[32] People from the Pella area set up a new colony in northwest Iowa and in 1882 founded the Northwestern Classical Academy.[33] Churches in Wisconsin founded the Wisconsin Memorial Academy in Cedar Grove, which opened in 1900 under the sponsorship of the Classis of Wisconsin and endorsement of the Particular Synod of Chicago.[34] By 1902 the academy in Harrison, South Dakota, was in operation.[35] A number of Reformed congregations were organized in Oklahoma during the early part of the twentieth century and founded the Cordell Academy

---

[30] Jeanne M. Jacobson, Elton J. Bruins, and Larry J. Wagenaar, *Albertus C. Van Raalte: Dutch Leader and American Patriot* (Holland, MI: Hope College, 1996), 69ff.

[31] *The Acts and Proceedings of the General Synod of the Reformed Protestant Dutch Church in North America, 1861-1865* (New York, 1865), 10:622. Even though Scholte wanted no part of the RDC, he requested help for the "school in Pella." This request may be an indication that many followers of Scholte had deserted him and turned to Dr. Albertus C. Van Raalte for guidance. One reason given for the request was: "There is a school now in operation at Pella, which only needs a teacher of the classics and higher mathematics that it may become a feeder of the new Western College."

[32] Corwin, *A Digest*, 511.

[33] Ibid., 468.

[34] Ibid., 830.

[35] Edward H. Scheuur, *After Lewis and Clark: The History of the Classis of Dakota* (self-published, 2004), 39-40. The academy was a "Christian institution of learning designed to prepare boys and girls for college or to fit them directly for various stations in life by laying the basis of a sound liberal Christian education." Because his father was the sole teacher in the academy during the four years of its existence, D. Ivan Dykstra gave extensive information on the Harrison Academy in his book: *'B.D.': A Biography of My Father, The Late Reverend B. D. Dykstra* (Grand Rapids: Eerdmans, 1982), 50-63. The curriculum of the academy consisted of English language and literature, Latin, Greek, New Testament, history, physics, and botany (56). Rev. Dykstra also conducted daily chapels and preached for churches without pastors.

in 1906 in Cordell, Oklahoma.[36] All of these schools were established with the intention of offering a Christian education for the children of the Dutch and German immigrants who had become part of the RDC. Other academies were established on domestic mission fields.

III. The Involvement of the Reformed Dutch Church in the Founding of Colleges.

The founding of colleges by the RDC was not related to the educational polity formulated at the Synod of Dort but sprang out of the felt need of the American Dutch churches for higher education. Queens College opened its doors in 1771 in New Brunswick, New Jersey, "for the education of youth in the learned languages, liberal and useful arts and sciences, and especially in divinity, preparing them for the ministry and other good offices."[37] In 1825 the name was changed to Rutgers College. A need for higher education in the Schenectady area and the competition in communities of that time to have a college led to the founding of Union College in 1795.[38] New York University was founded in 1831 to meet the needs of a growing urban population. At that time, New York City had two hundred thousand inhabitants but only two colleges: Columbia College and the College of Physicians and Surgeons.[39]

Colleges, however, were not founded by the RDC without controversy. Leaders in the denomination who led the movement to found colleges were split over the issue of where ministers should receive their training. One side, called the "Coetus," wanted them trained in America; the other group, named the "Conferentie," wanted candidates for ministry to continue to receive their theological education in the Netherlands and be ordained there. By the eighteenth century, progressive, visionary ministers in the RDC saw the necessity for the church in America to have its own educational institution for training ministers. Presbyterians founded a school in Princeton, New Jersey, for

---

[36] Corwin, *A Manual*, 5th ed., 97. Corwin lists a number of academies that were part of the domestic mission program of the church at this time: McKee Academy formed in 1905 and Annville Institute in 1910, both in Kentucky; Southern Normal and Industrial Institute at Brewton, Alabama, organized in 1919.

[37] William H. S. Demarest, *A History of Rutgers College, 1766-1927* (New Brunswick, NJ: Rutgers College, 1924), 75. Demarest, president of Rutgers College 1906-24, wrote a succinct history of Queen's College in an essay in Corwin, *A Manual*, 105-18.

[38] *Encyclopedia of Union College History*, 296.

[39] Thomas J. Frusciano and Marilyn H. Pettit, *New York University and the City: An Illustrated History* (New Brunswick, NJ: Rutgers University Press, 1977), 1.

this purpose in 1746, and Episcopalians founded Columbia College in 1754 on Manhattan Island. Congregationalists had two schools—Harvard and Yale—for theological education.[40] The divisiveness over ministerial education between the Coetus and Conferentie groups was finally healed at the Union Convention in 1771, organized by John H. Livingston.[41]

Ministers of the RDC were intimately involved with the founding of Queens College, Union College, and New York University, but the history of their development was quite different from each other and from that of Hope, Central, and Northwestern Colleges, institutions that are still connected to the denomination. Queens College, whose purpose was the training of ministers, probably remained with the RDC the longest.

Queens College had a slow and difficult start, but it grew out of a growing need for ministers in the RDC. Ministers debated the issue at a convention in 1738 and again in 1755, with Theodorus Jacobus Frelinghuysen taking a leading role, and a plan for an academy was finally approved. A charter for the school was granted in 1766, but classes did not begin until 1771 after financial and location issues for the school were settled. The Revolutionary War had intruded.

The search for a president was also long and difficult. John H. Livingston was chosen by the denomination in 1784 to be its professor of theology and, in addition to serving as pastor of the collegiate church in Manhattan, taught theology to students in Manhattan and Brooklyn. In 1810 Livingston severed all the ties he had in New York and moved to New Brunswick to open a seminary in conjunction with Queens College and to become its president, a position he held until his death on January 25, 1825. During this period, the theological department dominated. The literary department in fact was discontinued for periods of time and then finally revived in 1825, and the college was renamed Rutgers College. Henry Rutgers, a leader in the RDC, a trustee of Queens, and a liberal supporter of good causes, gave a substantial sum ($5,000) to the college, resulting in new and growing strength.

In time, space became an issue. Both the theological seminary and the undergraduate college had occupied the same building for

---

[40] Reed, *A History of Christian Education*, 297.

[41] For a summary of the struggle of the Coetus and Conferentie factions over the issue of ordination, see Elton J. Bruins, "The New Brunswick Theological Seminary 1884-1959" (PhD diss., New York University, 1962), 1-12. A copy can be found in Van Wylen Library, Hope College, Holland, MI. See also Demarest, *A History of Rutgers College*, 28-29.

thirty years. An increased number of students and faculty had made the situation intolerable. A substantial gift from Ann Hertzog of Philadelphia made it possible to build a separate hall for the seminary, and in 1856 the Peter Hertzog Theological Hall was dedicated, named in memory of Mrs. Hertzog's husband.[42] The denomination continued to support both the college and the seminary since they were both vital for providing ministers to the churches.

The reputation of the college was enhanced under the presidency of Theodore J. Frelinghuysen, who served from 1850 until his death in 1862. Chancellor of New York University prior to his presidency at Rutgers, Theodore Frelinghuysen was a lawyer by profession, a US senator, and the vice-presidential candidate on the Whig ticket in 1844, when Henry Clay was the nominee for president.[43] He was a leader in American religious life as well, serving on the boards of the American Bible Society, the American Tract Society, and the American Board of Commissioners for Foreign Missions. His father, Frederick Frelinghuysen, was appointed the first tutor at Queens in 1771 and was one of many Frelinghuysen family members who were involved in the early history of Queens College, the predecessor of Rutgers College.[44]

After Frelinghuysen's death, two significant changes took place. The denomination sold the land on which the campus was situated to the college. Rutgers College thus achieved a quasi-independent status, although three-fourths of the board members were required to be members of the RDC. The second change was that the college became a state college, an indirect result of the Morrill Act (land-grant act), passed by Congress in 1862.[45] The state of New Jersey assigned to Rutgers College the responsibilities and benefits of the land-grant act. They received state monies in the amount of $116,000 to develop its scientific work, but with it came responsibilities, such as buying a farm and equipment for it. The school continued to receive private

---

[42] Demarest, *A History of Rutgers College*, 379-82. Corwin, *A Digest*, 508.
[43] Robert V. Remini, *Henry Clay: Statesman for the Union* (New York: W. W. Norton, 1991), 645. Hermann K. Platt, in his biographical sketch of Frelinghuysen in *American National Biography* (New York: Oxford University Press, 1991), wrote: "In 1844, after Frelinghuysen had been out of politics for six years [as a US senator and the mayor of Newark, NJ] the Whig nominating committee chose him as Henry Clay's running mate in the presidential election. His unblemished moral reputation was considered attractive to the Christian reform wing of the party" (457). His nickname in the senate was "Christian Statesman," and he was known for his "deep Christian piety" (456).
[44] Demarest, *A History of Rutgers College*, 23-46.
[45] Ibid., 405-8.

monies, such as a gift from Ralph and Elizabeth Voorhees that provided a new library for Rutgers in 1903.[46] Rutgers was designated a college of the state in 1917 and subsequently declared a university. Rev. Dr. William Henry Steele Demarest was the last RCA head, from 1906 to 1924, of Rutgers University. In a very short time, all ties to the church had ended. Scholarship funds (in the amount of $250,000), which had been contributed by RDC church members during the nearly hundred years Rutgers was a church school, remained at Rutgers. During the 1950s, Dr. A. Livingston Warnshuis was able to get the trusteeship of these funds changed from the university to the RCA for the purpose of providing funds for students at Rutgers who were preparing to enter the Reformed Church ministry.[47]

Union College in Schnectady, New York, was never officially a college of the RDC; its "direct ancestor," however, "was the Schenectady Academy, a school founded at the initiative of the Dutch Reformed Church in 1785."[48] Union College was also related to the denomination by RDC members who studied there, such as Philip Phelps Jr. The first initiative for the founding of a college at Schenectady came in 1779, from an elder in the Dutch Reformed Church there, John Cornelius Cuyler. At the recommendation and encouragement of Rev. Dirck Romeyn, who became pastor of Schnectady's First Dutch Reformed Church in 1784, the consistory established an academy in 1785. In 1792, in a statement addressed to the New York State Board of Regents, those petitioning for a college in Schenectady reported that in support of that campaign "The town of Schenectady had promised 5,000 acres, various individuals had pledged a total of 700 acres and 1,000 pounds ($2,500), and the Dutch church had offered the academy building and 250 pounds for library books."[49] When even more money was pledged, the college was chartered in 1795—the first college to be chartered by the New York State Board of Regents, much to the displeasure of the citizens of the city of Albany who had vied for that distinction.

Since the efforts to found the college were community wide, present college historians consider the college to be the nation's oldest nondenominational college, even though the RDC minister Romeyn

---

[46] Demarest, *A History of Rutgers College*, 493. The Voorheeses were generous with Hope College as well and funded the building of Voorhees Hall in 1907.
[47] Norman Goodall, *Christian Ambassador: A Life of A. Livingston Warnshuis* (Manhasset, NY: Channel Press, 1963), 162-63. Court action was necessary to wrest these funds from the university.
[48] Somers, *Encyclopedia of Union College*, 628.
[49] Ibid., 296-97.

is considered by some to be its founder, and members of that church were vital in its founding. No Union College president has ever been a member of the RDC, although Romeyn did propose at one time Rev. William Linn of the Collegiate Church as a candidate for the presidency. Several Reformed Church ministers, such as Prof. William V. V. Mabon of New Brunswick Seminary and Rev. William N. P. Dailey, a prominent nineteenth century RDC minister, were graduates of Union College. In fact, Dailey claimed that "up to the year 1840 there were as many graduates of Union College in New Brunswick Seminary as there were from Rutgers."[50]

New York University was founded in 1831 to meet the needs of a burgeoning urban scene.[51] "By the beginning of the 1830s, New York City had become the principal capital market in the United States . . . and began to rival the European capitals in commerce and trade, especially in banking, warehousing, and insurance enterprises."[52] Three groups of individuals saw the need for a university: New York City merchants, democratic theorists, and clergymen. Democratic theorists, a group which included Albert Gallatin, former secretary of the treasury under presidents Jefferson and Madison, were eager to instill democratic ideals in youth. Among the clergymen who advocated for an urban university education were three Episcopalians, one Presbyterian, and one Dutch Reformed minister, Rev. James R. Matthews, pastor of the South Reformed Church on Garden Street. The new school was to be nondenominational, although its first three presidents were Dutch Reformed ministers.

Nine prominent citizens met in Matthews' parsonage in 1829, one of several gatherings to discuss plans for a university. Myndert Van Schaick, a lawyer of Dutch descent, was one of the nine. "The new venture was financed through the offering of stock to the public."[53] Subscribers numbered 175 persons. Gallatin was elected president of the governing board but resigned in 1831; Matthews was chosen as the university's first chancellor, a position he held for eight years. One of the first faculty members was Samuel F. B. Morse, a well-known painter and sculptor and inventor of the telegraph in 1844.[54] The university was

---

[50] William N. P. Dailey, "Union College and the Reformed Church in America," in Corwin, *A Manual,* 5th ed., 142.
[51] Information about New York University was taken from Frusciano, *New York University.*
[52] Frusciano, 1.
[53] Frusciano, 8. Brackets and capitals were in the original.
[54] Ibid., 21-22, 47.

first called University of the City of New-York; this was changed in 1896 to New York University.[55]

The intention of the founders of the university was that it would be nonsectarian. It was, however, to be "a Christian university [which would] hold up with unshaken firmness a Standard against Infidelity, and encourage its pupils in the acquisition of a Christian hope, and the practice of the duties of a Christian life."[56] In light of this, it was not surprising that the first chancellors and presidents of the governing board were clergymen. Although avowedly Christian, the school was open to everyone, regardless of religious or nonreligious affiliation, and the first Jewish student enrolled soon after the beginning of the university. Many students, however, attended New York University in order to prepare for the Reformed Dutch Church ministry, just as they did at Union College. Samuel Merrill Woodbridge, a long-time professor at New Brunswick Theological Seminary, graduated from NYU in 1838. He served as a distinguished church history professor from 1865 until 1901.[57]

Rev. James Matthews served as chancellor until 1839 and was succeeded by Frederick Frelinghuysen, who served until he became president of Rutgers College in 1850. In addition to being the 1844 Whig party candidate for the vice presidency, he was an abolitionist, a former senator from New Jersey, and the mayor of Newark.[58] The third Reformed Dutch Church member to become chancellor was Rev. Isaac Ferris, who resigned his pastorate of the Market Street Reformed Church to do so.[59] He took the position at the urging of Myndert Van Schaick and served as chancellor from 1853 until 1870, the most successful of the first three presidents. He was an able fundraiser, eliminating debt, raising faculty salaries, and acquiring funds for endowment, and the university expanded considerably under his leadership.

"Religious influence on university life [NYU's] generally declined in proportion to civil and secular life as the university expanded in the late nineteenth and early twentieth century," [60] as was typical of many American colleges and universities that began with strong Christian assumptions. "NYU's council reflected this secularity far less than other older colleges in the north east and continued to include a substantial

---

[55] Ibid., 37, 129.
[56] Ibid., 15. Brackets in original.
[57] Corwin, *A Manual*, 5th ed., 597-98.
[58] Frusciano, 35.
[59] Ibid., 46.
[60] Ibid., 142.

number of clergymen among its members for some time."[61] Today New York University is a distinguished, modern, urban university, prominent in higher education in America and completely secular in outlook.

Based on the history of Rutgers University, Union College, and New York University—institutions that did not continue their relationship with the RCA but became independent of it—a logical conclusion might be that the denomination was a failure in establishing institutions of higher education. This, however, would not be a correct conclusion. The Reformed Church in America continues to have close ties with three Christian colleges it founded: Hope, Central, and Northwestern. All three schools are thriving and stem from the nineteenth-century Dutch emigration to America of the Afgescheidenen, or Separatists, who broke with the mother Reformed Dutch Church in 1834. Two key leaders who brought their followers to America were dominies Albertus C. Van Raalte and Hendrik P. Scholte: Van Raalte to Holland, Michigan, and Scholte to Pella, Iowa—both in 1847. These leaders' work and interest in Christian education, not only based on Dortian principles but also for the new spurt of growth it would give, led to the founding of these three colleges.

Within a year of founding Holland, Van Raalte was at work organizing the Classis of Holland, which was made up of all Dutch immigrant congregations in the Middle West until 1854 when the Classis of Wisconsin was founded. After 1854 it was comprised of all immigrant congregations east of Lake Michigan; Wisconsin Classis included all the churches west of Lake Michigan. In addition Van Raalte was the major force in the uniting of Holland classis with the old Reformed Dutch Church, an action which was accomplished in 1850.[62] In 1851 he established Pioneer School for the education of students, most of whom were interested in entering the ministry. The RDC soon took the fledgling institution under its wing and granted it support. In 1857 the school was organized into an academy called Holland Academy. That same year, Van Raalte began fundraising to construct the school's first permanent building, Van Vleck Hall.

Providentially, Van Raalte was able to persuade Rev. Philip Phelps Jr., pastor of the Reformed Church in Hastings-on-Hudson,

---

[61] Fruscianco, 142.
[62] For a history of this union, see Elton J. Bruins, "1850—The Union of 1850: The Classis of Holland Joins the Reformed Protestant Dutch Church," in Robert P. Swierenga and Elton J. Bruins, *Family Quarrels in the Dutch Reformed Churches in the Nineteenth Century* (Grand Rapids, MI: Eerdmans, 1999), 36-60.

New York, to become the principal of the academy when ill heath forced John Van Vleck to resign the position. Both Phelps and Van Raalte had a vision of establishing a Christian college, a church-supported institution based on Dortian principles. Hope College got its start with the inauguration of a freshman class in 1862. Phelps was the sole instructor that first year, putting his education at the Albany Academy and Union College to good use. Each year he added another class, another year of instruction, and more instructors to help. "On 14 May 1866, Hope College was incorporated under the terms of the Michigan General College Law," and in July 1866, the first class of eight young men graduated from Hope College.[63] Phelps and Van Raalte immediately begged the denomination to allow theological education to take place at the college, a plea responded to positively by the church, and the foundation of Western Theological Seminary was laid. Academy graduates no longer had to travel to the Theological Seminary in New Brunswick, New Jersey, for their theological education. Seven of the eight graduates in 1866 continued their education in the same town and in the same building in which they had received their collegiate training.

The origins of Central College, in Pella, Iowa, were quite different. The very independent Rev. Hendrik P. Scholte refused to unite his flock with the Reformed Dutch Church, and instead founded an independent Christian Church of Pella. Some seceders though wanted to join the RDC, and by 1856 the majority of Scholte's followers had turned to Van Raalte for ecclesiastical leadership. In response, Van Raalte visited Pella, preached and organized the first Reformed Church congregation in Pella, which then became a member of the Classis of Holland. The new congregation, impressed by Van Raalte's leadership, called him to become its first pastor. He declined. After extending calls to some ministers in the Netherlands, the church called Rev. Pieter J. Oggel, Van Raalte's son-in-law, who accepted and became the first pastor of the First Reformed Church, Pella, in 1860.

---

[63] Elton J. Bruins, "Hope College: Its Origin and Development, 1851-2001," *Origins* 19, no. 1 (2001): 4-13. The two standard histories of Hope College are: Preston J. Stegenga, *Anchor of Hope: The History of an American Denominational Institution, Hope College* (Grand Rapids, MI: Eerdmans, 1954) and Wynand Wichers, *A Century of Hope, 1866-1966* (Grand Rapids, MI: Eerdmans, 1968). A religious history of the college is James C. Kennedy and Caroline J. Simon, *Can Hope Endure?: A Historical Case Study in Christian Higher Education* (Grand Rapids, MI: Eerdmans, 2005). Quote is from Wichers, 68.

A church-related academy was established in Pella within four years of its settlement, but Scholte, who aspired to also found a college, received help from the Baptist denomination to achieve this goal. The Baptists founded the Central University of Iowa in 1853 in Pella, with the help of many seceders, including Scholte himself, who participated by donating land or money.[64] Its imposing name, however, did not bring it immediate success. It took some time to get underway, and it was decimated when many students enlisted in the army during the Civil War. Several decades later, when the Baptists wanted to consolidate its educational interests in Iowa to Des Moines, they offered to transfer Central College to the Reformed Church in America on condition that a Christian college would be maintained there. At the time, there were fifty-five students in the academy and sixty-six in the college, one-third of which were from Reformed families. Central became affiliated with the RCA in 1916 and continues to be to the present day—a second jewel in the crown of RCA colleges.

The history of Northwestern College in Orange City, Iowa, was more like that of Hope College.[65] In 1869 a group from Pella made the trek to Sioux County in Northwest Iowa to establish a new colony. Other settlers followed, until a well-established colony developed. The center of the colony was a town called Orange City, a name that clearly had a relationship with the Netherlands. The area attracted many Reformed Church members, who brought with them their interest in Christian education and a desire to establish an institution similar to Holland Academy.

During the 1870s, Henry J. Hospers, former mayor of Pella and a leader in the new colony, and Rev. Seine Bolks, first pastor of First Reformed Church of Orange City, kept the vision of an academy alive. Bolks had studied under Van Raalte in the Netherlands and came to the United Sates with him. He witnessed the beginnings of Holland Academy and Hope College, and like Van Raalte, was instrumental in organizing Northwestern Classical Academy in 1882. Its chief purpose was "to train the mind and character of young people that they might serve both church and society."[66] The academy thrived in

---

[64] There is no published history of Central College. Material about Central was drawn from *The Acts and Proceedings of the One Hundred and Tenth Regular Session of the General Synod of the Reformed Church in America...*, June 1916, 762-66.

[65] George De Vries Jr. and Earl Wm. Kennedy, "The Reformed Church in America and Higher Education (with special reference Northwestern Academy and College)," *Reformed Review* 23, no. 3 (spring 1970): 184-95.

[66] De Vries and Kennedy, 191.

the late 1890s under the leadership of its second principal, Rev. James F. Zwemer, a dynamic pastor and successful fundraiser. It took more time for Northwestern Academy to develop into a college than Holland Academy, but in September 1928, the Northwestern Junior College (a two-year college) began with a class of thirty students. In 1957 the board of trustees and the RCA approved the school's development into a four-year institution. Northwestern College is now a thriving Christian college.

All three Reformed Church colleges—Hope, Central, and Northwestern—are today intentional about maintaining their ties with the denomination. It is therefore unlikely that these schools in the foreseeable future will fall away from the aegis of the Reformed Church, as Rutgers, Union, and New York University all have. A positive attitude on the part of the denomination, and a realization of how valuable the three colleges are to them, may well ensure a long partnership of these colleges with the church.

IV. Dort Revisited: Samuel B. Schieffelin's Attempt to Revive Church-Sponsored Schools

Samuel B. Schieffelin was one of the most prominent Reformed Dutch Church members of the nineteenth century and a good friend of Van Raalte. Unfortunately, he is virtually unknown in Reformed Church circles today. Therefore, some biographical information about Schieffelin is necessary to understand the extent of his influence in the RDC of his day.

Schieffelin was born in New York City in 1811, son of Henry Hamilton and Maria Theresa (Bradhurst) Schieffelin. They were members of the Fifth Avenue Presbyterian Church, New York, where Samuel was baptized.[67] By the mid-1800s, Schieffelin was an active member of the RDC, however, and served on the denominational Board of Domestic Missions and Board of Education.[68] He wrote and published religious literature, including "The Foundations of History" (1863), "Milk for Babies: A Bible Catechism" (1864), and "Music in Our Churches" (1881).[69]

The Schieffelin family was heir to a very successful wholesale drug business founded by Jacob Schieffelin, Samuel's grandfather,

---

[67] *New York Genealogical and Biographical Record* 108, no. 2 (April 1977): 98.
[68] *The Twenty-Third Annual Report of the Board of Domestic Missions of the Reformed Protestant Dutch Church* (1855) and *First Catalogue and Circular of Hope College 1865-66*.
[69] *National Cyclopaedia of American Biography* (New York, 1897), 4:521, s.v. "Schieffelin, Samuel Bradhurst."

in 1780, in New York City. Samuel was engaged in the drug business, along with his three brothers. In addition to his service to the church, he was a member of the National Academy of Design and a trustee of the American Museum of National History. He was a very generous donor to various RDC causes and gave many gifts of money and books to Hope College, a result of his friendship with Van Raalte.[70] The first edition of the *Hope College Remembrancer* (1867) was dedicated with gratitude to Samuel B. Schieffelin "whose sympathies and liberalities have been enlisted in behalf of Hope College."[71]

Schieffelin became very interested in developing a system of denominational church schools, or parochial education. In 1851 he gave a small amount ($100) to the board of education to investigate the possibility of establishing such schools.[72] This gift inspired little interest, but that changed when Schieffelin in 1852 placed a large sum ($7,000) in a trust fund in the care of the Board of Direction of the Reformed Dutch Church for the purpose of establishing "some general parochial school system" in the denomination.[73] The money was given with the stipulation that, if such a system was not established within two years, he would withdraw the funds and give them to the parochial school system of the Presbyterian Church. The committee that dealt with this proposal in 1853 noted that several Classes have with unanimity "regarded the establishment of such schools as inexpedient" and declined to deal with it further, suggesting Schieffelin give the money to Holland Academy.[74]

On 1 March 1854, Schieffelin sent a letter to RDC pastors which stimulated much more interest in his goal to establish parochial schools.[75] The letter was lengthy and carefully worded. In it he first deplored the history of the question, that the church had failed in her duty to the children of the church by not following educational policies decreed by the Synod of Dort and devoting attention to Christian day

---

[70] Corwin, *A Digest*, s.v. "Schieffelin, Samuel B."
[71] The dedicatory statement in its entirety reads: "To Samuel B. Schieffelin, Esq., whose sympathies and liberalities have been enlisted in behalf of Hope College, from its germinal to its present position, this first commencement number of the Hope College Remembrancer is most gratefully dedicated." It was written by President Philip Phelps Jr., editor of the *Remembrancer*.
[72] Corwin, *A Digest*, s.v. "Parochial Schools."
[73] The Board of Direction handled endowment funds for the denomination.
[74] Corwin, *A Digest*, 479-80.
[75] Samuel B. Schieffelin to the RDC, "A Letter on Parochial Schools," 1 March 1854, General Synod Papers 1849-1859, RCA Archives, New Brunswick Theological Seminary, New Brunswick, NJ (microfilm, Joint Archives of Holland, Hope College, Holland, MI).

school education but instead supporting public schools. "The duty of the Church to teach has been fixed upon her by her great Head, and the requisition covers the whole period of human life, from infancy to old age. . . . Has she not, during all this period [since Dort], too generally dropped the reigns from her hands and abandoned oversight, direction, and control to the world?" Schieffelin contended that many of the problems the church was facing in his time were due to her failure to sponsor church schools as directed by the Synod of Dort. The Presbyterians had established at least one hundred such schools by this time, and he thought the RDC should be as intentional about establishing a system of parochial education as the Presbyterians.

About two-thirds of the way through the letter, Schieffelin gets to the heart of the matter—the compelling reason for him as to why the church was duty bound to establish parochial schools. The "Romanists," the real threat to the American public education system, "are endeavoring to get hold of the public school-money, to use for their own sectarian purposes." The Roman Catholic Church knew the importance of educating their young children. "The Papists have now in the city of New-York, besides their fashionable schools, about twenty-eight schools, connected with, and bearing the names of, their churches, under the charge of sixty priests, and having over ten thousand scholars, and amongst them some children of Protestants,—their teachings and their reading-books being especially suited to train them up Papists." Schieffelin clearly felt it was incumbent upon the RDC to set up its own parochial school system. If the Roman Catholic Church was able to do it, why should not the Reformed Dutch Church?

Schieffelin's letter brought action in 1854. The church accepted Schieffelin's gift and adopted a "Plan for the Establishment and Sustaining of Parochial Schools in the Reformed Dutch Church." Every school applying for funds from the Schieffelin Fund must be under the care of a Consistory of a RDC church and subject to the supervision of the Classis. "The Holy Scriptures shall be used in such school as a text-book for daily instruction in religion, and the Catechism approved by our Church shall be taught at least twice a week in addition to the usual branches of early education." The teacher must be a member of the Reformed Dutch Church. Rules followed governing the application for grants from the Schieffelin Fund, such as the application needing the approval of the local Classis and the congregation being bound to take offerings for the support of the school.[76]

[76] Corwin, *A Digest*, s.v. "Parochial Schools."

The Educational Endeavors of the Reformed Dutch Church   29

Edward Tanjore Corwin, distinguished nineteenth-century minister and historian, in his essay on parochial schools, notes that a number of congregations took advantage of this funding, and "In 1858 sixteen [schools] were in operation [and] Christian School books began to be published." When Van Raalte and his own congregation began a parochial school in 1857, he may have been able to acquire monies from the Schieffelin Fund.[77] Van Raalte earlier had cast his lot with public education because the immigrants were too poor to fund congregational schools. Possibly he found that the public school was losing its Christian emphasis. Van Raalte's Christian school, sponsored by the First Reformed Church, lasted only about ten years. It seems unusual that Van Raalte was not successful in this attempt because one of the reasons for the Separatists to emigrate was for the avowed purpose of establishing Christian schools.

Corwin, however, concluded, "It began to appear it was chiefly the Holland and German churches which availed themselves of the aid of this Fund." In spite of all of the effort and funding given by Schieffelin for the establishment of parochial schools, they did not flourish. Interest in parochial schools diminished. Corwin suggests that other causes had captured the interest of the churches, and the "Public School system seemed all sufficient." In any case, Schieffelin could not overcome the tendency of the Reformed Dutch Church to rely on the public school system for the education of their children.

The flagging interest of the RDC in a parochial school system may have led to Schieffelin's generosity to the Holland Academy and nascent Hope College. All his gifts, interest, and efforts at least had an effect at the academy level and certainly on Holland Academy. Schieffelin had found a faithful cohort in Van Raalte who worked diligently to establish Christian education at the academy and college level in the Holland Colony.

The Sunday school movement may also have tended to dull the enthusiasm for Christian Day Schools.[78] RDC congregations adopted this movement for Christian education within the local church, beginning as early as 1826. By the end of the nineteenth century, all efforts to follow the Dortian model for Christian education had virtually

---

[77] It seems more than coincidental that Van Raalte organized a school in 1857, when Schieffelin's funds were available to assist local congregations to establish church schools.

[78] See Corwin, *A Digest*, s.v. "Sunday Schools," for information on the adoption by the RDC of the Sunday school movement.

ended. In the twentieth century, the last of the academies closed or were secularized. From the history of early educational endeavors of the Reformed Church in America (as the church became known in 1867), there is a lesson that perhaps the three remaining RCA church colleges can learn.[79] Unless Hope, Central, and Northwestern Colleges are fully intentional about being Christian institutions of higher learning, their future as Christian institutions is bleak. The secularization that Rutgers, Union, and New York University have experienced is always a threat that the RCA church colleges will face, but, we pray, our three colleges will never be deterred from recognizing the importance of the relationship between the Christian faith and learning.

---

[79] Kennedy and Simon in *Can Hope Endure?* trace the efforts of Hope College to reclaim its intentionality to be a Christian college.

CHAPTER 3

Emotional Intelligence as It Impacts Pastoral Leadership

Cornelis G. Kors

Gregg Mast is my colleague, friend, and pastor. He has often been the calm in the midst of a storm. When conversations become complicated, and tension levels run high, he is apt to contribute a perspective that results in solutions and alleviates anxiety. Gregg is intelligent and pragmatic when it comes to addressing problems; he has good common sense, and when he speaks, people stop and listen.

Gregg knows who he is and has an uncanny ability to read the dynamics of a situation and understand what he must say and do. He is confident and self-aware and demonstrates self-control when others ride the waves of emotional upheaval and create chaos where order is needed. Gregg remains calm in the center of conflict and controversy. Drawing from an internal source, he tends to keep conversations objective, balanced, focused, and fair. Parker J. Palmer would refer to this as his "inner teacher" at work. Palmer, in his book *A Hidden Wholeness*, states: "We must find a way to live in the continuing conversation, with its conflicts and complexities, while staying in close touch with our inner teacher."[1] My personal assessment of Mast is that

---

[1] Palmer, Parker J., *A Hidden Wholeness: The Journey Toward an Undivided Life* (San Francisco: Jossey-Bass, 2004), 127.

his "inner teacher" is grounded in not only a high IQ but also a high EI/EQ (emotional intelligence / emotional quotient). His ministry, in its many forms as preacher, teacher, and president has been successful in large part because of his strong emotional health and maturity, that is, emotional intelligence.

Gregg will often mention the importance of emotional intelligence. On many occasions while working alongside him, I have observed him identify and recognize high EI in an individual or system. He has often suggested that emotional intelligence might be the distinguishing factor of good pastoral leadership. According to Gregg, it might even be more significant than any other single characteristic, including intellectual capacity. This places him in good stead; experts in the emotional intelligence field say the same. Daniel Goleman, who has written volumes on EI, says that, when it comes to the emotional and rational mind, "In many or most moments, these minds are exquisitely coordinated: feelings are essential to thought, thought to feeling. But when passions surge, the balance tips: it is the emotional mind that captures the upper hand, swamping the rational mind."[2]

Brené Brown, a social scientist, in speaking of the most resilient individuals she has studied, asks: "What do these people with strong relationships, parents with deep connections to their children, teachers nurturing creativity and learning, clergy walking with people through faith, and trusted leaders have in common?" The answer for her is "They recognize the power of emotion, and they're not afraid to lean into discomfort."[3]

Research provides convincing statistical evidence regarding the importance of EI and the weighted advantage of emotional intelligence over intellectual intelligence:

> When emotional intelligence was first discovered, it served as the missing link in a peculiar finding: people with the highest levels of intelligence (IQ) outperform those with average IQs just 20 percent of the time, while people with average IQs outperform those with high IQs 70 percent of the time.[4]
>
> A study of PhDs spanning 40 years at the University of California at Berkeley concluded that well-developed EI was four

---

[2] Goleman, Daniel, *Emotional Intelligence: Why it can matter more than IQ* (New York: Bantam Books, 1995), 9.
[3] Brown, Brené, *Rising Strong* (New York: Spiegel & Grau, 2015), xix.
[4] Bradberry, Travis, and Jean Greaves, *Emotional Intelligence 2.0* (San Diego: Talent Smart, 2009), 9.

times more powerful than strong IQ in predicting who succeeded in their chosen field.[5]

This takes on greater meaning as one considers the impact of EI on pastoral leadership. Peter Scazzero writes, "It is impossible to be spiritually mature while remaining emotionally immature... emotional health and spiritual maturity are inseparable."[6] He states, "Christian spirituality, without an integration of emotional health, can be deadly—to yourself, your relationship with God, and the people around you."[7]

The Reformed Church's Heidelberg Catechism identifies the importance of emotions as it confesses our faith and relationships. Reformed theologian Scott Hoezee states: "Although a catechism may seem to be aimed at one's head, the Heidelberg Catechism also aims at the heart. Along with *comfort*, the words *assurance* and *joy* occur often, particularly in those questions and answers that address the Christian faith and the utter assurance provided by that faith through the love of Jesus Christ the Lord."[8]

Emotional intelligence is demonstrated in many places in scripture. From Cain and Abel, where hate and jealousy result in an irrational act, to Psalms and Proverbs, where fear, frustration, joy, and lament are expressed, to the epistles, where caution, control, and love are encouraged, emotions are at the forefront of relationships. Scripture places emphasis on both vertical relationships, manifested in emotion toward God, and horizontal relationships, centered on emotion toward others. A demonstration of mature emotional health is Acts 24:10ff, a highly emotional scene where Governor Felix offers Paul the opportunity to make a statement in defense of erroneous charges originating with Ananias the high priest. Paul remains calm and objective and says, "I cheerfully make my defense" (vs. 10). He clearly manages his emotions and gives evidence of a high EI. Peter writes in 1 Peter 4:7 "Therefore be clear minded and self-controlled so that you can pray. Above all love each other deeply" (NIV). The directive is to turn inward and manage one's own emotional state, while also developing and nurturing relational emotions.

---

[5] Jordan Eric, *Emotional Intelligence Mastery* (San Bernardino: Pine Peak Publishing, 2016), 8.
[6] Scazzero, Peter, *Emotionally Healthy Spirituality* (Grand Rapids, MI: Zondervan, 2006), 12.
[7] Ibid., 7.
[8] Hoezee, Scott, *Speaking of Comfort* (Grand Rapids, MI: CRC Publications, 1998), 12.

In Psalm 51:6ff, David takes similar steps by first turning inward, processing his internal "stuff," drawing from wisdom and intentionally claiming joy and gladness:

> You desire truth in the inward being;
> > Therefore, teach me wisdom in my heart.
> Purge me with hyssop, and I shall be clean;
> > wash me, and I shall be whiter than snow.
> Let me hear joy and gladness;
> > let the bones that you have crushed rejoice. (NRSV)

Emotional intelligence and emotional quotient have become major topics in business, church, society, and even entertainment. The movie *Inside Out* (2015) highlighted and popularized the importance of emotions. The movie allowed us to recognize the inner self and the various emotions residing inside each of us. Teachers have utilized the movie to illustrate the role of emotion in our lives. Adolescents have felt legitimized through the characters of the movie and found a means for expressing what they are experiencing internally. The creators of the movie had twenty-six emotions to choose from and finally selected anger, fear, joy, sadness, and disgust.

In walking through bookstores and airports, one will observe best sellers such as *Emotional Intelligence 2.0* by Travis Bradberry and Jean Greaves prominently displayed. The final list of emotions included in their book consists of "happy, sad, angry, afraid, and ashamed." Bradberry and Greaves identify personal and social competence as categories or grids for these emotions. According to them, "competence" is based on the ability to "manage" emotional tendencies and behaviors in self and others.[9] The ability to manage emotions has been determined by those who study emotional intelligence as a key to success in personal and relational life. For the pastor, I would include "professional life."

Daniel Goleman, in his book *Emotional Intelligence* suggests there are eight main families of emotions:

1. Anger (fury, hostility, irritability, annoyance)
2. Sadness (grief, self-pity, despair, dejection, loneliness)
3. Fear (anxiety, edginess, nervousness, fright, terror, apprehension)
4. Enjoyment (joy, relief, contentment, delight, thrill, euphoria, ecstasy)
5. Love (acceptance, trust, devotion, adoration)

---

[9] Bradberry and Greaves, 24.

6. Surprise (shock, amazement, wonder)
7. Disgust (contempt, scorn aversion, distaste, revulsion)
8. Shame (guilt, remorse, humiliation, embarrassment, chagrin)[10]

Emotions, no matter how one chooses to categorize them, are expressed and experienced by individuals in a wide variety of combinations. By recognizing their own emotions, pastoral leaders can manage their responses empathically and objectively, assessing situations and appropriately acknowledging the inner processes of others. I would suggest that the higher the emotional intelligence of the individual, the greater is their capacity to be an effective presence to others. It is a "presence" that best represents Jesus.

Emotional intelligence is important to those in ministry because it can serve as a compass leading to Christian and moral behavior. It includes empathy, kindness, and ethical sensitivity. Whereas intellectual maturity leads to increased capacity of knowledge, emotional maturity leads to increased relational capacity, fine-tuned Christian values, and ethical behavior. Daniel Goleman describes emotional intelligence as "a collection of capacities having to do with knowledge of emotions, control of emotions, and sensitivity to one's own or other's emotional states."[11] This translates into a capacity for deepening relationships, to function well in community and to effectively create a culture of trust.

A team led by Goleman has identified two domains and four competencies for thinking about emotional intelligence and leadership. These categories, although not theological as such, are apropos to the specific topic of pastoral leadership. Goleman, Boyattzis, and McKee identify the domains as personal competence and social competence.[12] They suggest that one's personal emotional health and maturity, or high EI, can drive the emotions of those they lead in directions that are empathic, healthy, and mature. In other words, they drive the system to be emotionally healthy and mature.[13]

Goleman et al. identify two domains, self-awareness and self-management, as part of personal competence. Within social competence, they identify two more domains: social awareness and relationship management. I would propose that being highly functional in these four competencies is critical for pastoral leaders and their ability to

---

[10] Goleman, *Emotional Intelligence*, 199-200.
[11] Gardner, Howard, *Intelligence Reframed* (New York: Basic Books, 1999), 69.
[12] Goleman, Daniel, Richard Boyatzis, and Annie McKee, *Primal Leadership* (Boston: Harvard, 2013), 39.
[13] Ibid., 6.

effectively minister. Academic training and intellect notwithstanding, without emotional intelligence consisting of self-awareness, self-management, social awareness, and relationship management, pastors will remain limited in their capacity to care for a congregation and bring the unconditional love of Jesus to others.

Self-awareness

Goleman et al. identify the following as critical components of self-awareness in understanding leadership:

1. Emotional self-awareness: reading one's own emotions and recognizing their impact; using "gut sense" to guide decisions;
2. Accurate self-assessment: knowing one's strengths and limits; and
3. Self-confidence: a sound sense of one's self-worth and capabilities.[14]

Robert Quinn suggests "We may greatly increase the likelihood of changing the world if we look within, clarifying our own values as we go, and then disciplining ourselves to more live those values."[15]

Emotional self-awareness requires that one is willing to be honest with oneself and, in the words of Henri Nouwen, to "see yourself truthfully." Nouwen advises that to be honest about the inner self, you must be willing to discover who you are and what your emotions are saying: "You have to start seeing yourself as your truthful friends see you."[16] Also, perhaps more important for the pastoral leader, "You have to be willing to live your loneliness, your incompleteness, your lack of total incarnation fearlessly."[17] In order to know God and to bring others into relationship with him, we must know ourselves. John Calvin wrote: "Our wisdom ... consists almost entirely of two parts: the knowledge of God and the knowledge of ourselves. But as these are connected together by many ties, it is not easy to determine which of the two precedes and gives birth to the other."[18]

The authentic and confident pastor must be open to introspection and dealing with the inner life as it involves our emotions and our spirituality, and our spirituality is the foundation of our pastoral

---

[14] Ibid., 39.
[15] Quinn, Robert E., *Change the World: How Ordinary People Can Accomplish Extraordinary Results* (San Francisco: Jossey Bass, 2000), 57.
[16] Nouwen, Henri J. W., *The Inner Voice of Love* (New York: Random House, 1996), 53.
[17] Ibid., 54.
[18] Calvin, John, *Institutes of the Christian Religion* (Grand Rapids, MI, Eerdmans, 1957), 1:37.

ministry. Reading and monitoring one's own emotions and spiritual journey is necessary if one is going to assist others in integrating their emotional journey with their spiritual journey. We must know our own heart. "To become a pastor is to embrace the invitation to enter deep into yourself. It is to accept a paradoxical view of reality, recognizing that you can only engage the outer world through your inner landscape. Becoming is about seeking personal inner transformation or revitalization before you seek it for others."[19] From 2 Corinthians 10:5: "We take captive every thought [emotion] to make it obedient to Christ" (NIV).

By knowing ourselves, we give permission to love ourselves and to have self-compassion. According to Christian counselor and professor of pastoral care, Chuck DeGroat, "Self-compassion frees us from the slavery of narcissistic self-promotion and self-perfection. Self-compassion frees us to pay attention to the inner conversations we're always having, as we debate which voice will decide the moment, the day, the future. Self-compassion allows us, in the end, to be imperfect."[20]

The counseling model known as "Internal Family Systems" (IFS) has brought meaning and new understanding as it provides a window into self-awareness and the possibilities of internal conversations. Psychologists, such as Richard Schwartz and Jay Early,[21] have written valuable contributions on this topic, recognizing the need for individuals to turn their focus to inside of their being and turn their attention to internal "thoughts, emotions, fantasies, images, and sensations."[22] Early and Schwartz speak of internal relationships with different thoughts and emotions as they live within each individual. They present it as if we all have multiple personalities that can be identified separately and dealt with as individual entities. Nor do they live only inside of us; they relate to one another. "We have ongoing, complex relationships with many different inner voices, thought patterns, and emotions that are similar to relationships we have with other people. What we call 'thinking' is often our inner dialogues with different parts of us."[23]

---

[19] Hamman, Jaco J., *Becoming a Pastor: Forming Self and Soul for Ministry* (rev. and updated) (Cleveland, OH: Pilgrim Press, 2015), 47.
[20] DeGroat, Chuck, *Wholeheartedness* (Grand Rapids, MI: Eerdmans, 2016), 46.
[21] Early, Jay, *Self-Therapy* (Larkspur, CA: Pattern System Books, 2009).
[22] Schwartz, Richard C., *Introduction to the Internal Family Systems Model* (Oak Park, IL: Trailheads Publishing, 2001), 2.
[23] Ibid., 5.

Self-management

Goleman et al. identify the following as critical components of self-management in understanding leadership:

1. Emotional self-control: keeping disruptive emotions and impulses under control;
2. Transparency: displaying honesty and integrity; trustworthiness;
3. Adaptability: flexibility in adapting to changing situations or overcoming obstacles;
4. Achievement: the drive to improve performance to meet inner standards of excellence;
5. Initiative: readiness to act and seize opportunities; and
6. Optimism: seeing the upside in events.[24]

Self-management begins with self-awareness. The challenge to look within oneself first is best given by Jesus:

> And why do you look at the speck in your brother's eye, but do not perceive the plank in your own eye? Or how can you say to your brother, "Brother, let me remove the speck that is in your eye," when you yourself do not see the plank that is in your own eye? Hypocrite! First remove the plank from your own eye, and then you will see clearly to remove the speck that is in your brother's eye. (Luke 6:41-42 NRSV)

In my professional role, I lead interviews for candidates. In my opening remarks, I often tell the candidate to "Relax, and just be yourself," and then I usually add, "But that is easier for me to say than for you to do." What happens if they have not gone on the quest to discover who they really are? Self-management is one of the most difficult tasks we are assigned as human beings. And yet, it is one of the most important. As Thomas Armstrong so wisely says, "Perhaps the real problem with arriving at a solid definition of the self lies in the fact that the object of our search is the same entity that is doing the searching."[25]

New situations often produce emotions we have not experienced, and thus we find ourselves inadequately prepared with an appropriate response—not only have we not defined said emotion, but we also find ourselves without the management skills to respond appropriately.

---

[24] Goleman et al., *Primal Leadership*, 39.
[25] Armstrong, Thomas, *7 Kinds of Smart* (New York: Plume, 1993), 130.

George Barna speaks of pastoral leaders and their ability to manage and minister out of their self-awareness. He states:

> God cannot trust you with the leadership of His most beloved creation, nor with the wise use of His precious vision, unless you understand yourself inside out. Great leaders know who they are at the most intimate levels of self-knowledge. Anything less would render them dangerous.[26]

The pastoral leader who neither knows and loves themselves at a deep personal level nor possesses self-control and discipline, is capable of harming themselves and their flock. Jaco Hamman, a psychologist and pastoral counseling professor states: "Without first integrating the love and hate in your own person, those you serve will experience you as ruthless and aloof, emotionally disconnected from your own issues and from their problems."[27] Transparency with self and others will provide a means of self-management.

Jack Hayford suggests that our "human disposition finds it easier to spend time 'tweaking systems' than prioritizing honest-to-God introspection and constant availability to transformation."[28] In other words, we can easily put our energy into managing circumstances around us, being defensive about how we have always acted and responded to certain situations, and not be true to the values and beliefs we hold deep inside. This takes on special concern if we have not identified and recognized our emotional attachment to those values. There is much at stake in being honest with God and our inner self as pastoral leaders. Objectivity and transparent introspection will lead us in a positive direction, keeping us true to our values and properly motivated in our leadership. In Hayford's words, we need to ask, "Am I maintaining 'integrity of heart?'"[29] He concludes, "At the core of everything a person does lies an inner value system—a commitment to the objectives dictated by a grid of convictions and personal priorities. These values that guide decisions and motivate action are life's 'heart' issues."[30]

Our values or heart issues best lead how we function in pastoral leadership. According to Robert Quinn, "When we align ourselves

---

[26] Barna, George, *Leaders on Leadership* (Ventura, CA: Regal Books, 1997), 52.
[27] Hamman, Jaco J, *Becoming a Pastor: Forming Self and Soul for Ministry* (Cleveland, OH: Pilgrim Press, 2007), 64.
[28] Barna, *Leaders on Leadership*, 63.
[29] Ibid., 68.
[30] Ibid., 71.

with our values, we know where we need to go. The purpose we need to fulfill becomes clear. Whatever suppressed or hidden purpose we may have had rises into our consciousness."[31] Since values, or heart issues, are centered in our emotional make-up, it is natural for us to react and respond emotionally. Recognizing emotion leads to feeling it. We need not fear our emotions or attempt to overrule them with intellect. I once had a candidate in our program whose solution to every pastoral situation was found in quoting the Heidelberg Catechism. He may have used the correct words but was unable to adequately care for and counsel the individual to whom ministry was needed. He drew from his intellect but lacked the expressed empathy to touch upon the heart issue. A more beneficial approach would have been for him to look inward to his own emotions and attempt to determine if they were the emotions the counselee was likely feeling. In other words, he would have been better off to play the role of empathetic comforter rather than instructor.

Quinn provides a meaningful analogy in his explanation of what was discovered at a medical school as they prepared and trained future doctors.

> Instead of providing only traditional answers, this facilitator asks questions that prod students to use their own inner resources for seeking explanations and solutions. Each student is thus encouraged to engage emergent reality and is expected to establish a caring, interactive, and impactive relationship with the patient as a real person with an illness rather than a "case number" or disease to be treated.[32]

The "inner resources" are the emotions that give meaning to the situation. If a patient is experiencing fear about an impending operation, the doctor's purpose should first and foremost be to recognize that precise fear and address it before explaining the technicalities of the surgery. In the case of ministry, if a grieving parishioner is anxious about a loved one's salvation, in part due to their own questions of faith, the pastor should first embrace the parishioner's anxiety and not provide a theological explanation of soteriology. It is all about knowing emotions, one's own and those of others. Ronald Richardson would add, "If we can hear their stories as being about their own anxieties

---

[31] Quinn, *Change the World*, 62.
[32] Ibid., 67.

and how they try to maintain a sense of security or safety by having an other-focus, then we may be a resource to them in thinking through their issues."[33]

Social awareness

Goleman et al. identify the following as critical components of social-awareness in understanding leadership:

1. Empathy: Sensing others' emotions, understanding their perspectives, and taking active interest in their concerns;
2. Organizational awareness: Reading the currents, decision networks, and politics at the organizational level; and
3. Service: Recognizing and meeting follower, client, or customer needs.[34]

Social awareness involves the ability to observe and recognize the circumstances and environment of others. Goleman et al. suggest: "Of all the dimensions of emotional intelligence, social awareness may be the most easily recognized."[35] A pastoral leader has a front-row seat to the behavior, culture, and ethos of his or her community. Those out of touch with their emotive self or unaware of emotional systems are incapable of tending to people's needs and leading change in ways that will be effective or relevant. The pastor is compelled to be aware of the community's behavior as well as the emotions that drive their own actions. Peter Steinke, discussing systems theory as taught by Edwin Friedman and Murray Bowen, states: "No emotional system will change unless people in the system change how they function with one another."[36] An emotional reaction by the pastor has the capability to trigger a series of subsequent responses in others. The pastor can choose whether the trigger is positive or negative.

When pastors are emotionally healthy and comfortable in their own skin, and if they love their own person, they will be able to express God's love to others. Emotional health "concerns itself primarily with loving others well. It connects us to our interiors, making possible the seeing and treating of each individual as worthy of respect, created in

---

[33] Richardson, *Becoming a Healthier Pastor*, 23.
[34] Goleman et al., *Primal Leadership*, 39.
[35] Ibid., 49.
[36] Steinke, Peter L., *A Door Set Open: Grounding Change in Mission and Hope* (Herndon, Virginia: Alban Institute, 2010), 4.

the image of God, and not just as objects to use."[37] Emotional health fosters trust between individuals and a trust of God and His plan for our lives.

Empathy toward others is most valuable if we are able to show empathy to ourselves. Nurturing the self, although appearing as selfish and narcissistic, is necessary and requires hard work on our part. "Being able to nurture the core of your being—your inner space—is a capacity you need to achieve as you lead the body of Christ with effectiveness and fruitfulness."[38] Hamman uses the expression of "concern" as a component of empathy and suggests that the lack of concern limits you to a ministry that is reactive and seldom proactive.[39] Healthy ministry demands one act in proactive ways, showing empathy, anticipating the needs of congregants, and responding accordingly. This engenders trust. It does not mean diagnosing the congregational dynamics and assigning categories or labels to any or all observations.

Patrick Lencioni borrows the expression: "fundamental attribution error" to describe what arises in social settings and within leadership teams when labeling and projection of emotions occurs.[40] "At the heart of the fundamental attribution error is the tendency of human beings to attribute the negative or frustrating behaviors of their colleagues to their intentions and personalities, while attributing their own negative or frustrating behaviors to environmental factors."[41] Lencioni provides examples of this behavior, but allow me to draw from the church and life of the pastor. For instance, if I were to see an elder at the close of a service scowling at the worship leader and wagging her finger in his face, I am likely to conclude that she has an anger problem and needs some counseling. In contrast, if I were to find myself scowling and wagging my finger at the worship leader, I am likely to conclude that my behavior is caused by an uncooperative staff member who did not bother to choose songs appropriate for that Sunday and at worst, I am just having a tough day.

Lencioni goes on to say: "Of course, this kind of misattribution, where we give ourselves the benefit of the doubt but assume the worst about others, breaks down trust on a team."[42] He suggests that to

---

[37] Scazzero, *Emotionally Healthy Spirituality*, 47.
[38] Hamman, *Becoming a Pastor*.
[39] Ibid., 66.
[40] Lencione, Patrick, *The Advantage: Why Organizational Health Trumps Everything Else in Business* (San Francisco: Jossey Bass, 2012), 32.
[41] Ibid.
[42] Ibid., 33.

correct this type of misattribution takes "a measure of judgment and emotional intelligence."[43] High EI would allow a person to engage the system—whether a team, consistory, or congregation—in a way that more accurately reflects one's own emotions. That person would be able to openly name the emotions driving the situation because they have actively searched within and understand themselves. It is interesting to note that Hamman and Lencioni warn that most organizations tend to naturally cling to artificial harmony. I suggest that "artificial harmony" is created when leaders do not have a strong enough EI to name reality. High emotional intelligence allows people to acknowledge realities, even if it means conflict and disagreement.

Lencioni admits that "Nowhere does this tendency toward artificial harmony show itself more than in mission-driven nonprofit organizations, most notably churches."[44] When people can disagree amicably with emotions under control, a trust is built. Trust is at the heart of Christian ministry and pastoral functioning. "In a similar way that trust enables conflict, conflict allows a team to move on to the next critical behavior of a cohesive team: achieving commitment." Goleman et al. claim that "Empathy makes resonance possible; lacking empathy, leaders act in ways that create dissonance. Empathy builds on self-management, but that means expressing emotions as appropriate, not stifling them."[45] The pastoral leader, by exercising smart emotional intelligence and being authentically empathic, can facilitate a unified faith community and achieve commitment to God and fellow believers.

Relationship management

Goleman et al. identify the following as critical components of relationship management in understanding leadership:

1. Inspirational leadership: guiding and motivating with a compelling vision;
2. Influence: wielding a range of tactics for persuasion;
3. Developing others: bolstering others' abilities through feedback and guidance;
4. Change catalyst: initiating, managing, and leading in a new direction;
5. Conflict management: resolving disagreements;

---

[43] Ibid., 35.
[44] Ibid., 44.
[45] Goleman et al., *Primal Leadership*, 50.

6. Building bonds: cultivating and maintaining a web of relationships; and
7. Teamwork and collaboration: cooperation and team building.[46]

The pastor is the inspirational leader for a community of faith. Inspiration, although having many distinctions, tends to be defined and formed by emotions. Congregants will often look to the pastor for emotional cues regarding life together. The pastor's emotional reactions are often seen as the most authentic since they are housed in what is perceived as the most educated and spiritually informed person. Congregants will emulate the pastor's emotional reactions, thus making the pastor's demeanor pivotal in determining the behavior of the community. How the pastor manages emotions will often determine how the congregants live out their emotions. Goleman et al. write:

> But the impact on emotions goes beyond what a leader says... even when leaders were not talking, they were watched more carefully than anyone else in the group. When people raised a question for the group as a whole, they would keep their eyes on the leader to see his or her response. Indeed, group members generally see the leader's emotional reaction as the most valid response and so model their own on it—particularly in an ambiguous situation, where various members react differently. In a sense, the leader sets the emotional standard.[47]

That places an enormous responsibility on the pastoral leader. Not only do congregants see the pastor's emotional state as the one to adopt for themselves, they will also base their relationship with God in the same source. Scazzero states: "Emotional health is not only about ourselves and our relationships, it impacts our image of God, our hearing of God's voice, and our discernment of his will."[48] An example that comes to mind is one I have observed in various Reformed settings. If the pastor delights in the celebration of the Eucharist and presents it as an opportunity for renewal and spiritual strengthening, the body of believers will experience their relationship with God as edifying, nurturing, and renewing. If the pastor is a strict gatekeeper and emphasizes unworthiness and the need for repentance to avoid the punishment of a wrathful God before participating, the body of

---

[46] Goleman et al., *Primal Leadership*, 39.
[47] Ibid., 8-9.
[48] Scazzero, *Emotionally Healthy Spirituality*, 47.

believers will walk away feeling inadequate and unworthy, perhaps not even participating.

Emotional intelligence is a resource and a tool for the pastoral leader, who is in relationship with others and with God. As the leader relates to parishioners, the ability to grow emotionally will often coincide with the attainment of the gift of empathy. The capacity to show empathy is crucial if one desires to gain the trust of others. "Empathy *can* be learned,"[49] and I would suggest it becomes an integral part of one's emotional makeup as one recognizes the emotions of self and others. When one places themselves in another's shoes or does as Jesus commanded, that is, to do to others as you would have them do to you, it becomes natural and habitual. Once learned and assimilated into one's emotional DNA, it can serve as a valuable pastoral tool. The expression of empathy can be crucial in counseling situations. It can also show itself in the impromptu conversation in the church parking lot, where many pastoral encounters occur. It can bring simple healing in the modern context through a social media comment. A caring comment directed at one individual in a Facebook post can not only touch the heart of that person and bring healing, it might also touch thousands of others who happen to be a part of their friendship network. The capacity to show empathy, to be in touch emotionally, is not limited to pastoral encounters; it can also be expressed in sermons, especially with good illustrations and storytelling.

High emotional intelligence is often demonstrated through storytelling. As pastors, we face the challenge to inspire faith, to impact behavior in positive ways, and to "frame events and possibilities so as to help [our] followers think differently about the world and their places in it."[50] I would conjecture that emotional intelligence equips the pastor with the capacity to discern what stories to communicate clearly, so that they touch the matters of the heart of the listener. So that the listener, as Gardner would describe, is impacted in such a way that he or she is able to embody the story in his or her own life.[51]

Developing and improving emotional intelligence as pastoral leaders

Emotional intelligence is the ability of an individual to recognize and label one's own emotions and feelings. "By understanding what

---

[49] Jordan, *Emotional Intelligence Mastery*, 7.
[50] Garner, *Intelligence Reframed*, 126.
[51] Ibid.

emotional intelligence really is and how we can manage it in our lives, we can begin to leverage all of that intelligence, education, and experience we've been storing up for all these years."[52] If you are, like me, high on the "feeling" scale of the Myers-Briggs, it is a challenge to recognize and name my emotions before I have committed myself to expressing what I am feeling. A developed EI allows me to hesitate in the middle of a conversation and name a feeling such as anger, embarrassment, frustration, or irritation and manage my response. Then, as Eric Jordan says: "Once you can recognize your own feelings to a degree of certainty, you will then move to develop the ability to see emotions and feelings in others for what they are."[53] This is true for us as individuals as we function in our family of origin, as well as in groups. The power of a surge of uncontrolled emotions has the potential to be extremely harmful, especially in the context of the church. We increase our capacity to do effective ministry by developing and maturing our EI. More highly developed EI allows for emotional separation and maturity. Richardson says, "By gaining that kind of maturity, we can then think more clearly in the other powerful emotional systems we are part of, such as the church. The more objectivity we can gain in a high-anxiety and intense emotional area, like our families, the better we can function in these other systems."[54]

As for the pastoral leader, there are additional benefits to developing emotional intelligence. Jordan suggests that you can develop for yourself a

> personal ability to rein in or direct your emotions, to call on certain emotions, for instance, so that they help you perform better. Many of us understand that when we are experiencing strong anger and are explosively out-of-control, we cannot think clearly. If we cannot think clearly, we cannot make good decisions or act effectively.[55]

The angry and reactive pastor is incapable of expressing grace or bringing healing to broken situations. Pastoral leaders function best by being self-controlled, and that requires close monitoring of one's emotions and the expression of them. A developed EI allows the person to be reflective, as opposed to reactive, to bring comfort and empathy, rather than critique and judgment.

---

[52] Bradberry & Greaves, *Emotional Intelligence 2.0*, xvi.
[53] Jordan, *Emotional Intelligence Mastery*, 2.
[54] Richardson, *Becoming a Healthier Pastor*, 61.
[55] Jordan, *Emotional Intelligence Mastery*, 2.

Jordan adds another benefit to the improved EI:

> Your ability to not only manage your own strong emotions or expressed emotions, but to regulate them at will. This includes the ability to let go of, or even dissolve strong feelings—in the moment. Related to this is your interpersonal ability to help others manage or regulate their own feelings, such as calming down a tearful child, or helping a person through a period of grief or mourning.[56]

Developed or "smart" emotions provide the pastoral leader the ability to exercise self-control, to be less likely to be detoured by the reactivity of others, and to assist those they lead in controlling and coming to terms with their emotions.

Armstrong identifies twenty-five possible ways to develop intrapersonal (emotional) intelligence.[57] Of the twenty-five, I would suggest the following fifteen are especially pertinent for the pastoral leader:

1. Do individual counseling or psychotherapy work as a client.
2. Learn to meditate.
3. Write your autobiography.
4. Record and work with your dreams on a regular basis.
5. Read self-help books.
6. Establish a quiet place in your home for introspection.
7. Take a battery of tests designed to assess your special strengths and weaknesses in a broad range of areas.
8. Keep a daily journal or diary for recording your thoughts, feelings, goals, and memories.
9. Study the biographies and autobiographies of great individuals with powerful personalities.
10. Engage in daily self-esteem-enhancing behaviors (e.g., using positive self-talk, affirming your successes).
11. Attend the house of worship of your choice regularly.
12. Find out what your personal "myth" is and live it in the world.
13. Keep a mirror handy to look into when you are in different moods or states of mind.
14. Take ten minutes every evening to mentally review the various thoughts and feelings you had during the day.

---

[56] Ibid., 3.
[57] Armstrong, *7 Kinds of Smart*, 145.

15. Spend time with people who have a strong and healthy sense of self.[58]

Many of Armstrong's suggestions will lead a person to be alone and reflective. Meditation, journaling, and soul-searching are mostly solo activities that cultivate the capacity to experience oneself and God in more authentic ways. Intentional time alone is important as one seeks to develop emotional intelligence. Jaco Hamman would advance the concept of being alone to a higher level. He proposes one learn to be alone in the "presence of others." He suggests, "cultivating the capacity to be alone in the presence of others will impact your ministry in significant ways." This capacity "will help you become an empathic and compassionate presence. Empathy is that capacity to contain your own world and enter into the experiential world of another."[59] Hamman also provides both background and means for "living with the destructiveness of others, dialoging with your inner saboteur, and keeping appropriate sexual boundaries."[60] These are emotion-driven dimensions of the pastor's make-up that require self-awareness and self-control. It implies that pastors must develop the capacity to withdraw into their own person when surrounded by others whose lives may be in disarray and confusion and sort out the emotions of the situation. This will allow the pastor to bring calm, reason, and perhaps the voice of God to an otherwise explosive and destructive interaction.

Theologically, we need to be aware of the "inner saboteur" and recognize that in contrast to the saboteur, the power of God, through the Holy Spirit, operates internally within each Christian. "To each is given the manifestation of the Spirit for the common good. For to one is given through the Spirit the utterance of wisdom and to another the utterance of knowledge according to the same Spirit" (I Cor. 12:7-8, NRSV). The Heidelberg Catechism, Q&A 53 informs us regarding this internal resource as follows:

> Q. What do you believe concerning "The Holy Spirit?"
>
> A. First, that the Spirit, with the Father and the Son, is eternal God.
>
> Second, that the Spirit is given also to me, so that, through true faith, he makes me share in Christ and all his benefits through true faith, comforts me, and will remain with me forever.[61]

---

[58] Ibid., 145-46.
[59] Hamman, *Becoming a Pastor* (rev.), 144.
[60] Ibid.
[61] *Our Faith: Ecumenical Creeds, Reformed Confessions, and Other Resources* (Grand Rapids, MI: Faith Alive, 2013), 87.

A major resource for the pastor, in all aspects of ministry, and especially in the realm of emotions, is the Holy Spirit dwelling within. The Spirit can be an active and driving force in the development and maturation of emotions. The pastor has access to the internal movement of the Spirit through prayer.

Many experts in the emotional intelligence field argue that EI can be developed, improved, and tuned. Well-founded data suggests that over the course of life and vocation, people develop more strength in emotional intelligence competencies.[62] There is, however, no reason to think that a person's development can bring them over certain thresholds such as taking them from an active pew sitter to lead pastor of a congregation. But "if the right model is used, training can actually alter the brain centers that regulate negative and positive emotions."[63] Attention to the inner self and one's emotions can create a script of "mindfulness," the creation of a habit where one identifies, monitors, and controls emotions. "Mindfulness is a skill that helps people keenly focus on the present moment and drop distracting thoughts (such as worries) rather than getting lost in them, thus producing a calming effect."[64] Once a reasonable level of self-awareness is accomplished, and a clear picture of reality exists, "an antidote to the inertia of habit"[65] is created. Habit, whose reputation is normally one of stagnation and monotonous routine, when centered in mindfulness and grounded in a strong EI, is capable of producing the "power to evoke and articulate one's personal self-image and the shared ideals that flow from it—and so lead others in that same direction."[66] Habit can foster confidence in the leader, resulting in consistent responses. As responses become more predictable and "hard wired," individuals will lean into the emotional system created by the pastoral leader and gain a sense of health and stability. Trust is created.

Hamman also discusses the significance of mindfulness in the life of the pastor. He states, "Become mindful of your dreams, your feelings and thoughts, the smells and tastes of food, your relationships, the pieces of scripture you use, how you use language, and what motivates you. Be conscious of your own presence."[67] He stresses that the capacity

---

[62] Goleman et al., *Primal Leadership*, 101.
[63] Ibid., 103.
[64] Ibid., 103.
[65] Ibid., 126.
[66] Ibid., 126.
[67] Hamman, *Becoming a Pastor* (rev.), 139.

to monitor and control the "inner self" is critical to the pastor. In a similar sense, the concept of "mindfulness" is deeply imbedded in the self-therapy model of Internal Family Systems (IFS) mentioned earlier.

IFS and self-therapy assist the individual in identifying the various emotional parts, or personalities that reside in them. If one is in need of healing, the naming of the various parts can serve as a step toward healing. It also allows for the identification and management of emotions.

> Unlike many forms of therapy, IFS doesn't pathologize people. When we have problems in life, IFS doesn't see us as having a disease or deficit. It recognizes that we have the resources within us to solve our problems, though these resources may be blocked because of unconscious reactions to events in the past. IFS is designed to be self-led. It empowers you to take charge of your own growth because your true Self, not a therapist, is the agent of healing and wholeness. This makes IFS a natural vehicle for self-therapy."[68]

I include IFS because it is a self-therapy process available to pastoral leaders. It is accessible and affordable, and it recognizes the importance of self-awareness and emotional power. It is a practical tool for improving emotional intelligence.

With resources such as *Emotional Intelligence 2.0*, *Emotional Intelligence Mastery*, *7 Kinds of Smart*, and *IFS*, pastoral leaders have the means to positively impact their ministry and the life of their congregation. These resources include assessment tools and step-by-step exercises for improving emotional intelligence. Although not included in this essay, there are other resources available, such as Peter Scazzero's "*Emotionally Healthy Spirituality Course.*"

Goleman et al. repeatedly recommend that leaders take advantage of these worthwhile tools that improve emotional intelligence. "Strong leadership development processes are focused on emotional *and* intellectual learning, and they build on active, participatory work: action learning and coaching, where people use what they're learning to diagnose and solve real problems in their organizations."[69]

Being prepared to be emotionally aware and mature will empower pastoral leaders to lead the church in what has traditionally been and

---

[68] Early, *Self-Therapy*, Loc 250.
[69] Goleman et al., 234.

continues to be, a state of emotional chaos. Movements in the Reformed Church in America such as coaching networks and the Ridder Church Renewal Process have shown the effectiveness of this type of training. Thank you, Gregg Mast, for leading the way.

CHAPTER 4

Natural Theology, Historical Data, and Sexual Ethics: Controversy in the Interpretation of Romans 1

James Brownson

I am pleased to offer this reflection in honor of Gregg Mast's retirement from New Brunswick Theological Seminary. Gregg has been a good friend for many years, a gifted leader, and a tireless advocate on the issues addressed in this paper.

In my book *Bible, Gender, Sexuality: Reframing the Church's Debate on Same-Sex Relationships*,[1] I argue that Paul's discussion of same-sex relationships in Romans 1:24–27 presupposes an understanding of same-sex behavior that is driven by excessive and self-centered desire, a desire that refuses to be content with normal heterosexual relationships but rather is driven by an unquenchable thirst for the exotic.[2] Here is the text from Romans that I focus on:

> Therefore God gave them up in the lusts of their hearts to impurity, to the degrading of their bodies among themselves, because they exchanged the truth about God for a lie and worshiped and served the creature rather than the Creator, who is blessed forever! Amen. For this reason God gave them up to

[1] *Bible, Gender, Sexuality* (Grand Rapids, MI: Eerdmans), 2013.

degrading passions. Their women exchanged natural intercourse for unnatural, and in the same way also the men, giving up natural intercourse with women, were consumed with passion for one another. Men committed shameless acts with men and received in their own persons the due penalty for their error.

I further argue that the disposition narrated in these verses does not mesh well with the contemporary experience of gay and lesbian persons, whose sexual desire is not commonly driven by such a thirst for the exotic, but usually by simple attraction. Most gay and lesbian people have never experienced any sort of significant attraction to persons of the opposite sex. Hence, while some gay and lesbian persons may be driven by excessive or self-centered desire, not content with more normal gratification (particularly in contexts driven by promiscuity), this focus on excessive desire that we find in Romans 1 is problematic when applied to *all* gay and lesbian persons, especially those who seek to discipline sexual desire through long-term commitments to each other. Of course, the same distinction between excessive and self-centered desire on the one hand, and more moderated desire on the other, also applies to heterosexual persons.

Not all people, however, agree with this argument. N. T. Wright provides a good example of those who take a different perspective. In his book, *Paul for Everyone: Romans*, Wright offers a succinct counter argument to this way of looking at Romans 1.[3] He offers the following discussion that is relevant to this topic:

> Nor is it the case, as is sometimes suggested, that in the ancient world, homosexual relationships were normally either part of cult prostitution or a matter of older people exploiting younger ones, though both of these were quite common.
>
> Homosexual "marriages" were not unknown, as is shown by the example of Nero himself. Plato offers an extended discussion of the serious and sustained love that can occur between one male and another. The modern world has put various names on this phenomenon ("homosexual"; recently, "gay"; and its female counterpart, "lesbian"). These imprecise labels refer to a wide

---

[2] See particularly the chapters on lust and desire (149–78) and nature (223–55).
[3] *Paul for Everyone*, pt. 1, chs. 1-8 (Louisville, KY: Westminster John Knox Press, 2004), 19–24. Wright has reiterated this sort of argument in a YouTube video as recently as March 25, 2014. See https://www.youtube.com/watch?v=xKxvOMOmHeI and another video in 2009: https://www.youtube.com/watch?v=YpQHGPGejKs.

range of emotions and actions which it would be foolish to think only came to light in recent generations.

Paul's point, then, is not simply, "We Jews don't approve of this"; or, "Relationships like this are always unequal and exploitative." His point is, "This is not what males and females were made for."[4]

Wright is working here at a fairly popular level of discourse and does not go into detail to support his argument, but the main lines of his analysis are fairly clear and embraced by others as well. I want to identify several aspects of his argument and then evaluate them more thoroughly.

First, I want to evaluate Wright's argument, that since homosexual marriages were known in Paul's day, Paul must have rejected them, making it impossible under any circumstances for Christians to look sympathetically at gay or lesbian marriages today. Second, I want to further evaluate Wright's argument that, in Paul's view, same-sex relationships are "not what males and females were made for," and that this is what makes these relationships always morally wrong in Paul's mind. What is at stake in Wright's argument here is the underlying rationale that shapes Paul's argument in Romans 1.

I turn first to the question of whether Paul would have been aware of homosexual marriages that occurred in his time, particularly the same-sex marriages of the Roman emperor Nero. I remain unconvinced that the argument about Nero's marriages is relevant. I devoted a good bit of time in my book to discussing Nero's predecessor, Gaius Caligula, whose gay exploits as emperor Paul may well have had in mind in Romans 1.[5] But Nero had probably been emperor for only a short time when Paul wrote Romans in the mid- to late 50s, according to most scholars. The dates for Nero's same-sex marriages (the first probably took place in 64) make their relevance to the interpretation of Romans (written in the mid- to late 50s) quite unlikely. These marriages simply had not happened when Romans was written. In fact, there is no record of any same-sex marriages occurring in the Roman Empire at or before the time Paul's letter to the Romans was written. So it is rather problematic, at least on this count, to assume that Paul had same-sex marriages in mind in Romans 1.

But this only raises a more critical question: was Paul aware of the discussion in Plato's *Symposium*, and the speech in that document

---

[4] *Paul for Everyone*, 22.
[5] Ibid., 156ff.

by Aristophanes which seemed to presuppose something like an inherent, same-sex sexual orientation? Is this knowledge presupposed and rejected in Romans 1? In Wright's quote above, he seems clearly to assume this is the case.

It certainly is the case that the speech by Aristophanes in Plato's *Symposium* seemed to presuppose something at least akin to the modern notion of sexual orientation. In his speech, he claimed that initially, all humans existed in binary, spherical pairs of three sorts: male-female, male-male, and female-female. These were created in this fashion by the gods. But when these binary spherical figures began to conspire against the gods, Zeus and the other gods decided to cut these paired beings into separate halves to diminish their power. After this action by Zeus and the other gods, humans were left longing to be reunited with their original other half. This, according to Aristophanes in his speech in Plato's *Symposium*, was the origin of erotic love or desire (Greek ἐρῶς—a word that is only rarely used positively in the Greek tradition).

But it is worth noting first, that even in the speech by Aristophanes, we see the dynamics of excessive desire. Those men and women who were originally part of a male-female pair (i.e., those with heterosexual desire) were said by Aristophanes to be the source of "adulterers" (Greek μοιχοί).[6] So even in its original context, this vision articulated by Aristophanes was not intended to portray the origin of marriage but rather of sexual desire, *particularly when that desire was present in excess*. Moreover, in Aristophanes' speech, the products of the original male-male bonds (i.e., those with gay desire) were said to be "boy-lovers" (Greek παιδεραστής, from which we get the word "pederast"),[7] suggesting that, even for Aristophanes, a nonegalitarian and pederastic relationship was in view, rather than one of mutuality and equality. So this speech can scarcely be construed, even in its original context, as one that spoke about the modern notion of sexual orientation or gay marriage, at least in categories that most folks would find relevant and meaningful today.

But I have not yet explored Paul's knowledge and use of these categories. So let us return again to Wright's quote cited above:

> Nor is it the case, as is sometimes suggested, that in the ancient world, homosexual relationships were normally either part of cult prostitution or a matter of older people exploiting younger

[6] Section 191D–E.
[7] Section 192B.

ones, though both of these were quite common. Homosexual "marriages" were not unknown, as is shown by the example of Nero himself. Plato offers an extended discussion of the serious and sustained love that can occur between one male and another.[8]

As I have already observed, it is unlikely that the vast majority of readers in the ancient world, even in the Greek tradition, would understand Aristophanes to be speaking of marriage or of any sort of "serious and sustained love." Adulterers certainly do not qualify for such a description. Aristophanes was speaking of sexual desire and its origin, not of marriage. But let us try to assess what Paul would have thought of this speech by Aristophanes if he had been aware of it.

What is most critical to understand is that, from a Jewish perspective (in which Paul was shaped), the speech by Aristophanes in Plato's *Symposium* represents an alternative creation story. Different gods were at work, in comparison to Genesis 1-2, and human beings were created within a completely different narrative. Thus, from Paul's perspective, one simply had to choose between the speech by Aristophanes and the account in Genesis; both simply could not be true. Paul, of course, sided with the Genesis account, believing that the God to whom Jesus points us is the God described in the Genesis stories.

Consequently, like most other Jews and Christians of his time, Paul had to come up with a different explanation for the origin of same-sex behavior. Because Plato's *Symposium* was not a narrative that could be accepted by Jews or Christians, given its alternative vision of creation and alternative deities, this story could not be used to explain the origin of same-sex behavior or desire.

What then was the origin of same-sex desire for these Jews and Christians who could not embrace the vision found in Plato's *Symposium*? Why did some men want to have sex with other men or boys? As I argue in my book, the alternative origin of such desire embraced by Jews and Christians in the ancient world can be clearly found in a vision of *excessive* desire. That vision was also already present in the larger culture. The Roman orator Dio Chrysostom, for example, who wrote shortly after Paul's time, speaks of same-sex eroticism as the manifestation of insatiable lust:

> The man whose appetite is insatiate in such things, when he finds there is no scarcity, no resistance, in this field, will have contempt

[8] Ibid., 22.

for the easy conquest and scorn for a woman's love, as a thing too readily given—in fact, too utterly feminine—and will turn his assault against the male quarters, eager to befoul the youth who will very soon be magistrates and judges and generals, believing that in them he will find a kind of pleasure difficult and hard to procure. His state is like that of men who are addicted to drinking and wine-bibbing, who after long and steady drinking of unmixed wine, often lose their taste for it and create an artificial thirst by the stimulus of sweating, salted foods, and condiments.[9]

The early Jewish philosopher and theologian Philo, writing a bit earlier than Paul, makes a similar equation between same-sex eroticism and self-centered lust that refuses any boundaries. He comments on the story of Sodom and Gomorrah:

> The land of the Sodomites, a part of the land of Canaan afterwards called Palestinian Syria, was brimful of innumerable iniquities, particularly such as arise from gluttony and lewdness, and multiplied and enlarged every other possible pleasure with so formidable a menace that it had at last been condemned by the Judge of All. The inhabitants owed this extreme license to the never-failing lavishness of their sources of wealth, for, deep-soiled and well-watered as it was, the land had every year a prolific harvest of all manner of fruits, and the chief beginning of evils, as one has aptly said, is goods in excess. Incapable of bearing such satiety, plunging like cattle, they threw off from their necks the law of nature and applied themselves to deep drinking of strong liquor and dainty feeding and forbidden forms of intercourse. Not only in their mad lust for women did they violate the marriages of their neighbours, but also men mounted males without respect for the sex nature which the active partner shares with the passive; and so when they tried to beget children they were discovered to be incapable of any but a sterile seed.[10]

Note that in both of these contemporaneous texts I have cited, there is a clear echo of the language found in Romans 1:27, which

---

[9] Dio Chrysostom, *Dio Chrysostom*, trans. J. W. Cohoon and H. Lamar Crosby, Loeb Classical Library (London/New York: W. Heinemann/G. P. Putnam's Son's, 1932), 7:152; 1:373.

[10] *De Abr.*, 133–35; cited from Philo, *Philo*, trans. F. H. Colson, 9 vols., Loeb Classical Library (Cambridge, UK: Cambridge University Press, 1935), 6:69f.

speaks of men who, "giving up [or to translate more accurately, "leaving behind"] natural intercourse with women, were consumed with passion for one another." There is a similar connection between idolatry, excessive lust, and perversion in the *Wisdom of Solomon*, a Jewish apocryphal text dating from a period not long before Paul's writings:

> For the idea of making idols was the beginning of fornication, and the invention of them was the corruption of life; . . . For whether they kill children in their initiations, or celebrate secret mysteries, or hold frenzied revels with strange customs, they no longer keep either their lives or their marriages pure, but they either treacherously kill one another or grieve one another by adultery, and all is a raging riot of blood and murder, theft and deceit, corruption, faithlessness, tumult, perjury, confusion over what is good, forgetfulness of favors, defiling of souls, sexual perversion, disorder in marriages, adultery, and debauchery. For the worship of idols not to be named is the beginning and cause and end of every evil.[11]

Let us review the argument that is emerging here: whether or not Paul knew of the speech by Aristophanes in Plato's *Symposium*, he would not and could not have accepted its vision of how humans came into being, and thus he would also have rejected this narrative as an acceptable explanation for the origin of same-sex desire. Instead, Paul embraces two basic observations that are well documented in multiple sources among some Roman writers, and especially among Jews and Christians in the ancient world. As seen in the *Wisdom of Solomon*, Jews and Christians made a close connection between idolatry and excessive or self-centered desire (quite apart from speculation about the origin of same-sex desire). Moreover, as noted earlier in the quotes, both from Dio Chrysostom and from Philo, Roman and Jewish writers also developed an alternative explanation of the origin of same-sex desire. They stated that same-sex desire was driven by excessive lust which was not content with mere heterosexual gratification but was driven by a thirst for the exotic.

This is why Paul focuses so much on the language of lust and passion in Romans 1:24-27. Look again at the key quote where I have italicized the references to lust and passion in Paul's depiction of same-sex desire:

[11] *Wisdom*, 14:12, 23-28.

> Therefore, God gave them up in the *lusts* of their hearts to impurity, to the degrading of their bodies among themselves, because they exchanged the truth about God for a lie and worshiped and served the creature rather than the Creator, who is blessed forever! Amen. For this reason, God gave them up to *degrading passions*. Their women exchanged natural intercourse for unnatural, and in the same way also, the men, giving up natural intercourse with women, were *consumed with passion* for one another. Men committed shameless acts with men and received in their own persons the due penalty for their error.

Here is the same threefold linkage between excessive lust/passion, idolatry, and same-sex desire. Paul is clearly operating with standard Jewish categories found in many other ancient documents. And this is, of course, exactly what one might look for at this point in Paul's overall argument in the letter. The rhetoric of Romans makes it clear that Paul expects, at this point in the letter, for his readers to be fully and completely agreeing with him, judging such excessively self-centered, overly passionate, and idolatrous pagans to be deserving of the judgment of God. That is what makes the opening of Romans 2 such a powerful rhetorical ploy: "Therefore you have no excuse, whoever you are, when you judge others; for in passing judgment on another, you condemn yourself, because you, the judge, are doing the very same things."[12] So Paul is making a standard kind of argument in Romans 1, fully expecting that his readers—both Jews and Christians—would wholeheartedly agree with his linkage between idolatry, excessive passion, and same-sex behavior.

So let us return again to the final portion of Wright's quote, with which this study began:

> Paul's point, then, is not simply "We Jews do not approve of this"; or "Relationships like this are always unequal and exploitative." His point is, "This is not what males and females were made for."[13]

In light of the exploration pursued thus far, it seems evident that Wright's explanation is not so much wrong as it is incomplete. He leaves out what for both Paul and his readers would have been the most important point: the link between idolatry (Paul's primary focus in Romans 1, see verse 23) and excessive and self-centered passion and

---

[12] Romans 2:1 (NRSV).
[13] Ibid., 22.

the tendency, because of that excessive passion, to "suppress the truth" about God and to descend into greater and greater corruption. One might even grant that Paul's point included the notion that "This is not what males and females were made for," but this cannot be at the center of Paul's concern. At the center of Paul's concern in this chapter is the link between idolatry and excessive, self-centered passion. It is that linkage that causes people to "suppress the truth," even including perhaps the truth about "what males and females were made for."

But this, of course, raises the dilemma already cited when trying to understand the contemporary experience of gay and lesbian persons and to relate this experience back to Paul's perspective in Romans 1. Paul centrally links same-sex behavior in Romans 1 with excessive desire. All the participants in the contemporary debate over same-sex relationships might well agree that whenever people are motivated by excessive and self-centered desire (whether gay or straight), that this is evidence of their alienation from God. But what interpretation should be made of gay and lesbian persons who have never had significant desire for persons of the opposite sex and whose desire for persons of the same sex may or may not be driven by excessive passion or selfishness?

Wright wants to say that Paul's focus on excessive passion is peripheral, and Paul's focus on the "structural" differences between men and women is fundamental. Hence, in his view, even though Paul's language about excessive or self-centered passion may not apply to the experience of contemporary gay and lesbian Christians, the "structural" argument against same-gender sexuality must continue to be understood as binding. My response, however, is to return to the language of Romans 1. I find that the references to excessive passion occur multiple times there and are amply documented in other sources from the same period. I do not, however, find the "structural" argument explicit in Romans 1 as the grounds for a rejection of same-sex desire. From my perspective, therefore, Wright seems to focus on what is peripheral and/or absent and to neglect what seems obvious in the text. This, I would argue, is simply bad exegesis.

But what about the language of "nature" in Romans 1? Is not that, in some sense, an appeal to "structure" and to biology, rendering it applicable, regardless of sexual orientation? Even though Wright does not mention this directly, it seems to be presupposed in what he says. Yet even here, Wright's case is problematic. I refer the reader to my chapter on nature for a full discussion of these issues,[14] but let me

---

[14] *Bible, Gender, Sexuality*, 223-55.

here refer back to the use of the word "nature" in the quote I discussed earlier from Philo:

> The land of the Sodomites, a part of the land of Canaan afterwards called Palestinian Syria, was brimful of innumerable iniquities, particularly such as arise from gluttony and lewdness, and multiplied and enlarged every other possible pleasure with so formidable a menace that it had at last been condemned by the Judge of All. The inhabitants owed this extreme license to the never-failing lavishness of their sources of wealth, for, deep-soiled and well-watered as it was, the land had every year a prolific harvest of all manner of fruits, and the chief beginning of evils, as one has aptly said, is goods in excess. Incapable of bearing such satiety, plunging like cattle, they threw off from their necks the *law of nature*[15] and applied themselves to deep drinking of strong liquor and dainty feeding and forbidden forms of intercourse. Not only in their mad lust for women did they violate the marriages of their neighbours, but also men mounted males without respect for the sex nature which the active partner shares with the passive; and so, when they tried to beget children, they were discovered to be incapable of any but a sterile seed.[16]

Note in Philo's comments how the abandonment of the "law of nature" leads to "deep drinking of strong liquor" and "dainty feeding," as well as "forbidden forms of intercourse." In other words, "nature" is what teaches moderation and propriety, and the abandonment of nature is part and parcel of an excessive indulgence of desire and passion. Hence, in the ancient world, appeals to "nature" were not primarily, and certainly not exclusively, concerned with biology (that makes no sense of Philo's references to drinking or feeding) but rather to a comprehensive ethic focused on moderation, propriety, and self-control. Biology is not excluded, as is evident in the reference to "sex nature" a few lines after the reference to the "law of nature" above. But these biological references are clearly subordinate to an overall emphasis on moderation and self-control. This focus on moderation is entirely consistent with Paul's usage of this word in Romans 1 and brings our focus back from "structural" considerations to concerns focusing on

---

[15] Greek τῆς φύσεως νόμον, using the same Greek word (φύσις) we find in Romans 1.
[16] *De Abr.*, 133–35; cited from Philo, *Philo*, trans. F. H. Colson, 9 vols., Loeb Classical Library (Cambridge, UK: Cambridge University Press, 1935), 6:69f.

excessive passion. And this, of course, brings up again the difficulty in applying this to all gay and lesbian persons, particularly since modern folk know more about the cause of same-sex behavior than did those ancient Christians and Jews. Most people now recognize that same-sex behavior is not driven by *excessive* passion but by a desire that is ordered differently in the brains and bodies of LGBT folks, in comparison with the brains and bodies of straight people.

This does not mean that Christians must return to the speech of Aristophanes to develop an etiology of same-sex desire. This is unacceptable for Christians today, as it was for Christians in the ancient world. But it does mean that folks today should call into question what Jews, Christians, and others in the ancient world simply assumed: that same-sex desire or behavior arose from excessive, self-centered, and overly exotic passions. Wherever, in the contemporary world, we see same-sex behavior (or heterosexual behavior) driven by excessive or self-centered passion, particularly in promiscuous contexts, then the teaching of Paul is directly applicable, and such behavior should be viewed as evidence of humanity's alienation from God. But where such excessive or self-centered passion is not evident and where straight, gay, or lesbian persons seek to discipline their desires by biblical principles of moderation, by living out the biblical link between sexuality and kinship (as I argue in my book[17]), then we ought not to assume that Paul's argument in Romans 1 applies to their lives, and we should not, on that basis, categorically reject their experiences of intimacy.

---

[17] See *Bible, Gender Sexuality* (Grand Rapids, MI: Eerdmans, 2013), especially 86-90.

CHAPTER 5

Bodies of Joy: German Gospel Choirs and the Church

Fritz West

German gospel choirs stimulate the German church and its congregations.[1] The reforms of the Roman Catholic Church enacted by the Second Vatican Council (1962-65) offer a parallel. Pope John XIII (1958-63) began the council with a consideration of the liturgy. He had other options. Of the three aspects of revelation entrusted to the church—doctrine, order, and liturgy—John could have begun with doctrine, as did the First Vatican Council (1870), or order, as did the Council of Constance (1414-18). He started with the liturgy, knowing as a pastor that the whole liturgical complexus of sacred signs, gestures, and rites imparts to the assembly the other two legs of the stool.[2] The dictum *lex orandi statuat lex credendi* conveys the reality that the

---

[1] This article is based primarily on interviews of persons involved in or with knowledge of the European gospel choir movement conducted in February of 2014: Peter Dych, Mark W. Lewis, Thomas Risager, and Peter Steinvig in Denmark; Martin Bartleworth, Adrienne Morgan-Hammond, Angelika Rehaag, Nikolaus Schneider, and Elke Wisse in Germany. Given the currency and culture of this movement, most literature is found in digital format on the web.

[2] Massimo Faggioli, *True Reform. Liturgy and Ecclesiology in Sacrosanctum Concilium* (Collegeville, MN: Liturgical Press, 2012), 10-18.

liturgy shapes what a Christian believes.[3] The liturgy also projects an ecclesiology. The Constitution on the Sacred Liturgy, with the image of the assembly gathered about the altar where the priest ministers, representing the bishop, posits a conciliar image of the body of Christ to contrast with the monarchical church. In its worship, the church projects its understanding of faith and order.[4]

Gospel choirs, whose singing is an aspect of worship, similarly convey understanding of belief and order. After reviewing how the German gospel choir movement emerged, I will reflect upon "bodies of joy." When singing gospel music, both a choir and its members become "bodies of joy," with implications for the life of the church.

Emergence

For many, mention of African American music in Germany brings Dietrich Bonhoeffer (1906-1945) to mind. While visiting Union Theological Seminary in the 1930s, he was impressed by the spirituals he heard sung in Harlem's "Negro" churches. Bonhoeffer brought back to Germany phonograph records by gospel choirs and quartets, which he had played for colleagues and students.[5] Although Bonhoeffer witnesses to the appeal that African American music has for German sensibility, he neither introduced it to the German people nor initiated the present-day gospel choir movement.

Black music from America was brought to Germany by the Fisk Jubilee Singers in the 1870s. Fisk University, one of dozens of schools founded to educate freed slaves during the Reconstruction Era (1865-

---

[3] Prosper of Acquitaine, *Liber praeteritorum sedis apostolicae episcoporum auctoritates de gratia dei et libero voluntatis arbitrio* VIII, PL 51:209-10.

[4] Constitution on the Sacred Liturgy, ch. 3, notably §C ¶33, §E ¶41 and 42.

[5] Dietrich Bonhoeffer, *Barcelona, Berlin, Amerika 1928-1931*, Hrsg. Reinhart Staats und Hans Christoph von Hase, et al., Dietrich Bonhoeffer Werke, 10. Bd. (München: Chr. Kaiser Verlag, 1991), 224, 274-75 [ET=Dietrich Bonhoeffer, *Barcelona, Berlin, New York: 1928-1931*, Dietrich Bonhoeffer Works (Minneapolis: Fortress, 2008), 10:269-314, 315] and Dietrich Bonhoeffer, *Illegale Theologen-Ausbildung Sammelvikariate 1937-1940*, Hrsg. Dirk Schulz, Dietrich Bonhoeffer Werke, 15. Bd. (München: Chr. Kaiser Verlag, 1998), 454 [ET=Dietrich Bonhoeffer, *Theological Education Underground 1937-1940*, Dietrich Bonhoeffer Works (Minneapolis: Fortress, 2012), 10:457-58]. For his playing Negro spirituals for colleagues, vide Eberhard Bethge, *Dietrich Bonhoeffer. A Biography* (Minneapolis: Fortress Press, rev. ed. 2000), 208; for his playing it for students at Finkenwalde, vide Wolf-Dieter Zimmermann, *I Knew Dietrich Bonhoeffer* (New York: Harper & Row, 1966), 64-65. Andrew Root, *Bonhoeffer as Youth Worker* (Grand Rapids, MI: Baker Academic, 2014), 83-84.

77),[6] was nearly bankrupt when George L. White (1838-1895), a white northern missionary serving the school as both treasurer and music director, struck upon the idea of a touring choir. When an eclectic repertoire of abolitionist, temperance, popular songs, and spirituals attracted only modest numbers, the group was inspired to sing their "jubilee." They had experienced the Jubilee promise of God fulfilled (Leviticus 25)—some while enslaved—that every fifty years, debts would be forgiven and slaves freed. With their jubilee style of singing, which used four-part harmony to develop the melody lines of spirituals, the group conveyed to audiences the sorrow and the hope that they had known.[7] From 1871 to 1878, the original Fisk Jubilee Singers toured the United States and Europe, including Germany, successfully raising money for their struggling alma mater.[8] In Europe, black music—first spirituals and later gospel—continued to be sung in the jubilee style even after World War II, influentially through the Golden Gate Quartet (1931-), which moved to Paris in 1959.[9] In the same period, Europeans increasingly heard gospel, the genre of black music that emerged in the early twentieth century.[10] Mahalia Jackson (1911-1972) and other black gospel singers toured Europe widely[11]; the Armed Forces Radio Network and black American GIs brought spirituals, jazz, and gospel to occupied Germany. In the 1960s, Langston Hughes' *Black Nativity* toured Europe, including a broadcast on German television.[12]

Although all these factors, along with folk music in the 1970s, prepared for the present-day German gospel choir movement,[13] the origin

[6] Fisk University, Nashville, Tennessee, was founded in 1866 by the American Missionary Association, an organization dedicated to the abolition of slavery and the education of freed men and women. Clara Merrit DeBoer, "Blacks and the American Missionary Association," in *Hidden Histories in the United Church of Christ*, ed. Barbara Brown Zikmund (New York: United Church Press, 1984), 1:81-94.
[7] Donna M. Co, "Religious Songs of the Negro," in *Encyclopedia of American Gospel Music*, ed. W. K. McNeil (New York/London: Routledge, 2010), 312a-313b; and Sherry Sherrod DuPree, "Spirituals," in *Encyclopedia*, 366a-369a.
[8] Andrew Ward, ed., *Dark Midnight When I Rise: The Story of the Jubilee Singers Who Introduced the World to the Music of Black America* (New York: Farrar, Straus, and Giroux, 2000), esp. 338-72.
[9] Robert Darden, "The Golden Gate Quartet," 141b-143a, in *Encyclopedia*.
[10] Mel R. Wilhoit, "Performance Styles," 293a-294b in *Encyclopedia*.
[11] Richard Carlin, "Mahalia Jackson," 199a-200b, in *Encyclopedia*.
[12] Robert M Marovich, *A City Called Heaven: Chicago and the Birth of Gospel Music* (Urbana, IL: University of Illinois Press, 2015), 249; and https://en.wikipedia.org/wiki/Black_Nativity, accessed 12/28/2016.
[13] Interview: Nicholas Schneider, Berlin, Germany, February 2014. In the German Protestant Church, a YMCA songbook containing folk and African American music was widely used in youth gatherings and groups. On occasion this music made its way into congregational worship services. *Die Mundorgel: Ein Liederbuch für Fahrt und*

of gospel choirs was Scandinavian. Influential choirs, like the Joybells (1963-) and Choralerna (1968-81) in Sweden, the Oslo Gospel Choir (1988-) in Norway, and the Kefas Gospel Choir (1975-) in Denmark, spread the good news, while annual workshops, held in Stockholm, Sweden (1988-), Oslo (early 1980s-) and Porsgrunn, Norway (1980s-2000), and Copenhagen, Denmark (1992-2015), provided training for singers and choir directors. These workshops established a pattern still in use: one or two days of workshops and rehearsals, initially always led by a American black gospel singer, ending with a concert performed by the workshop participants. Hundreds attended these workshops, thousands their concerts.[14]

From Scandinavia, the gospel choir movement circled the globe, spreading first to Western European countries with a Protestant history (Germany, the Netherlands, Switzerland, and the United Kingdom), and later—more modestly—to countries with a Catholic history (Austria, France, Italy, and Spain). With the end of the Cold War, gospel singing became more common in former Soviet satellite countries, the Baltics and those in Eastern Europe. The Gospel Fellowship International in Denmark has helped "more than 30 gospel music pioneers in Serbia, Bulgaria, Belarus, Ukraine, Czech Republic, and in Poland . . . start gospel choirs."[15] An unsystematic Google search finds gospel choirs in sub-Saharan Africa, primarily in former British colonies where English is spoken.[16] In Japan and Australia, gospel choirs are well established.[17]

Lager (Köln: Evangelisches Jungmännerwerk, Kreisverband, 1970). ET: *Mouth Organ: A Songbook for on the Road and in Camp*, translation mine; and https://de.wikipedia.org/wiki/Mundorgel_(Liederbuch), accessed 12/17/2016.

[14] For the Scandinavian roots of European gospel: Mark W. Lewis, *The Diffusion of Black Gospel Music in Postmodern Denmark*, Asbury Theological Seminary Series in World Christian Revitalization Movements in Intercultural Studies 3 (Lexington, KY: Emeth Press, 2010), 47-76 and www.berlin-gospel-web.de.gospelineuropa.html, accessed 1/16/2017. For Sweden: http://www.gospelflava.com/articles/gospelaroundtheworld-sweden.html, accessed 12/17/2016; http://home.swipnet.se/choir-Brandstrom/Choralerna/Historik/choralerna-historik.htm, accessed 12/15/2016; and http://www.joybells.se/english, accessed 1/17/2017. For Norway: http://www.oslogospelchoir.net/about-us, accessed 12/15/2016; and http://www.gospelflava.com/articles/gospelaroundtheworld-norway.html, accessed 12/15/2016. For Denmark: Lewis, *Diffusion*, 47-76, http://sn.dk/Greve/En-dansk-gospel-pioner-fylder-60-aar/artikel/502593, accessed 12/15/2016; and http://kefas.dk/wp-content/uploads/2014/09/KEFAS_PR_English2016-2.pdf, accessed 1/1/2017.

[15] http://www.hanschristianpresents.com/support/, accessed 12/19/2016.

[16] For example, http://answersafrica.com/african-gospel-music-videos.html, accessed 12/19/2016. Otherwise Google searches for "gospel choir" and individual countries regularly brings up sites and YouTube videos.

[17] Melvin L. Butler, "Globalization of Gospel," 139-41, in *Encyclopedia*; http://www.

This music, however, did not migrate without change. "The globalization of gospel ... involves not only the worldwide spread of this music but also its localization by musicians and audiences situated around the globe and the steady appropriation of global sounds by North America-based gospel musicians."[18]

The first gospel choir in Germany predates the movement: the Paul Robeson Choir, formed out of a youth center in the Friedrichhain neighborhood of East Berlin (1963-).[19] The affiliation with Paul Robeson (1898-1976), which the choir specifically requested, and Robeson personally granted, was telling. While Robeson's communist leanings certainly played a role, so did his reputation as a black civil rights leader. Over the years, Dr. Martin Luther King Jr. has enjoyed similar esteem throughout Germany, with church members of the erstwhile Deutsche Demokratische Republik (East Germany) feeling a particular affinity.[20] Gospel choirs began forming in the former Bundesrepublik Deutschlands (West Germany) during the 1970s. Edwin Hawkins' (1943-) hit recording of "Oh Happy Day" (1967) sparked the movement, and Bonhoeffer's love for African American music lent an imprimatur. The number of choirs increased rapidly in the West during the 1980s, in former East Germany—more modestly— in the 1990s, after the fall of the wall.[21]

---

gospelflava.com/articles/gospelaroundtheworld.html, accessed 12/19/2016; and E. Patrick Johnson, *Appropriating Blackness* (Durham and London: Duke University Press, 2003), 160-218.

[18] Butler, "Globalization of Gospel," in *Encyclopedia*, 141.

[19] http://www.paul-robeson-chor.de/ and http://www.paul-robeson-chor.de/chorannalen/paul-robeson/, accessed 12/15/2016. In the latter article, one reads, "In the GDR [German Democratic Republic], Paul Robeson was appreciated as an artist and civil rights activist. He visited East Berlin several times and received the honorary doctorate of the Humboldt University in 1960. In the same year, the Academy of Arts of the GDR called him a corresponding member. After his last appearance in East Berlin in 1963, the former youth choir Friedrichshain asked him to bear his [sic] name. Paul Robeson received his honorary membership for lifetime and the membership card No. 1. Paul Robeson himself sang songs such as "Ol 'Man River" and "Deep River." She [sic] and other well-known spirituals still belong to the repertoire of the Paul Robeson choir" [translation mine].

[20] http://www.berliner-zeitung.de/berlin/sophienkirche-berlin-wo-schon-martin-luther-king-predigte,10809148,23322094.html, accessed 12/17/2016; and http://www.spiegel.de/einestages/martin-luther-king-in-ost-berlin-a-948492.html, accessed 12/17/2016.

[21] Bernd Grimmel, "Gospelmusik in Deutschland," http://bernd-grimmel.beepworld.de/gospelindeutschl.htm, accessed 1/13/2016; Bernd Grimmel, "Gospel Around the World: Germany (Part I: History)," http://www.gospelflava.com/articles/gospelaroundtheworld-germany1.html, accessed 1/13/2016; and Bernd Grimmel and Sebastian Hensch, "Gospel Around the World, Germany (Part II: Influences),"

As a 2009 survey of German gospel choirs demonstrates, gospel music and choirs are now woven into the warp and woof of German religious and cultural life.[22] There were then three thousand gospel choirs with one hundred thousand members, with further growth expected.[23] The average age of singers is forty-two: 29 percent falling between the ages of twelve and thirty and 37 percent between ages thirty-one and fifty.[24] Their education level is above average: 56 percent hold at least an advanced degree from a technical college,[25] and 80 percent of participants are women, 10 percent higher than other mixed German choirs.[26] Gospel choirs sing traditional gospel (83 percent), African gospel (61 percent), contemporary gospel (60 percent), and Christian pop (52 percent).[27] Practically all choirs (98 percent) sing in English, though 60 percent also use German and 48 percent another language.[28] Gospel choirs have a significant relationship to the church. Three-quarters of the choirs have some relationship to a congregation, either as a congregational choir or as a community choir sponsored by

---

http://www.gospelflava.com/articles/gospelaroundtheworld-germany2.html, accessed 1/13/2016.

[22] Petra-Angela Ahrens, *BeGeisterung durch Gospelsingen. Erste Bundesweite Befragung von Gospelchören* (Hannover: Sozialwissenschaftliches Institut der EKD, 2009), downloadable from https://www.si-ekd.de/downloads/22877.html, accessed 12/17/2016. This survey, whose title freely translates as InSpiriting through gospel singing, and which—in collaboration with the Creative Kirche—was sponsored by the Protestant Church in Germany, gathered data on gospel choirs in Germany nationwide. All quotes from this survey cited below are translations of mine from the German.

The primary focus of the survey is gospel choirs and the church. This is by no means a necessary connection. Seventy-seven percent of the gospel choirs in Germany are church related, 23 percent are not (pp. 16-18). Although the survey takes these independent choirs into account in the sample as a whole, it does not analyze them as a distinct a group. Thus questions like, How is the "good news" message of gospel music understood by choirs independent of the church? Does gospel music have a converting power in this setting? and Does the common life of the nonchurch choirs have a religious dimension? are not addressed. Since my focus is church-related choirs, this omission does not lessen the utility of this survey for this article.

[23] Ahrens, *BeGeisterung*, 5. These numbers can only be guesstimates. Statistics are hard to come by since choirs come and go, are often local phenomenon with a low profile, and the term "gospel choir" is at times ambiguous.

[24] Ibid., 10-11.
[25] Ibid., 12.
[26] Ibid., 10-11.
[27] Ibid., 21.
[28] Ibid., 20.

a congregation.[29] Choirs often meet on church property (61 percent),[30] and worship is the most common venue for singing in public (60 percent).[31]

The explosion of gospel choirs in Germany calls for an explanation. One aspect is common to all gospel singers rooted in Western culture: gospel music provides a socially acceptable form of *ecstasis*; it allows persons to break through the *stasis* of decorum and constraint generally found in Western culture in order to express one's feelings freely. As joy follows, there is a catharsis of release and rejoicing. To be sure, release is also engendered by performances of other musical genres influenced by African American culture, as for example, in rock concerts. Such release, however, is not socially acceptable to everyone, including many elderly in the church. Some place the raw rebellion, overt sexuality, and incipient violence of rock music beyond the pale. Although gospel music pushes the envelope of church etiquette, its Christian content and relative restraint renders it more acceptable for use in worship.[32] In addition, however, gospel music may also address a specifically German cultural need. Martha Bayles (1948-) argues that, despite German's long and strong musical tradition, its history constrains the use of indigenous music forms for expressing emotion. "The Germans . . . are, for compelling historical reasons dating back to the Third Reich, overly rationalistic and distrustful of emotion and communal enthusiasm." German folk music and the romantic tradition, both emotionally expressive, are tainted for their Nazi associations. For its part, twentieth-century German art music either subordinates feeling (Serialism) or deems it disruptive (Expressionism). German popular music, on the other hand, is mostly imported, primarily American and British pop. "Rather than deplore this situation," Bayles contends, "one might ask which of the many imported musical styles best addresses the need of thoughtful young Germans to grapple with their problematic history while at the same time get on with their lives. . . . Enter gospel music, a music that looks backward at a traumatic history but also forward to a hopeful future." In a happy conjuncture of cultural forms, so Bayles maintains, gospel music in Germany has found a home in a venerable musical tradition: the choral society, a place for both feeling

---

[29] Ibid., 16-17.
[30] Ibid., 6.
[31] Ibid., 23.
[32] Lewis, *Diffusion*, 58, 93-116; Johnson, *Appropriating Blackness*, 187-88; interview: Peter Steinvig, Ørsted, Denmark, February 2014.

and fellowship. "The German people feel a lot of sadness because of all they have been through. Gospel music helps them feel joy."[33]

The embodiment of joy

Let us return to the parallel between the conciliar reforms of Vatican II and church-related German gospel choirs. John XXIII placed liturgical reform at the top of the agenda, aware that worship reflects, shapes, and conveys the doctrine and order of the church. In the life of the German church, gospel music—worship both in itself and in the liturgy—shapes the faith and order of the choir. This happens as a singer's experience of his physical body informs the social body of the choir. Gospel music is a kinesthetic form in which feelings of both release and joy are felt in and expressed through the free use of one's body. Here one finds an interplay of cultures. Just as gospel music sung in the black style provides an occasion for using one's body freely, so both the message (sorrow and joy) and the medium (kinesthetic choral singing) provide a path for Germans to release and rejoice. This experience of the physical body has implications for the social body. First of all, the shared experience of physical spontaneity creates a powerful bond of social cohesion among choir members.[34] Second, the kinesthetic release provides avenues to think about the choir's social body and engage with it. While gospel singing brings vibrancy and vitality to worship, gospel choirs challenge the boundaries the historic church has maintained around belief, membership, and leadership.[35]

The baseline for my argument is the structure, social and musical, of Western classical musical performance.[36] Imagine a performance of Tchaikovsky's (1840-1893) ballet *Swan Lake*. The setting is a theater transected by a proscenium arch and the orchestra pit that together separate the area for performing from that for seating. In front of the orchestra pit are the stalls: rows of seats fixed to a sloped floor, and ranged above the stalls, one may find balconies with more seating. The event begins with persons taking their places in both sections

---

[33] Martha Bayles, "Music; Gospel Speaks a Language Germans Understand," *New York Times* (Oct. 21, 2001). Vide Amerikanischer Blick auf Gospelmusik in Deutschland - ein Artikel aus der New York Times (englisch / deutsch), at http://www.berlin-gospel-web.de/archiv_frame.html, accessed 1/16/2017.

[34] Ahrens, *Begeisterung*, 7.

[35] Mary Douglas, *Natural Symbols* (New York: Vintage Books, 1973), 93-112.

[36] Since contemporary popular music has modified these structures under the influence of Black American culture, I am taking classical performance as "traditional."

of the theater. In front of the proscenium arch with its curtain, the orchestra assembles in the pit to tune up and practice while members of the audience move toward their reserved seats. The performance starts with the conductor of the orchestra assuming the podium, then turning to the audience and bowing. After the audience acknowledges her with applause, the overture is performed. Simultaneously, behind the curtain, members of the ballet company take their places, ready to start the dance. When the curtain is raised following the overture, the dancers perform to the music the orchestra plays, while the audience sits in silence. Not a sound is heard in the stalls or balconies until the ballet ends and the curtain drops, but only for a moment. Then the audience begins to applaud. Shortly thereafter, the curtain is raised again, revealing the ballet company gathered on stage for the curtain call, ready to step forward and curtsy or bow—in ascending order according to their "stardom." To show greater approval, the audience may increase its applause. It recognizes the conductor and orchestra in a similar fashion. To show special recognition for the whole production, the audience may give a standing ovation. Then the curtain comes down, and all go their separate ways: audience, musicians, and dancers.

Such a performance is highly structured, socially and musically. The space reflects social structure. The seats of the audience, from expensive box seats to (relatively) cheap "nose bleed" seats, broadly reflect social class. Inversely elevation marks status among the performers as well, with the musicians barely visible in the pit, the conductor a bit higher, and the dancers on stage. Further the performing and seating areas divide the performers who play and dance from the audience members who watch and listen, publicly expressing their feelings only after the curtain falls. This division separates amateurs from professionals, patrons from artists, ballet lovers from performers. Moving from social to musical relationships, western musical notation is also highly structured. The musicians play the music Tchaikovsky wrote; the conductor interprets the master within the parameters of his score. Finally, music and dance are separable. In the Western musical tradition, dance is distinct from music, something superadded. Although Tchaikovsky composed *Swan Lake* as a ballet, the music can be performed apart from the dancing as an integral orchestral piece.

Worship in German Protestant congregations follows similar patterns. As in the theatre, the space is divided. Traditionally the chancel (regarded as the front) is distinguished architecturally from the nave oriented toward it. Typically elevated, the chancel is ordered for liturgical function, organized minimally around pulpit, font, and table. The nave has a level floor filled with pews, sectioned by aisles to allow for movement. This pattern pertains *mutatis mutandis*, even in modern configurations, for instance a church in the round, where function may communicate structure as well as architecture. In the church, the pairing of worshippers/worship leaders parallels that of amateurs/professionals in the theater. Both pairs contrast as inactivity/activity. As an audience sits quietly while artists perform, worshippers are seated in the nave, while worship leaders, ordained or authorized, perform liturgical functions in the chancel. The congregation is relatively passive, responding only when invited to stand, sing, recite, contribute, come forward, commune, or assume a posture of prayer. The leaders in the chancel are more active: reading, preaching, and offering liturgical leadership from various locations, in various postures, and with a variety of gestures. Finally, the worship and music are structured. The music is structured according to the Western musical tradition. The worship employs liturgical forms and songs in an order and with rituals and texts provided by the church (mostly). The duration of worship is limited to an hour or so.

Gospel music in worship "violates" structures traditional to Western culture:

Communal song

In black worship, gospel music is a communal choral event. There are few moments when a singer or choir performs, that is, sings alone to a silent, listening audience, in hopes of applause. The choir functions as the congregation's song leader, welcoming all to sing.

Charismatic selection

In the black church, the criteria for determining who leads from who follows is charismatic rather than professional. Although musicians are gifted and may be trained and professional, they need not be. Directors and soloists arise out of the community, recognized by their charism for singing. In the black church, the boundary drawn by the edge of the dias is low.

Clapping and applause

First the definitions: one applauds in approbation, usually following a performance; one claps along with the music. In a black church using gospel singing, the congregation claps both to join in the music and to encourage the musicians, similar to shouts like "Amen" and "Praise the Lord." The applause following a gospel song in worship, while surely showing approbation, brings this grateful encouragement to its conclusion.

Musical transmission

Gospel music is oral-aural. When taught, it is lined-out, though it is as often "caught" as "taught." Further, the rhythmic syncopation and note bending used in gospel elude Western musical notation. Since Western notation can only approximate the way gospel is actually sung, teaching a gospel song from a printed score requires a disclaimer: "This is the way it is written; this is the way it is sung."

Music and dance

Gospel is a dance form integral to the music sung, a kinesthetic choral performance of body and voice. Gospel singing combines music and dance in organic forms: the physical bodies of the choir members and the social body of the choir. As choral dance, gospel music is infectious, moving members of the congregation to join in.

We have here two distinct worship traditions, one Western and the other African American. To compare them is instructive; to combine them presents challenges and opportunities.

Now imagine a gospel choir singing during the worship service of a German Protestant congregation. After a concert of the Westend Gospel Singers from Eberswalde, Germany, held at First Congregational United Church of Christ, River Falls, Wisconsin, a visiting African missioner was moved to comment. Having lived in Germany, he related what we had just seen in concert to what he had experienced there in worship: elderly congregations, moving very little, and singing mostly German chorales. Gesturing toward the choir, he exclaimed: "Now look at this! A choir aged 14 to 50, singing gospel music while clapping and swaying."[37] When gospel is first introduced into German Protestant congregational worship, it can be met with resistance from clergy, musicians, and parishioners.[38] Its kinesthetic choral form can be held to transgress the etiquette and decorum of structured worship. The

---

[37] Personal experience of the author, Sunday, October 2006.
[38] Interview: Nicholas Schneider, Berlin, February 2014.

exuberant singing, the free physical movement, and the clapping violate "inviolate" forms, desecrate "sacred" structures, and disturb the pious and prayerful. To some German ears, gospel music sung in English sounds like pop, not sacred music; like radio, not church; appropriated from the world of black Americans, it is culturally unfamiliar. For members of gospel choirs, on the other hand, and the many coming to hear them sing, gospel is vibrant and fresh.

The phrase "embodied joy" describes the kinesthetic dimension of singing gospel music. One need only visit the website of a German gospel church choir to witness the free combination of body and song that gospel singers experience.[39] This kinesthetic form is appropriated from black gospel singers and choirs. Appropriation goes beyond emulation, for the singers engage with black gospel music organically; they strive to embody the spirit of the music.[40] In response to the question, "What about gospel music moves you personally?" respondents surveyed were nearly unanimous in answering "simply to have fun."[41] Close behind came the "rhythmic sound" (94 percent) and "the elation I feel singing in harmony with other voices" (93 percent)[42]; ninety-five percent gave their reason for participating "the joy of singing and making music."[43] Angelika Rehaag illustrates the connection between body and joy. After seeing the movie *Sister Act* (1992), members of a church choir she directed asked her to start a gospel choir. After some hesitation, she starting slowly with a project choir and was inspired to attend the Stockholm Gospel Festival in the summer of 1993. "This was where the Spirit hit me so badly." In a workshop on directing, she got caught up in the energy and joy. "While not letting go of the classical style [of

---

[39] For an example, vide the online magazine *Berlin Gospel Web*, http://www.berlin-gospel-web.de, accessed 1/16/2017.
[40] Johnson, *Appropriating Blackness*, 1-16 and 198-218. Although generally impressed by the gospel movement of members of the Australian choir, Johnson found some to be "rock and clap challenged" (167). An illustration of appropriation in the German context is found in two videos involving the Glory Gospel Singers, an American black gospel group that travels internationally to perform concerts and conduct workshops (glorygospelsingers.com/, accessed 12/31/2016). Both videos present performances of "O Happy Day," by Edwin Hawkins, the first showing the Glory Gospel Singers performing it alone in concert in Monteruda, Germany (https://www.youtube.com/watch?v=UAF6qQCR21g, accessed 12/31/2016), the second showing the Glory Gospel Singers singing it with the Westend Gospelsingers of Eberswalde, Germany, after having conducted a workshop with that choir (https://www.youtube.com/watch?v=liNaAYzZD9s, accessed 12/31/2016).
[41] Ahrens, *BeGeisterung*, 35.
[42] Ibid.
[43] Ibid., 26.

directing], but getting more into the free style [of black gospel choir directing], I was directing like having both of my hands in electric outlets." When conducting gospel music, she feels jolted as by an electrical charge.[44] Most anyone listening to or singing gospel music can attest to a physical response.

The joyful abandon gospel singers experience kinesthetically impacts their social body, the choir. Just as gospel leads singers to transgress the boundaries of decorum customary in worship, it also frees them vis á vis boundaries and structures of faith and order. The boundaries defining this social body are low. There is no creed such as the Apostles' Creed, no confession such as the Augsburg, no initiation such as baptism, no catechism such as Luther's, no membership preparation such as confirmation. Anybody who wishes to sing gospel music in the social setting of a congregation-related choir is welcome. Consequently these choirs are religiously heterogeneous. No matter the affiliation of the congregation, the distribution among members falls out 57 percent German Protestant Church, 6 percent other Protestant denominations, 28 percent Roman Catholic Church, 9 percent no religious affiliation, and 1 percent members of other faiths. The formal affiliation, however, does not tell the whole story. In practice choir members may be active or inactive church members, sympathetic outsiders, persons uninterested in or even hostile to the church, New Age adherents, practicing or nonpracticing adherents of world faiths, agnostics, atheists, or spiritual but not religious. Accordingly the boundaries of gospel choirs are porous. Persons come and go without institutional expectations or constraints.

Petra-Angela Ahrends, who authored the survey of German gospel choirs, considers the capacity of gospel choirs to entertain this homogeneity a mark of strong social cohesion. Fully 91 percent are moved by singing gospel music because it "binds together persons who are radically different,"[45] whereas 92 percent indicated that they participate in a gospel choir "because here I experience community with like-minded people."[46] Setting these two statements side by side, one can discern communities united in their commitment to be open to and engaged with others, without regard to biology or background. Ahrens writes, "Gospel choirs succeed in inspiring persons to sing

---

[44] Interview: Angelika Rehaag, Krefeld, Germany, February 2014, http://www.gospelacademy.com/angelika.php, accessed 1/2/2016.
[45] Ahrens, *BeGeisterung*, 35.
[46] Ibid., 26.

'good news' who explicitly reject—if anything, dismissively—churchy or religious motivations, who do not feel themselves tied to the church or a congregation."[47] The fact is, some choir members do not believe what they sing. To be sure, many Christians of conviction participate in gospel choirs.[48] But what brings an agnostic to perform "Give me Jesus," or a liberal Protestant to rejoice in being "washed in the blood of the Lamb," or choir members who are Muslim or Hindu or Buddhist to join in singing any gospel song? When E. Patrick Johnson explored this question with the Café of the Gates of Salvation Gospel Choir in Sydney, Australia, the spirit of the language trumped its content. Persons discerned generic religious values in specific Christian language, such as "retranslating the word 'Jesus' to mean 'my highest welfare,' or 'freedom.'"[49] A vast majority of those responding to the German survey—be they Christian or not—participate in a choir because "Gospel music gives me new strength for everyday life" (84 percent).[50] The skeptic might think that persons who are not Christian betray their convictions for the sake of singing and belonging. This, however, gainsays the religious power of the social body of a choir. For that body is "in-spirited"; all are imbued with the spirit of gospel, Christians with the Holy Spirit. Doctrinal distinctions pale in comparison to the spiritual power felt in the kinesthetic choral dance of gospel music. The feeling of belonging in a joyous body of persons with a liberal spirit overshadows in some the antinomy between their convictions and Christian language.

In light of these realities of choir life, the support that the German Protestant Church gives gospel choirs is ironic.[51] The low boundaries of gospel choirs counter the disciplines of faith and order the church has historically upheld: the baptized and the unbaptized, the confirmed and the unchurched, believers and unbelievers. Whereas the church employs these binary criteria to determine whether a person

---

[47] Ibid., 7.
[48] Ibid. Pagination shown in brackets. When explaining the reason for participating in a gospel choir, we find these explicitly religious responses: "that gospel music expresses my religious feelings" (63 percent) [26 and 35], "that it brings me closer to God" [35], or "that inspires others persons with the Good News" (64 percent) [26 and 35], while 44 percent of those "felt more strongly connected to the church as a result their participation in a choir" [28-29].
[49] Johnson, *Appropriating Blackness*, 164-78, esp.166 and 173.
[50] Ahrens, *BeGeisterung*, 35.
[51] The movement has received encouragement from the highest levels of the German Protestant Church, including two recent chairpersons of the national Council of the Protestant Church in Germany, Margot Käßmann (2009-10) and Nikolaus Schneider (2010-14).

is "in" or "out," members associate freely within a gospel choir. In general the German Protestant Church overlooks these anomalies of choir life to co-opt its vibrancy. Reflecting on the survey, Ulrich Fischer, bishop of the Protestant Church in Baden, said, "To sing in a gospel choir is also attractive for persons who otherwise involve themselves in congregational life hardly at all. The study confirms our perception that gospel choirs realize the living out of the *oikoumene* in the church's congregations; they integrate and establish community between confessions and generations."[52] German gospel choirs are "of" but not "in" the church. They are of the church in that they are sponsored and even encouraged by it and invited to sing in worship. They are not, however, in it. Gospel choirs play by different rules of faith and order.

Martin Bartelworth, leader of the Creative Kirche,[53] employs insights from Fresh Expressions for understanding gospel choirs as a form of church.[54] Fresh Expressions, a church renewal movement in the United Kingdom, seeks to gather unchurched persons into new congregations rather than to create structures to draw them into existing ones.

> Many existing churches operate with a "you come to us" mindset. "Would you like to join us?" is an invitation to come to "our" church, set out as we like, at a time that fits us, in a style that we have pre-arranged. The flow is from outside-in: from the world into the congregation.
>
> Fresh expressions have a "we'll come to you" mindset instead. They start not with an invitation ("Come to us on our terms") but with an offer (*"We're willing to come to you, serve you,*

---

[52] *EKD Pressemitteilung* (Wednesday, June 17, 2010, 11:00 a.m.), 1 (https://www.si-ekd.de/download/090616_pm_gospelx.pdf, accessed 12/21/2016, translation mine). Petra-Angela Ahrens voices a similar opinion in the introduction to the German survey. "It says a lot for gospel music that [its] emotional qualities open up an avenue to religious understandings, even if not formulated explicitly in the language of the Christian church. That in-spirits both those who feel close to the church and those who keep their distance." Ahrens, *BeGeisterung*, 7, translation mine.

[53] The Creative Kirche supports and promotes gospel music and singing in the German church. The organization has a publishing house; it commissions gospel oratorios (Die Zehn Gebote, Amazing Grace, and Luther Pop-Oratorio), sponsors an annual gospel Kirchentag, and supports gospel churches. While explicitly serving the church, the performances of their oratorios exhibit some of the structures characteristic of western performance, notably the professional/amateur divide. http://www.creative-kirche.de, accessed 12/28/2016.

[54] http://www.freshexpressions.org.uk, accessed 12/28/2016; and https://en.wikipedia.org/wiki/Fresh_expression, accessed 12/28/2016.

and stay with you. If you want, we'll also help you to be church in a way that suits you—in your style, not ours.") The aim is not to provide a stepping stone into [the] existing church, but to form new churches in their own right. The flow is from the congregation to people outside—not inward, but outward.

For example, the skateboard and BMX[55] subculture in Essex, the cafe culture in Kidsgrove, artists and "creatives" in London, university students in Southampton, surfers in Cornwall, and British Asian people in Birmingham have formed Fresh Expressions churches.

In gospel choirs, Bartelworth sees the church meeting and offering something of value to the unchurched. True, church-related gospel choirs are congregation-sponsored groups rather than church plants. They rehearse on church property and sing publicly primarily in worship. Also, to form gospel choirs, the church does not venture out to the places where people with alternative lifestyles gather. On the other hand, in gospel, the church offers music that—as we have seen—has the power to draw unchurched persons onto the "foreign territory" of a church-sponsored choir. Further, German Protestant congregations give gospel choirs the latitude to shape their own common life, to create a church with the church, if you will, an *ecclesiola* within the *ecclesia*. While this is not a New Expression church,[56] for Bartelworth, it is a new expression of church.[57]

The phrase "gospel is church" has wide currency in the movement. Thomas Risager, pastor of the Methodist Church in Odense, Denmark, lifts up the early Christian community in Jerusalem to explain this phrase. He contends that gospel choirs are Spirit-filled communities similar to the one Acts 2:42 describes: "They devoted themselves to the apostles' teaching and fellowship, to the breaking of bread and the

---

[55] BMX, an abbreviation for bicycle motocross, is a cycle sport performed on BMX bikes. https://en.wikipedia.org/wiki/BMX, accessed 12/28/2016.

[56] Germany offers a few examples of nascent gospel churches. The Creative Kirche, for example, actively supports the Worship Café in Witten, Germany. For a YouTube video of a service, see https://worship-cafe.jimdo.com/worship-café/, accessed 12/28/2016. Other gospel congregations have been sponsored by Erlösergemeinde in Hannover (www.gospelkirche-hannover.de/, accessed 12/28/2016); Evangelisch-Lutherische Markusgemeinde in Hildesheim (www.markusgemeinde-hildesheim.de/pages/gospelkirche/, accessed 12/28/2016); and by Markuskirche in Karlruhe (www.gospelkirche-karlsruhe.de/, accessed 12/28/2016). The Petrikirche in Rostock sponsored the Rostock Jugendkirche (http://www.jugendkirche-rostock.de, accessed 12/18/2016).

[57] Interview: Martin Bartelworth, Witten, Germany, February 2014.

prayers" (RSV). In gospel choirs, one finds these four features: teaching (minimally in explaining the songs, sometimes through an opening reflection), commensality (as choirs regularly and joyfully socialize around tables laden with refreshments and food), fellowship (as a choir supports its own members), and prayer (as choirs care for one another and the least of this world).[58] One example must suffice. In great distress, an impoverished choir member called Risager. His life had taken a turn for the worse, and he had to drop out of the choir. His marriage had ended abruptly, and he was out on the street, with three school-aged children in tow. He had found an apartment but had no furniture, no clothes, no household items, no food. He did not know what to do. He knew only that he had to devote all his energy to sorting out his life. Good-bye, choir. But not for Risager, who immediately shared the fellow's plight and what needed to be done on the choir's Facebook page. Within two days, food filled the refrigerator, household items stood on the cupboard's shelves, clothes hung in the closets, and the apartment was fully furnished—including "a TV, play station, games, everything." From each according to their ability, to each according to their need (Acts 11:29).[59]

The generosity of this example is neither remarkable nor unusual; many a congregation has provided for one in need. What is remarkable is how it came to pass. The response was *social* and *spontaneous*. Risager did not need to contact a committee of the church or spend hours on the phone soliciting members for help. No organizational effort was needed. He merely made the need known, and the choir came through spontaneously.

To Clarence Jordan (1942-1970), founder of Koinonia Farms, a group acting in love and justice is the risen Body of Christ. He said once, "Never did Paul or Peter or Stephen point to an empty tomb as evidence of the resurrection. The evidence was the Spirit-filled fellowship."[60] For Jordan, Luke-Acts is a two-volume biography of Jesus Christ: the first telling how Jesus ministered in human form and the second recounting the ministry of his risen body, the Spirit-filled community of the church, carrying forward the preaching of Christ and challenging,

---

[58] Thomas Risager, *Sing unto the Lord. The Story of the Revitalization of an Old United Methodist Church through the Introduction of Gospel Music Ministry*, A Project Thesis Submitted in Candidacy for the Degree of Doctor of Ministry, Wesley Theological Seminary (Washington, DC, 2012), 29-72.
[59] Interview: Thomas Risager, Odense, Denmark, February 2014.
[60] Dallas Lee, *The Cotton Patch Evidence* (Americus, GA: A Koinonia Publication, 1971), 25.

healing, and praying. By embodying the joy of gospel music, choirs can also become Spirit-filled: teaching, feasting, supporting, and praying. In the language of the church—which would give pause to many a gospel singer—a choir can become the risen Body of Christ.

Conclusion

Returning to where I started, church-related German gospel choirs follow the path John XXIII forged with Vatican II. In vastly different ecclesial contexts, one finds worship projecting new forms of faith and order. The German Protestant church has shown great wisdom in accepting the anomalous forms gospel choirs employ. Congregations have cultivated relationships with individual choirs and the church's judicatories with leaders in the movement. It will be fascinating to see how the conversation between the historic church in Germany and this fresh expression develops. In the meantime, let us shout: *Deo gratias*!

CHAPTER 6

Ecumenical Liturgical Influences and the Reformed Church in America 1987–2004

Carol Myers

I have known Gregg Mast since he and Vicki were students at Hope College and babysat for our boys. It has been a distinct pleasure to watch his career unfold and to work with him as well. We served together on the worship commission, and he staffed the commission while I was moderator. I have always said, if I could come back, I would like to have Gregg's brain. You could call him and ask a complex and challenging question. After a brief pause, Gregg would offer a perfectly thought out three- or four-part reply. Brilliant, simply brilliant.

The Second Vatican Council (1962-65) had wide-ranging effects that went way beyond renewal in just the Roman Catholic Church. The council emphasized the primacy of Eucharist as the "summit toward which the activity of the Church is directed; at the same time, it is the font from which all her power flows."[1] This set in motion major changes to Roman Catholic liturgy. This emphasis raised the importance of lay people's participation. It brought vernacular language into the liturgy,

---

[1] Constitution on the Sacred Liturgy, *Sacrosanctum Concilium*, solemnly promulgated by His Holiness Pope Paul VI on December 4, 1963, chapter 1, 1.10.

had the whole congregation drink from the communion cup, and gave more importance to the reading of scripture in worship. The amount of scripture to be read during Mass was increased greatly by developing a multiple-year lectionary:

> The treasures of the Bible are to be opened up more lavishly, so that a richer share in God's word may be provided for the faithful. In this way, a more representative portion of holy Scripture will be read to the people in the course of a prescribed number of years.[2]

These ideas resonated with Christians beyond the Roman Catholic Church and led to broad liturgical renewal, particularly in mainline Protestant churches.

The development of the new Roman Catholic, three-year lectionary included consultation with North American Protestant biblical scholars. They, too, were less than satisfied with their own denominational lectionaries. The Episcopal Church, Presbyterians,[3] and Lutherans[4] each developed adaptations of and revisions to the new Roman Catholic three-year lectionary. Following trial use, these lectionaries were approved and eventually included in the Presbyterian *Worshipbook* (1972), the *Lutheran Book of Worship* (1978), and the Episcopal *Book of Common Prayer* (1979). These three derivative three-year lectionaries greatly expanded the amount of scripture read in Sunday services from the previously predominant one-year, two readings lectionary model, thus bringing much more biblical content to people in the pews.

In 1970 the Commission on Worship of the Consultation on Church Union (COCU)[5] began work on a lectionary to be used across denominations. This was to further church unity and to provide a revised lectionary for churches that either did not have one or had

---

[2] Sacred Congregation for the Sacraments and Divine Worship, *Lectionary for Mass*, introduction (Second *Editio Typica*), 1981; (London: Collins Liturgical Publications and Cassell Ltd; Dublin: Veritas Publications; Sydney: E. J. Dwyer Ltd., 1981) and *Liturgy Documentary Series* 1 (Washington, DC: Office of Publishing Services, United States Catholic Conference, 1982).

[3] The Joint Committee on Worship for the Cumberland Presbyterian Church, the Presbyterian Church in the United States, and the United Presbyterian Church in the United States of America.

[4] Inter-Lutheran Commission on Worship representing the Lutheran Church in America, the American Lutheran Church, the Evangelical Lutheran Church of Canada and the Lutheran Church—Missouri Synod.

[5] The Reformed Church in America had observer status, not full membership, in the Consultation on Church Union.

not done any recent lectionary revision. This effort, harmonizing the new Roman Catholic lectionary with the Episcopal, Presbyterian, and Lutheran variants, was published in 1974 as *A Lectionary*. Each Sunday and holyday had three readings: Old Testament, Epistle, and Gospel, with Acts taking the place of the Old Testament reading during the Easter season.

The Consultation on Common Texts (CCT)[6] assumed further development of the COCU lectionary. Their *Common Lectionary: The Lectionary Proposal by the Consultation on Common Texts* was first made available in 1981. When published in 1983, it was offered to the churches for three years of trial use, study, and comment, with a final version anticipated in 1987.

The Reformed Church in America (RCA) participated in that trial. In 1983 the Commission on Christian Unity of the RCA's General Synod encouraged use of the CCT *Common Lectionary* in the commission's *A Pastoral Handbook for Ecumenical Practice*. These *Common Lectionary* texts were printed for the first time in the RCA 1983-84 Plan Calendar.[7] This followed the commission's 1981 recommendation "that local congregations actively and consistently seek to share . . . through exposition from common lectionaries."[8] The Christian Unity Commission also encouraged the use of liturgical color as an expression of unity, saying "It would seem appropriate that if Reformed churches are going to use liturgical colors, then for the sake of Christian unity, we should respect the usage of those churches with the longest history of uniformity of color sequence. It would be poor manners simply

---

[6] Member churches of the Consultation on Common Texts (some only part of the time): American Baptist Churches USA, Anglican Church of Canada, Canadian Conference of Catholic Bishops, Christian Church (Disciples of Christ), Christian Reformed Church in North America, Church of the Brethren, Cooperative Baptist Fellowship, Evangelical Lutheran Church in America, Evangelical Lutheran Church in Canada, Free Methodist Church in Canada, International Commission on English in the Liturgy (an agency of 26 Roman Catholic national or international conferences of bishops), Lutheran Church–Missouri Synod, Mennonite Church, North American Lutheran Church, Polish National Catholic Church, Presbyterian Church (USA), Presbyterian Church in Canada, Reformed Church in America, Roman Catholic Church in Canada, The Episcopal Church, The United Methodist Church, Unitarian Universalist Christian Fellowship, United Church of Canada, United Church of Christ, United States Conference of Catholic Bishops, Wisconsin Evangelical Lutheran Synod.

[7] The Acts and Proceedings of the 1983 - 182nd Regular Session of the General Synod (hereinafter MGS [year]), 114-15, 145.

[8] Ibid., 111.

to design our own schema when we could be helped by others whose practice in this matter goes back far in history."[9]

In implementing these recommendations, the Plan Calendar introduced the changes with these words:

> *The Plan Calendar*, in its twenty-first edition, celebrates its coming of age with a new format, revised colors for the church year, and, for the first time, a lectionary for Sundays and special days in the Christian year.
>
> LECTIONARY: By request of the Commissions on Worship and Christian Unity, the Plan Calendar this year offers as a resource the ecumenical lectionary produced by the Consultation on Common Texts (CCT). The use of a lectionary is an ancient Reformed practice. Calvin used to preach through entire books of the Bible on consecutive Sundays as a means to ensuring the proclamation of the whole Gospel. (Those interested in following this scheme may consult the 1968 *Liturgy*.)
>
> The CCT lectionary present here represents the latest stage in the effort to harmonize the texts used by the various churches, an effort which began with the 1969 Roman Lectionary and led to the 1974 lectionary prepared by the Consultation on Church Union. It follows a three-year cycle.
>
> In addition to its use by the Reformed Church in America, the CCT lectionary will be in trial use for the next three years in the following churches: Presbyterian Church US, United Presbyterian Church USA, Lutheran Church in America, American Lutheran Church, Association of Evangelical Lutheran Churches, Episcopal Church, Methodist Church, Anglican Church of Canada, United Church of Christ, United Church of Canada, and the Roman Catholic Church through the National Council of Catholic Bishops of the US and the Council of Bishops in Canada. The plan calendars of the Presbyterians, Methodists, and the UCC will also feature this lectionary, with a more controlled trial being planned in some of the other churches.[10]

The *Revised Common Lectionary* came out in 1992, offering alternate tracks for the Old Testament reading during the time

---

[9] Ibid, 114.
[10] Hugh F. Gambaro, ed., *1983-4 Plan Calendar, Reformed Church in America* (New York, NY: Reformed Church Press, 1983).

following Epiphany and Pentecost/Trinity Sunday. Both tracks include a corresponding Psalm that is the congregation's response and meditation on the particular Old Testament reading.[11] One track paired the Gospel reading with a closely related Old Testament reading. The other offered semicontinuous Old Testament readings. Providing these alternates made the lectionary acceptable to more denominations by keeping the original thematically paired readings and also responding to comments, particularly from Reformed churches, that wanted more themes and narrative from Old Testament continuous readings. These two patterns are offered as equals; denominations and/or individual churches are asked to follow one or the other and not to mix the two.

The Revised Common Lectionary texts have been printed on the RCA Plan Calendar since 1992 through the present. These advantages[12] were listed to encourage use:

1. It covers a great breadth of scripture–the whole counsel of God.
2. It provides a sequence from week to week (frequently from the New Testament).
3. It relates the gospel of the New Testament to its Old Testament antecedents (including an appropriate Psalter passage).
4. It follows the Christian year, with its focus on Christ.
5. It speaks to the persons and work of the Trinity.
6. It protects the congregation from a narrow preoccupation with the New Testament to the exclusion of the Old Testament.

The Commissions on Worship and Christian Unity both commended the *Common Lectionary* for use in the RCA. As one consultant participant said, it is "by far the most successful and practical ecumenical progress in Christian worship since the Second Vatican Council."[13] From 1982 to 2002, the Revs. Daniel Meeter, Gregg Mast, and John Paarlberg represented the RCA at CCT.

Major English-speaking Christian churches throughout the world began renewing their liturgy by incorporating more contemporary, easily understood language for the prayers and other texts used

---

[11] The Consultation on Common Texts, *The Revised Common Lectionary: Includes Complete List of Lections for Years A, B, and C* (Nashville: Abingdon Press, 1992), page 11.

[12] This list was included in RCA Plan Calendars, summarized in *At Home with the Word* booklets, and is currently in the worship resource section of the RCA website, https://www.rca.org/resources/revised-common-lectionary.

[13] Ibid.

in worship. They realized this work should be done cooperatively, not separately by individual denominations.

The International Committee on English in the Liturgy (ICEL) is the Roman Catholic body charged "to achieve an English version of liturgical texts acceptable to the interested countries... bearing in mind the ecumenical aspects."[14] They began work on the texts traditionally used in Eucharistic services[15] with ecumenical groups in Great Britain, America, Australia, and beyond. This work was then collected and reviewed by an international and ecumenical group, the International Consultation on English Texts[16] (ICET), that was formed in 1969 out of the work begun by ICEL. The ICET texts were published for trial use in 1972, as *Prayers We Have in Common*, with comments due for revision in 1974.

Responding to comments and suggestions from the churches, ICET revised the texts. An example of the revision responding to such comment is shown in the Lord's Prayer. The 1972 edition began, "Our Father in heaven, holy be your Name." This was chosen because "hallowed" had gone out of use and was debased in some English-speaking areas. The new edition, however, reinstated "hallowed be your name," even though the word was somewhat archaic. The new edition of *Prayers We Have in Common* came out in 1975.

In succeeding years, as many churches were revising their orders of worship, it became clear that further work on the texts was needed. There was a growing emphasis on using broader liturgical language to

---

[14] International Consultation on English Texts, *Prayers We Have in Common* (Philadelphia: Fortress Press, 1972), 4.

[15] These texts are the Lord's Prayer, the Apostles' Creed, the Nicene Creed, *Gloria in Excelsis, Sanctus and Benedictus, Gloria Patri, Sursum Corda, Agnus Dei, Te Deum, Benedictus, Nunc Dimittis*, and the *Magnificat*.

[16] Members of the International Consultation on English Texts (ICET): John M. Barkley, Presbyterian, Ireland; A. O. Barkway, Anglican, Scotland; Eugene L. Brand, Lutheran, United States; Edgar S. Brown Jr., Lutheran, United States; Neville Clark, Baptist, England; R. Aled Davies, Presbyterian, England; Godfrey Diekmann, O.S.B., Roman Catholic, United States; H. P. R. Finberg, Roman Catholic, England; A. Raymond George, Methodist, England; John Hackett, Roman Catholic, Ireland; G. B. Harrison, Roman Catholic, United States; R. C. D. Jasper, Anglican, England; Percy Jones, Roman Catholic, Australia; J. C. Lusk, Presbyterian, Scotland; G. Mayes, Anglican, Ireland; Frederick R. McManus, Roman Catholic, United States; James Quinn, Roman Catholic, Scotland; John M. Shea, Roman Catholic, United States; Massey H. Shepherd Jr., Episcopalian, United States; Gerald J. Sigler, Roman Catholic, United States; Charles W. F. Smith, Episcopalian, United States (representing COCU); Stephen Somerville, Roman Catholic, Canada; David Thomas, Anglican, Wales; James M. Todd, Congregationalist, England; Harold E. Winstone, Roman Catholic, England. ICET was jointly chaired by R. C. D. Jasper and Harold E. Winstone.

make it clear that both male and female were created in God's image and that in Christ there is neither male nor female (Galatians 3.28). A new ecumenical body was established in 1985 to carry out this work, the English Language Liturgical Commission (ELLC). This group took the place of ICET, continuing to work on text revision, while also addressing other aspects of liturgy.

The ELLC's first task was to review the common texts that had been distributed in 1975. An extensive and very thorough process was adopted. All points and guidelines were submitted to ELLC member bodies,[17] who were to share them with all their member churches. Comment was to flow back through the system to the ELLC committee on revision. The first and foremost concern was to maintain the accuracy of the texts, avoiding misleading implications and keeping them true to the original meaning of the Greek and Latin. These principles guided their work: (1) only necessary changes; (2) inclusive language; (3) ease of saying, hearing, and singing; and (4) contemporary language. The ELLC published *Praying Together* in 1988.

In 1997 the RCA General Synod commended the ELLC *Praying Together* texts for the Lord's Prayer and the Apostles' and Nicene Creeds for use in RCA churches. The RCA worship commission also incorporated these texts, along with the *Sursum Corda* and the *Sanctus and Benedictus* as RCA sacramental liturgy was updated.[18]

The worship commission also embraced ecumenical Eucharistic developments in 1986[19] and 1988[20] by commending to the church, as

---

[17] Members of the English Language Liturgical Consultation (ELLC): Australian Consultation on Liturgy (ACOL), representing six churches; Canadian Churches' Coordinating Group on Worship (CCCGOW), five churches; Consultation on Common Texts (CCT), sixteen North American churches; International Commission on English in the Liturgy (ICEL), 26 conferences of Roman Catholic bishops in the English-speaking world; Joint Liturgical Consultation within New Zealand (JLCNZ), four churches; Joint Liturgical Group (JLG), nine churches in Great Britain; Liturgical Committee, South African Church Unity Commission, four churches.

[18] MSG, 1983, 145–48. The worship commission had recommended approving the use of earlier CCT texts in 1983, saying, "Having before it a continuing interest in Christian unity, the commission reviewed anew the versions of the Lord's Prayer and the Apostles', Nicene, and Athanasian Creeds prepared by the Consultation of Common Texts and already in use in many Christian churches. In the commission's judgment, RCA members would be served well through becoming familiar with these texts, and ecumenical relations between the RCA and other denominations would be enhanced if we acknowledged their validity for use." The recommendation, however, was amended to "permit" replacing "approve."

[19] MGS 1986, 168.

[20] MGS 1988, 218.

provisional forms for occasional use, both the World Council of Churches Faith and Order Commission's *The Lima Eucharistic Liturgy*[21] and the Consultation on Church Union's *The Sacrament of the Lord's Supper: A New Text—1984*.[22] General Synods adopted both recommendations.

In the midst of all this liturgical foment, the RCA, too, embarked upon liturgical renewal. The Commission on Christian Worship[23] has responsibility for advising the church of changes needed in the liturgy. To fulfill that charge, the commission reviews and revises various orders, being attentive to specific concerns that have been raised and also working toward the goal of having consistent liturgy.[24]

To aid in carrying out that mandate, in 1988 the commission developed both process[25] and principles to guide their liturgical revision. The process assured that prior to presentation to the church, the orders will have been through at least four drafts, including professional editing and a thorough review by the entire commission, meeting in session, at least twice. Orders are then sent to the General Synod for recommendation for a year of study, trial, and comment throughout the whole church. Following that period, the commission reviews all comments, makes necessary revisions, and brings them again to General Synod for recommendation to the classes for approval. This deliberate process assures careful liturgical development and thorough vetting by both the commission and the whole church. This process would assure orders would not come for approval prematurely as had

---

[21] The *Lima Eucharistic Liturgy* is a "liturgy developed by Max Thurion of the Taizé community. At the meeting of the Faith and Order Commission in Lima, Peru, in 1982, some revisions were made, and the liturgy was used for the first time on January 15, 1982, with J. Robert Wright, an Episcopal priest, as the celebrant. It embodies the eucharistic theology of *Baptism, Eucharist, and Ministry* (1982)." The Episcopal Church, Library, Glossary: http://www.episcopalchurch.org/library/glossary/lima-eucharistic-liturgy.

[22] MGS 1986, 168. "Following an inquiry from the church, the commission reviewed *The Sacrament of the Lord's Supper: A New Text–1984*, prepared by the Commission on Worship of the Consultation on Church Union. This liturgy, like the *Lima Eucharistic Liturgy*, is recommended for occasional use by the churches, particularly in ecumenical settings, but also, perhaps, within the context of a particular congregation's worship when the relationship to the universal church is being emphasized. Therefore, approval of this liturgy for use by RCA congregations ought not to be understood to imply regular use by adoption of the form."

[23] Gregg Mast served on the worship commission from 1982 to 1984 and staffed the commission from 1984 to 1988, while he served the RCA as Minister of Social Witness and Worship.

[24] *The Book of Church Order*, 3.1.5, Sec. 11.b.1 and MGS 1999, 188.

[25] MGS 1988, 206.

happened once when a first draft had been circulated by mail among commission members following the commission's winter meeting and then submitted to General Synod, without commission discussion, for recommendation to the classes for approval. These are the principles[26] that were adopted to guide liturgical revision:

1. Use of clear and concise language;
2. Vivid, biblical imagery;
3. Breadth of imagery for God and inclusive language for people;
4. Faithfulness to Reformed theology;
5. Congregational participation;
6. Historical sensitivity;
7. Attention to the aural nature of liturgy; and
8. Sensitivity to emerging ecumenical convergence.

These principles incorporate the same values that were informing liturgical renewal across the English-speaking world. They formed the basis for the next full cycle of liturgical revision that took place in the RCA from the late 1980s through the early years of the twenty-first century.

The fruit of this period of liturgical renewal was published in *Worship the Lord: The Liturgy of the Reformed Church in America* (2005). The volume is bound with a quality, simulated-leather Kivar cover, with three ribbon markers to facilitate use in worship. Orders included were those approved by General Synod and adopted by the classes,[27] those approved by General Synod and commended to the church,[28] and some of those approved by General Synod and commended for occasional use.[29] During this time, the worship commission was aided in its work

---

[26] Ibid, 206.
[27] Orders approved by classes: Preparatory Services (1995), Sacrament of Baptism (1995), Profession of Faith (2001), Ordination and Installation of Elders and Deacons (2001), Ordination to the Office of Minister of Word and Sacrament (2001), Reception into the Classis and Installation of a Minister of Word and Sacrament (2001).
[28] Orders commended to the church: Christian Marriage (2002), Christian Burial: A Service of Witness to the Resurrection (2002).
[29] Orders commended for occasional use: Commissioning Christians to the Ministries of the Church (2001), Recognition of Ministries in the Church (2001), Farewell and Godspeed for Pastor and Congregation (1994), Blessing—Prayer for Godspeed: A Service of Farewell (1993), The Lord's Supper in Home and Hospital (1990), Celebration for the Home (1994), Commissioning a Minister of Word and Sacrament into a Specialized Ministry (2001), Worship at the Closing of a Church (1994).

by the strong support of Gregg Mast and John Paarlberg, who both staffed the short life of the Office of Worship.

Liturgical life in the RCA was enriched by the winds of liturgical renewal in the wider ecumenical world. The RCA was blessed to have shared in this movement and benefitted from these connections with the wider church. To God be the glory.

CHAPTER 7

The Ministry of Word and Sacrament: Two Sermons

Renee S. House

During his forty-two years as a minister of Word and Sacrament in the Reformed Church in America (RCA), the Reverend Dr. Gregg Mast has fulfilled his vocation through a wide variety of ministry positions. He has served churches in South Africa, New Jersey, and New York; directed the RCA's offices of ministry, social witness, and worship; taught in a number of theological schools and still teaches; written and published in the area of liturgy and worship, the focus of his PhD studies; and, most recently, ministered as president of New Brunswick Theological Seminary (NBTS). Gregg has seen and experienced ministry from many sides now, but his great, persistent love is for the ministry that takes place on "the front lines," in the local church, where God's people are gathered and formed by Word and Sacrament. Gregg has done all that he has done over the years of his ministry for the sake of empowering the ministry and mission of local congregations in diverse contexts. I am grateful for the years I was blessed to labor with Gregg in the teaching ministry of NBTS, and I am grateful for his companionship in the four years since I left the seminary to become a parish pastor for the first time in my thirty years of ordained ministry. Gregg has "been there," and he has "done that" well. He once told me that he was able to write his weekly sermon in three hours on a Sunday morning. Perhaps this was not possible every week, but I have coveted the ability to do that just now and again. Even with a sermon fully prepared, I have trouble sleeping on Saturday night. With thanksgiving for Gregg's ministry and mentoring, I offer two sermons—one on the sacrament of baptism, the other on the sacrament of the Lord's Supper.[1]

"The You God Baptized: A Sermon on Baptism"

Galatians 3:23-28:

> Now before faith came, we were imprisoned and guarded under the law until faith would be revealed. Therefore the law was our disciplinarian until Christ came, so that we might be justified by faith. But now that faith has come, we are no longer subject to a disciplinarian, for in Christ Jesus you are all children of God through faith. As many of you as were baptized into Christ have clothed yourselves with Christ. There is no longer Jew or Greek, there is no longer slave or free, there is no longer male and female; for all of you are one in Christ Jesus.

With her permission, I begin this sermon about the grace of baptism with the story of a member of our church. She goes by many names, but I will call her Mary. I met Mary four months after I became the pastor of the Old Dutch Church. She had come to one of our many large community events, during which, the church was open for tours. I was on duty when Mary showed up. I told her about the history of the congregation and our commitment to welcome all people to share in our life as a community of Jesus Christ. Not long into this conversation, Mary haltingly explained that she was a member of the Catholic church across the street, but she did not feel welcome there and asked if she could become a member of our church. "Of course," I said, "everyone is welcome here." The next day, she was in worship with us. Within a few months, Mary became a member of the Old Dutch Church.

Mary is a transgender person. She was born with a typically male body, but at a very early age, she experienced herself as a girl and begged her parents to let her be a girl. She wanted to clothe her body

---

[1] These sermons were preached at the "Room for All Conference," held October 2015, at Central Reformed Church in Grand Rapids, Michigan, and have been edited for this publication.

in dresses, wear patent leather Mary Janes and bows in her hair, and do all the things that little girls do. She was born in 1953, at a time when gender identity and appropriate behavior for girls and boys were strictly defined. Mary's parents refused to let her express her identity as a girl. It just was not possible for them. They were trying to protect her in a society that had no room for someone like her.

As a young adult on her own, Mary gained the freedom to live out her identity as a woman. But it cost her nearly everything. Her family rejected her. The Catholic church in which she was baptized and confirmed and where she had made faithful use of the means of grace warned Mary that purgatory was her best hope after death, but hell was her more likely fate. For years she had been shamed, mocked, judged, ridiculed, and refused a place to work and live and worship in peace. By the time Mary came to the Old Dutch Church, she was living on social security disability, with her psyche shattered, her mental health depleted, and her spirit crushed.

She came to us hoping against hope that she could find a place to belong. A place where she could be welcomed and affirmed. For months and months after coming to us, Mary tried to hide the reality of her transgender self, even though this identity was immediately clear to anyone who met her. It was written in her body. It was evident in her voice, and she was too poor to afford complex hormone therapies or surgery that could have altered her appearance.

As a welcoming and affirming congregation, Old Dutch Church intends to be a place where you do not have to hide, a place where you can tell the truth of yourself and the truth of your life and not fear being shamed and rejected. In our early months with her, I and others kept extending the invitation for Mary to tell her whole story. We were sure it would be freeing for her. I soon realized that we were a bit too evangelical about this. After years of ridicule and rejection, Mary did not yet feel safe with us.

Then one day it happened. Mary asked me to go with her to a medical appointment, and the doctor pulled out the male anatomy chart to explain her condition. Driving home, we did not speak about it. A week later, when I said to Mary, "You know that I know." She said, "I know." Then with great relief, she told the whole struggling story of her life, although I barely understood a word she said because she was sobbing so hard. A week after that, she came and asked if she could be rebaptized. When I asked why, she said, "Because when I was baptized as a baby, I was not myself. Now I am myself, and I want to be baptized as myself at this church because the people here know me and love me."

Believe it or not, my first thoughts in response to Mary's request went straight to the Belgic Confession, Article 34. People who know me are not surprised that the "Belgic" would be at the front of my mind at such a moment. I was raised in a Midwestern Reformed Church in America congregation. I was thoroughly catechized and am deeply formed in the continental Reformed tradition. And Mary's request had me thinking about two things that the Belgic says about baptism. First, these words: "Anyone who aspires to reach eternal life ought to be baptized only once without ever repeating it—for we cannot be born twice." And second, "This baptism is profitable not only when the water is on us and when we receive it but throughout our entire lives."

The confession's prohibition against rebaptism is a polemic against the "damnable Anabaptists," as our old translations say, who rebaptize adults already baptized as infants. But the main point is not to condemn the Anabaptists. The point is to seal to you the truth of your baptism in the name of the Triune God. In baptism God claimed you as God's own. The font is the womb of God's grace from which you were reborn as child of God forever. At the font the Spirit joined you to Jesus, and in Jesus you received your true, and best, and most treasured self. And the point is that the Triune God did it all and does it all and will keep doing it. This is what makes the baptism of infants so powerful. Before you or anyone else knew the fullness of the "who of you," God sealed you with an infinite love that you did nothing to get and which neither you nor anyone else can ever undo.

The Belgic goes on to say, "This baptism is profitable not only when the water is on us and when we receive it but throughout our lives." The fact that Mary was sitting in my study at the Old Dutch Church asking to be rebaptized was sure proof that she did not need to be rebaptized. The fact that she did not tell the church to go to hell, the fact that she refused to walk away, the fact that she kept seeking a place where she could hear God say, "Mary, you are my beloved"—all of this is proof that her baptism was profitable even though the water had dried up years and years ago. Her baptism was working. The Spirit of God was holding Mary in union with Jesus Christ, bearing witness to Mary's spirit with a love that would not let her go.

On the day that Mary was baptized as an infant, before anyone knew how her life would unfold, God knew her completely and claimed her as God's own, claimed her whole person—body and soul—forever as belonging to God through Jesus Christ. And that is why, despite all of the judgment and all of the rejection that she had experienced from her family, society, and the church, the Spirit sustained Mary's faith in Jesus and kept her searching for a community of Christ in which she could hear and sing and taste and see and experience in her body and soul the amazing grace of God. The Spirit kept her searching for a church in which the transforming power of baptism was visible, not only in the lives of individuals but also in a community that was receiving its identity and its being as the first fruits of God's new creation. Pouring out from the little bang of Jesus' resurrection, the Spirit is always pressing with all of her might to order human relationships in a way that befits, reveals, and rejoices in God's brand new creation.

"As many of you as were baptized into Christ have clothed yourselves with Christ," says Paul. "You have clothed yourselves with Christ." Clothes are part of our cultural sign systems. They serve as social identity markers, as visible clues to a person's worth and power and rights and proper place in society. This was especially true in the first century. Slaves did not dress like free people. Women did not dress like men and vice versa. Jews and Greeks used different patterns, fabrics, and tailors.

But in the community of the baptized, says Paul, everybody is wearing Jesus. All of the socially constructed distinctions; all the differentiations in power, status, and worth that cause harm; all of the boundary and identity markers, symbolized by clothes and acted out in society—all of this has been put to death by Jesus Christ. A new eschatological community has come to life in Christ and has been gathered to be a sign and manifestation of God's new creation where the only identity that matters—for anybody—is that you and everybody who has passed through the waters of baptism is God's beloved, forever. Ain't nobody gonna take that away from you.

On the day that Mary asked to be rebaptized, we went into the sanctuary and she filled the baptismal font with fresh water. Holding hands in that water we blessed God for all the grace and all the love, and we cried for all the pain, and we pleaded for healing and for peace. We have kept praying like this with our hands in the watery womb of God's grace, and the Spirit has convinced Mary that God loves her and honors her and clothes her, and he has made her one with all of us in Jesus Christ.

Of late Mary's physical health has become fragile, and she asked to begin planning her funeral. We talked about Scripture and songs, but she was most eager to talk about what she would wear for her funeral. After much talking, Mary decided that she wants to be buried in a wedding dress, as the bride of Christ. A few days after we had this conversation a complete stranger appeared at the church with a lovely wedding dress, in Mary's exact size, and asked "I wonder if you know anyone who would like this dress?" With thanksgiving in my heart for the wonder of God's ways, I hung the dress on the back of my study door, careful to hide it behind my robes so Mary would not see it just yet.

Not long after the ivory bridal gown came as gift, I dreamt that Mary had died. In the dream, I carefully carried out all of her wishes. I brought photos to the funeral home so they could see how she wore her hair and makeup, and I included all her favorite hymns in the funeral service and draped the pulpit and table with white "resurrection" paraments. When I arrived at the church for her funeral, the casket was standing empty, and Mary was standing at the church door in her wedding dress. She was fully alive. Radiant and light like an angel. Welcoming a wild mix of interesting people such as I had never seen before. And I saw water running down her face, over her gown, and onto her arms. In disbelief, I just stood there, overwhelmed by a sense that past, present, and future had collapsed into a single moment. Mary's baptism, her dying, and her rising were happening all at once. Watching and wondering, I asked, "What is going on here? Am I in the church or am I standing in the middle of the new heavens and the new earth?" And Mary answered me, "Yes pastor, you are."

"How the Broken Body Heals: A Sermon on the Lord's Supper"

I Corinthians 11:17-2 (NRSV):

Now in the following instructions, I do not commend you, because when you come together, it is not for the better but for the worse. For, to begin with, when you come together as a church, I hear that there are divisions among you, and to some extent, I believe it. Indeed, there have to be factions among you, for only so will it become clear who among you are genuine. When you come together, it is not really to eat the Lord's Supper. For when the time comes to eat, each of you goes ahead with your own supper, and one goes hungry, and another becomes drunk. What! Do you not have homes to eat and drink in? Or do you show contempt for the church of God and humiliate those who have nothing? What should I say to you? Should I commend you? In this matter, I do not commend you!

> For I received from the Lord what I also handed on to you, that the Lord Jesus on the night when he was betrayed took a loaf of bread, and when he had given thanks, he broke it and said, "This is my body that is broken for you. Do this in remembrance of me." In the same way, he took the cup also, after supper, saying, "This cup is the new covenant in my blood. Do this, as often as you drink it, in remembrance of me." For as often as you eat this bread and drink the cup, you proclaim the Lord's death until he comes.
>
> Whoever, therefore, eats the bread or drinks the cup of the Lord in an unworthy manner will be answerable for the body and blood of the Lord. Examine yourselves, and only then eat of the bread and drink of the cup. For all who eat and drink without discerning the body, eat and drink judgment against themselves.

On the night he was betrayed, Jesus took a loaf of bread, and when he had given thanks, he broke it, and he gave it to Judas whose kiss would give him away. He gave it to Peter who would deny him with such conviction he could have passed a lie detector test. He gave it to all his disciples who would soon be dozing under the olive trees while he cried out in anguish to God. He gave it to all his disciples who would flee the scene of his execution. On the night he was betrayed, Jesus took the cup and when he had given thanks, he gave it to all his disciples—betrayers, deniers, dozers, and frightened fleers—and said, "This is the new covenant in my blood, given for you."

On the night the Corinthians gathered to share the Lord's Supper, the rich people came early because they were their own bosses and controlled their own schedules, which were full of leisure. And when the poor mother came after feeding her children the last crust of bread in the house, and when the famished male slave arrived having finished his back-breaking chores, the Lord's Supper was all gone. The bread all eaten. The wine all drunk. The poor were betrayed by the wealthy. And Jesus was betrayed too.

Paul accuses the rich Corinthians of unworthily eating and drinking this Holy Supper which Jesus gave in remembrance of himself. He warns them that with their table manners they have created a dangerous situation for themselves and for their community. And he exhorts them to examine themselves and to discern the body, lest they eat and drink judgment against themselves.

The Reformed Church in which I grew up did not mess with Paul's word. The church's quarterly administrations of the Lord's Supper were a serious and somber affair. They felt nothing like a celebration. The week before the Supper, the minister read the lengthy "Exhortation to Self-Examination" in a tone of voice that would have made the prophet Jeremiah sound like a relatively happy guy. Especially worrisome to me as a kid were the words: "For all who eat and drink this Supper without discerning the body, eat and drink judgment against themselves." Not wanting to take any chances, my grandpa, a good and faithful man, ate the bread and drank the cup only once in his whole lifetime, and that was at my brother-in-law's ordination in a Reformed Church out East, where he was beyond the judgment of the local board of elders and his fellow Christians.

On the Sundays the Supper was actually administered in the church of my childhood, the Lord's Table was piled high with silver trays, then covered by a huge white cloth. It looked like a casket holding a corpse. The air in the church felt thicker than normal. The lights seemed dimmer. As the elements were passed to the adults sitting in their pews, we kids got peppermints to eat. I was kind of grateful that I was not allowed to take the Supper. And I was hopeful that God's judgment would not come down on someone right there in church as they swallowed the last drop from their little cup. As a grown up, I have a clearer sense of the solemnity that surrounded the supper.

The people who raised me in the faith felt a double danger in taking the Supper. On the side of self-examination, they feared they would not be sufficiently righteous and worthy to receive it. And on the side of discerning the body, they feared they would not recognize and be sufficiently grateful for the great price Jesus paid with his own body to free them from their sin and make them righteous. It seemed that the Supper was all about recognizing God's great grace in Jesus Christ, while also trying to demonstrate that you were exactly the kind of person who did not need God's grace.

The danger that the people who raised me in the faith *did not* seem to recognize in the Supper was the danger of eating and drinking this food that is Jesus. They did not recognize the danger of taking Jesus in, the danger of being taken up into the life of this Jesus who happily ate with folk whom the religious self-righteous called "sinners." And who on the night he was betrayed went ahead and broke the bread of new life and poured the cup of salvation and gave it to a bunch of disciples whom he knew would give him up and sell him out. In this single gesture, the whole story of Jesus is told in a nutshell. Jesus is the one who in sheer gratuity and unquenchable love gives himself to the world to take away the sin of the whole world. From his incarnation to his death on the cross, Jesus is giving himself away in love.

Paul writes, "As often as you eat this bread and drink this cup, you proclaim the Lord's death until he comes." You proclaim the cross. What exactly does this mean? What are we proclaiming in the death and cross of Jesus? Theologian Michael Welker writes,

> The cross confronts us with the hideous knowledge that [the institutions of] religion, law, politics, morality, and public opinion—all institutions that are supposed to serve true piety, public order, universal justice, and the promotion of human community and what is good—can collaborate in driving the human beings who use them into ongoing falsehood, injustice, mercilessness, disintegration, and distance from God.[2]

And it is not only these external institutions and forces and systems that confront us with the human capacity to destroy life. It is also people on the inside who are good, well-meaning people—kin, neighbors, friends, and fellow disciples—who end up betraying Jesus and collaborating in ways that resist God's sovereignty, God's real presence, God's righteousness, and God's faithful love. Welker again:

> The proclamation of Christ's death on the cross pulls the rug out from under all religious, legal, political, and moral righteousness of human beings. In light of this proclamation, no one can boast, no one can point the finger at others, no one can separate from others, no one can elevate themselves and look down on others. In the death of Jesus, in the old rugged cross, this emblem of suffering and shame, all illusions are destroyed that human beings can by their own power deliver themselves from their own act of closing themselves off from God.[3]

And in closing ourselves off from God, we as human beings continually close ourselves off from the divine-human community that God is creating in Jesus Christ.

It happens at a supper table in Corinth where the rich betray the poor; in America where whites betray blacks and other people of color; in Uganda where activists for gay and lesbian rights rape the ones they

---

[2] Michael Welker, *What Happens in Holy Communion*, trans. John F. Hoffmeyer (Grand Rapids: Eerdmans, 2000), 105.
[3] Ibid., 106.

have come to liberate; and in the Body of Jesus Christ where in the name of Jesus queer people are judged and shamed and shut out. When you proclaim the death of Jesus, you proclaim the immensity of human evil and the impossibility that, on our own, human beings and human institutions can overcome the evil we create.

But you proclaim something else too. You proclaim the wonder of this crazy, vulnerable, dangerous love that is embodied in the one we call Jesus. You proclaim the foolish wisdom of trusting in God more than you trust in anything else. You proclaim the scandal of Jesus letting the intersecting powers and principalities do their worst, because he trusted that in the end, God would expose them for what they really were and defeat them for love.

But if this Holy Supper were only a proclamation of the death of Jesus, we would be lost. The world would be lost. If God had not raised Jesus from the dead, we would be a people most to be pitied. If there were no Easter, we would be a people and a world without hope. At this Table, we proclaim too the life of Jesus. We proclaim a love that is stronger than death. We celebrate good news.

But the good news of Easter is not only that Jesus, who was brutally, unjustly killed, is now alive again. The good news of Easter is not only that Good Friday was a hideous wrong that God has set right. The good news of Easter is not only that through Jesus all will be made alive, for ever and ever, world without end. The good news of Easter is also that when God raises Jesus from the dead, the world is flooded with a very particular kind of new life.

On Easter morning, what lives again is the life of this particular man named Jesus who willingly became the innocent victim of human betrayal and violence. What lives again is the life of this man who agreed to become the sacrificial scapegoat of the human thirst for blood. On Easter morning, what the world gets is the life of this God-man who spoke forgiveness to those who nailed him to the cross, who died as he lived, in utter, complete, self-giving love. Jesus did not return evil for evil, did not respond to violence with violence, did not exclude those who excluded him, and did not hate those who hated him. Jesus died as he lived, and he now lives as he died: pouring out perfect love for the stranger, for the enemy, for the excluded, for the little, the least, the lost, the lepers, the limpers, the unloved. Pouring out perfect love for you.

On the night he was betrayed, Jesus tore apart a loaf of bread, and he raised a cup of wine, and when he had given thanks, he gave it to all his disciples—betrayers, deniers, dozers, frightened fleers—and said,

"This is my body, broken and given for you. This is the new covenant in my blood, poured out and given for you." This is how the broken body of Jesus heals: by giving us what we need but cannot give to ourselves, a love that does not walk away from our sin and brokenness, a love that is stronger than all our fears, a love that is stronger than the deaths we as human beings experience and cause.

This is how your broken body is healed. This is how the broken body of the church is healed. This is how the broken body of the world is healed: by our receiving the nourishment of this dangerous, Holy Supper; by our consuming the dangerous life-giving, love-multiplying person of Jesus; and by our being consumed by the life, death, and resurrection of Jesus who trusted God more than he trusted anything else.

In Jesus Christ, the whole story we are carrying in our bodies, our sin and our betrayals, our shame and our radiance, all of our dying and all of our rising, is taken up and spread out on this banquet Table, where divine love places us beyond the reach of danger and nourishes our daring to live and love in, with, and through Jesus. To Jesus Christ, the crucified and risen Lord, to God the Father and Mother of us all, to the Holy Spirit, unquenchable breath of new life, to the triune God be all glory and honor, in the church and in the world, now and forever!

CHAPTER 8

"Worship as a Way of Seeing"

Carol Bechtel

Worship is a way of seeing the world in the light of God.[1]
Abraham Joshua Heschel

  I remember highlighting this quote by Abraham Joshua Heschel as a seminary student decades ago. At the time, I thought, "That is profound—I should remember it." It is, and I have. Yet over the years, I have come to realize that it is one of those statements that one must live into. Just as "deliver us from evil" from the Lord's Prayer takes on a whole new urgency when danger is no longer in the abstract, so Heschel's deceptively simple observation becomes more profound each time we look at it. The statement remains the same, but we do not.
  If life experience affirms the truth of Heschel's words, then it is natural to wonder what experiences led him to say these words in the first place. Absent the opportunity to ask the celebrated twentieth-century rabbi, philosopher, and theologian, who died in 1972, we may at least safely conclude that he knew well two Old Testament/Hebrew

---

[1] Abraham Joshua Heschel, *Man's Quest for God* (New York: Charles Scribner's Sons, 1954), xii.

Bible passages that seem to make the same point: Psalm 73 and the book of Job. In this chapter, I would like to explore these two texts to see if we can gain any wisdom as to why worship helps us to see the world in a new light—more specifically, in *God's* light.[2]

Psalm 73: memoir of a personal epiphany

Psalm 73 begins on an innocuous note: "Truly God is good to the upright, to those who are pure in heart."[3] It is so out of step with the rest of the psalm that one suspects the psalmist is quoting a popular proverb with which he disagrees. Indeed, the sentiment—and the theology—have much in common with a plethora of biblical proverbs. One example will suffice to represent the many. Proverbs 12:2 asserts: "The good obtain favor from the LORD, but those who devise evil, he condemns." Many psalms echo a similar assumption. "O fear the LORD, you his holy ones," urges Psalm 34:9, "for those who fear him have no want." Both examples drink deeply from the well of deuteronomic theology, which is aptly summarized in the "blessings and curses" of Deuteronomy 27 and 28. The if/then structure of these prescriptive promises is designed to motivate the faithful by way of both the carrot and the stick. Deuteronomy 28:1-2 holds out the carrot:

> If you will only obey the LORD your God, by diligently observing all his commandments that I am commanding you today, the LORD your God will set you high above all the nations of the earth; all these blessings shall come upon you and overtake you if you obey the LORD your God.

Deuteronomy 28:15 raises the stick:

> But if you will not obey the LORD your God by diligently observing all his commandments and decrees which I am commanding you today, then all these curses shall come upon you and overtake you.

These deuteronomic assumptions undergird the opening verse of Psalm 73. But our psalmist is having none of it. What at first may

---

[2] This effort seems a fitting tribute to the Rev. Dr. Gregg Mast to whom this festschrift is dedicated. Worship and a deep love for the gathered people of God have been at the heart of Gregg Mast's vocation.
[3] All biblical quotes are from the New Revised Standard Version unless otherwise indicated.

have seemed innocuous now seems naïve. And what is it that sets his theological teeth on edge? Simply this: experience. He observes, first, the prosperity of the wicked:

> For they have no pain; their bodies are sound and sleek.
> They are not in trouble as others are; they are not plagued like other people.
> Therefore pride is their necklace; violence covers them like a garment.
> Their eyes swell out with fatness; their hearts overflow with follies.
> They scoff and speak with malice; loftily they threaten oppression.
> They set their mouths against heaven, and their tongues range over the earth.[4]

Over against this is the suffering of the righteous—namely, his own. In his experience, God has not made good on God's promises. In the "Let's make a deal" language of deuteronomic theology, God has not held up God's end of the deal. And so, the psalmist complains in verses 13-14:

> All in vain I have kept my heart clean and washed my hands in innocence.
> For all day long I have been plagued, and am punished every morning.

In an unpublished sermon on this psalm, Ellen Davis writes,

> It makes perfect sense that God should encourage good behavior with prompt rewards and be equally conscientious in punishing the wicked. The only problem with this theory, popular among religious people of every age, is lack of evidence.[5]

Davis continues,

> As the psalmist sees, the wicked often do uncommonly well, by any objective measure:
> "In ordinary human affliction, they have no part" (v. 5). The wicked are rich, well placed, and, to add insult to injury, they are

---
[4] Psalm 73:4-9; my own preference for translating v. 9b is, "Their tongues *strut* over the earth."
[5] This sermon—to which I owe much—was preached on June 15, 1997. I am grateful to Ellen Davis for many things, but especially for permission to quote her here and perhaps to give this gem of a sermon a broader hearing.

healthy and good looking—whereas the righteous are poor, pale, and sickly from excessive study. This the psalmist sees, and it galls her. Following a strangled expression that probably stands for some ancient four-letter word, she cries: "In vain have I kept my heart clean and washed my hands in innocence" (v.13).[6]

It is enough to make one give up on God. Indeed, we get the sense that the psalmist is an eyelash away from doing just that. So, what stops him—or at least—slows him down?

First, there is his nagging sense of responsibility. In verse 15 the psalmist admits, "If I had said, 'I will talk on in this way,' I would have been untrue to the circle of your children." In other words, he is afraid that his outburst will cause others to doubt the goodness and justice of God.[7] It is one thing, evidently, to feel the footing of his own faith slipping but quite another to be responsible for taking others with him over the edge.[8]

Still, he says, "When I thought how to understand this, it seemed to me a wearisome task" (v. 16). The psalmist has, for all practical purposes, come to an existential impasse. He cannot understand how a good and just God could be so sloppy and irresponsible in meting out reward and punishment. And yet, in acknowledging this, we also ought to acknowledge that the psalmist is already several steps ahead of those who claim they understand it all. As we will see when we get to the story of Job and his friends, there is something to be said for admitting when we do not "get it." He may be disillusioned, but there are worse things. As Barbara Brown Taylor reminds us, if disillusionment literally means the loss of illusion, then "it is not a bad thing to lose the lies we have mistaken for the truth."[9]

Stunning as Brown Taylor's insight is, one suspects it would still be cold comfort to our psalmist. Like his ancestors on the edge of the Red Sea, he cannot go back, he cannot stand still, and he is afraid to go

---

[6] Davis chooses to refer the psalmist with feminine pronouns. I have opted to use masculine ones, but not out of any conviction one way or the other about the psalmist's gender. By not harmonizing the references, I hope to help readers keep an open mind.
[7] The author of Psalm 39 testifies to a similar crisis of faith but vows to "keep a muzzle on my mouth," not for the sake of other believers but out of concern for what the wicked might make of his words (Ps. 39:1-3).
[8] The author of Psalm 125 could be praying for our psalmist. He begs God to "do good to those who are good" so that "the righteous might not stretch out their hands to do wrong."
[9] Barbara Brown Taylor, *The Preaching Life* (Cambridge: Cowley Publications, 1993), 8.

forward. And yet, he *does* go forward—not into the Red Sea, but into the sanctuary of God. And that, as they say, makes all the difference.

At the center of this psalm, verse 17 acts as a hinge. Just when the task of theodicy seemed to this psalmist "a wearisome task" and a dead-end effort, he goes into the sanctuary of God. What does he experience there? We are not told precisely. What we *can* say, however, is that this experience is enough to counterbalance the experiences that had given rise to his earlier doubts. Whatever happens, it gives him a new perspective on the fate of the wicked and renews his faith in the justice and goodness of God. "Then I perceived their end," he says. In what can only be called a "God's-eye view" of the situation, the psalmist sees clearly for the first time:

> Truly you set them in slippery places; you make them fall to ruin. How they are destroyed in a moment, swept away utterly by terrors!

Hebrew verb tenses are notoriously slippery. We might prefer a translation that renders these verbs in the future tense—testifying that the wicked *will fall to ruin* and *be swept away* at some judgment day on the horizon. And perhaps that is the thrust of the psalmist's vision. Yet the fact that the NRSV opts for the present tense is both more powerful and more comforting. The sense of his vision is that justice is *as good as done*—for both the wicked and, presumably, the righteous. The present tense invites us to join the psalmist in God's "eternal now"—a perspective that is possible only when we stand beside him in the sanctuary.

Awash in the light of this God-given epiphany, the psalmist blinks at its unaccustomed brightness and rubs the sleep from his eyes. The first thing he notices is that the wicked have no more substance than a bad dream. "On awaking, you despise their phantoms," he says (v. 20). Next he looks back at his own doubts with wondering chagrin. "I was stupid and ignorant," he says in verse 22; "I was like a brute beast toward you." God, however, does not seem to be holding a grudge, since the psalmist goes on to celebrate that God holds his right hand, guides him with God's counsel, and receives him with honor (vv. 23-24).

In the first half of the psalm, the psalmist clamored for answers, doubting God's goodness and justice. In the second half of the psalm, he seems content to live without all the answers and is willing to trust in God's justice (see v. 27). Also restored is his faith in God's goodness. Like a tired child crawling up onto his father's lap, he sighs, "Whom have I in heaven but you? And there is nothing on earth that I desire other than you" (v. 25). The psalm concludes with both a new perspective and a new agenda. "For me," he says, "it is good to be near God; I have made the LORD God my refuge, to tell of all your works" (v. 28).

Ironically, the psalmist seems to have come full circle. Now he knows that, "God *is* good to the upright, to those who are pure in heart" (v. 1; italics mine). He may not be able to explain *why* this is, but thanks to the "hermeneutic of the sanctuary," he can now testify *that* it is. As Davis puts it, truism has been transformed into truth.[10]

Psalm 73 tells the story of a radical reorientation—a kind of religious conversion. Part of its power is that it reads like a memoir, inviting us to walk with the psalmist on his road of doubt until we, too, are "surprised by joy" in the temple courts. Whether we can walk with him along the path of renewed faith may depend in part on whether we are willing to enter the sanctuary ourselves. (Conversion, after all, is not something one can claim vicariously.) Still, the psalmist points us in the right direction. If we want to open our hearts to the possibility of this kind of conversion, we will need to make our way to the sanctuary.[11]

But how to proceed? As powerful as the "memoir" of Psalm 73 is, it is frustratingly short of specifics. When we read the psalmist's description of the wicked, we are not given names or dates. We wonder in vain about what particular experiences prompted his outburst against wicked people doing well. Perhaps it was a series of encounters that allowed him to make generalizations as to type, but we know nothing definite about any of them.

And yet the description drips with tantalizing detail. The bodies of the wicked are "sound and sleek" (v. 4). They wear pride and violence like favorite sweaters (v. 6). Their eyes "swell out with fatness" and their hearts "overflow with follies" (v. 7). We feel like we know these pompous degenerates—and indeed, we probably do. We see them on the news with regularity. They sit across from us at family reunions and in faculty meetings. They greet us at the grocery store and pass the peace with us at church. They may even look back at us from the mirror on occasion.

This, one suspects, is part of the brilliance of the psalms. Their language is vivid and evocative, without being tethered to any

---

[10] I owe the phrase "hermeneutic of the sanctuary" and the insight about moving from "truism to truth" to Ellen Davis's sermon (see above).

[11] For a particularly brilliant musical interpretation of Psalm 73, see "All My Life," Ken Medema's setting in *Psalms for All Seasons: A Complete Psalter for Worship*, edited by Martin Tel (Grand Rapids: Calvin Institute for Christian Worship; Faith Alive Christian Resources; Brazos Press, 2012), 448-51. This setting tracks the transformation from trite to true, helping the congregation to retrace the steps of the psalmist's internal conversion.

identifiable story. They are, in the words of one wise observer, "kind of like a blues song." And it is that very quality that allows us to fill in the blank with the details of our own lives. When we pray Psalm 51:3, "I know my transgressions and my sin is ever before me," it is not David's sins that are ever before us, but our own.

Of course, this reference to David illustrates the way people have tried to tie certain psalms to specific incidents. The superscription to Psalm 51 identifies it as a "psalm of David," and suggests that it springs from the time "when the prophet Nathan came to him, after he had gone in to Bathsheba." Though it does fit that situation like a glove, one cannot help but wonder if the superscription errs by giving the faithful too much information. Is this a prayer that only works when one has committed murder, adultery, and (arguably) rape? Given the popularity of this prayer over the centuries—yea, millennia—one thinks not.[12] Nevertheless, the urge to historicize the generic language of the psalms is a product of our natural curiosity about what prompted these prayers in the first place.

All of this is an excuse for going to the book of Job for the information Psalm 73 lacks. If we want to know more about what happened to the psalmist in the sanctuary, we will not find it by reading between the lines of Psalm 73. So why not look to a story that narrates a similar "conversion experience" to see if we can glean additional insights about why worship helps us to "see the world in the light of God"?

Job's story: the limits of human wisdom

Most people think the book of Job is about "why bad things happen to good people." They are only partly right. While this dilemma constitutes the presenting problem in Job's story, I would like to suggest that the central theme of the book is *the limits of human wisdom*.[13] To get at this, one must pay careful attention to the structure of the book's prologue.

The action of the prologue moves back and forth in an upstairs/downstairs pattern. All of Job's experiences—for good or for ill—take place "downstairs." God and the heavenly beings are the principal actors "upstairs." One of these heavenly beings—the accuser—asks the

---

[12] Someone once suggested that we read the superscription of Psalm 51 as illustrative. In other words, "If it worked in David's situation, how much more will it work in mine?"

[13] For fuller arguments of this thesis, please see Carol Bechtel, "Knowing Our Limits: Job's Wisdom on Worship," in *Touching the Altar* (Grand Rapids: Eerdmans, 2008), and *Job and the Life of Faith: Wisdom for Today's World* (Pittsburgh: Kerygma, 2004).

central question of the book: "Does Job fear God for nothing?" (1:9).[14] This sets in motion the cosmic bet designed to find out whether Job will still serve God if there is nothing in it for him.

If Psalm 73 left us wanting more detail, the prologue to Job gives us more detail than we know what to do with. Many have pointed out the problematics of a plot depicting God as hapless at best and diabolical at worst. (Though I suppose it would have been worse if God had been described as betting *against* Job.) Still, theological discomfort is the price we pay for a story that will work only if we know for certain that Job is innocent. How else, after all, would we know that Job has not, in fact, done anything to deserve his suffering? How else—when we read past the prologue—would we know that Job's friends are wrong?[15]

The upstairs/downstairs structure of the prologue gives us, as readers, an unprecedented peek into the real explanation for Job's suffering. We may not be entirely comfortable with the explanation provided, but it does offer one example of a situation where a righteous person suffers for a reason other than his own sin. This ought to give us pause the next time we are tempted to connect the cosmic dots with too much confidence. Sometimes the answer to the question, "What did I do to deserve this?" may be, "Nothing!"

It is crucial to remember that Job and his wife and friends know nothing at all about what is going on "upstairs." The only explanation for suffering that they know is the deuteronomic one.

Sin → Suffering

Obedience → Blessing

Of course, it should be noted that the original articulation of these "equations" in Deuteronomy 27 and 28 was intended as a prescription for how to behave, not a description for how to diagnose the causes of bane and blessing. In other words, the equations were designed to be read left to right and not right to left. When Job's friends insist that his

---

[14] It is important not to confuse this character with "Satan" as we encounter him in later Jewish and Christian literature. This is not a personal noun but a descriptive title for a character who acts as a kind of prosecuting attorney. The NRSV's decision to render the noun as "Satan" simply sows confusion.

[15] Calvinists are notoriously hard to convince of Job's innocence. "All have sinned and fall short of the glory of God," after all. Job's story does not dispute this. It does, however, present us with a character who scrupulously maintains his innocence through God's gift of the sacrificial system. He is even described as rising "early in the morning" to make sacrifices on behalf of all his children just in case they may have sinned (1:5).

suffering has been caused by some secret sin (as, for instance, in Job 4:7), they are, in essence, attempting to read the equations backwards: Job is suffering, *therefore*, it must be because he sinned. This might sound like the flip side of a song from the *Sound of Music*; that is, when Job's friends see him scraping his sores on the ash heap, they conclude, "Somewhere in your youth or childhood—you must have done something bad." While the Bible is replete with examples of others drawing similar conclusions, the book of Job functions as a kind of cautionary tale. At the very least, it suggests that we should proceed with fear and trembling but, perhaps better yet, that we do not try to make this theologically dangerous move at all.

Job is not the only one whose faith is put to the test in this scenario. If we take seriously the creation story's "one flesh" description, then Job's wife is "tested in every way" just as he is. She, too, has lost every last one of her children and all her worldly goods. Unlike Job's friends, she believes that Job is innocent of wrongdoing. But if Job is not guilty, then who is? Maybe *God* is. What most commentators fail to recognize is that her advice to "Curse God and die" in 2:9 articulates a very real—and understandable—reaction to a God who does not seem to be playing by God's own rules. If God is not just, after all, then the most merciful option may be to curse God and die.

Job, however, sees another option—an option very like the one taken by the author of Psalm 73. In the ensuing chapters, Job rails against God and his friends, insisting on his innocence and demanding an explanation for his unjust suffering. He wrestles with God and, in a line that has come to epitomize his tenacious faith, declares, "Though he slay me, yet will I trust in him."[16]

By the end of chapter 31, Job reaches the same existential impasse that our psalmist reached in just fourteen verses. We can well imagine Job saying "Amen!" to Psalm 73:13-14:

> All in vain I have kept my heart clean and washed my hands in innocence.
> For all day long I have been plagued, and am punished every morning.

---

[16] This is the way the KJV translates Job 13:15a. It is, in my judgment, a more faithful rendering of the Hebrew than the NRSV's "See, he will kill me; I have no hope." The NRSV's footnote does acknowledge "Though he kill me, yet I will trust in him" as a possibility. An even better option might be, "yet I will wait for him" or "hope" for him.

Yet, here again, Job's journey proves startlingly similar to that of the psalmist. In chapter 38, God finally "answer[s] Job out of the whirlwind."[17] Here at last is a description of what an encounter with God in such circumstances might be like. It is not, as they say, for the timid. Indeed, it brings to mind that famous passage from Annie Dillard about how worshipers have no idea what we are getting up to on any given Sunday morning. If we did, she maintains, the ushers would "lash us to our pews" and distribute "crash helmets."[18] And yet, it surely qualifies as worship—especially if we look to that word's etymological roots. Worship is *worth-ship*, after all, and chapters 38-41 are all about getting Job to acknowledge God's worth.

It should be said that God does not really answer Job's questions in the speech from the whirlwind. No explanation for the suffering of the innocent is forthcoming. Yet, that God does respond to Job is no small sign of respect. And indeed, if the main theme of the book of Job is the limits of human wisdom, then God's response is spot on.[19] "Where were you when I laid the foundation of the earth?" may be poor pastoral care, but it goes straight to the heart of the reality check Job needs. In a series of rhetorical questions, startling, not least for their sarcasm, God points out what should be patently obvious: God is God, and Job is not.

Like most Old Testament theophanies, this one comes with a full quota of terrifying special effects. Still we should not miss the beauty that swirls through the speech from the whirlwind. God's delight in the details of creation is palpable. Even the mighty leviathan gets a celebratory stanza (ch. 41). In fact, God's attitude toward this fearsome mythic sea monster may be the most telling thing of all. Mortals of Job's day would have trembled at the mention of leviathan's name. God, on the other hand, asks Job, "Will you play with it as with a bird" or "put it on a leash for your girls?" (41:5). The implication is that God can do these things without even breaking a sweat. (One wonders who God's "girls" are, but that is a rabbit trail I will save for another day.) This is whom Job is dealing with, and he will never be the same.

---

[17] God's response is delayed in the canon by an interruption from a hitherto unheard of person named Elihu. In chapters 32-37, Elihu attempts to do a better job of defending God than Job's friends have done. It is significant that, when God begins to speak in chapter 38, he pays no attention whatsoever to Elihu, brushing away his words as if they were a pesky gnat.

[18] Annie Dillard, *Teaching a Stone to Talk* (New York: Harper & Row), 40.

[19] The placement and content of chapter 28 serve to underscore that this is the book's true theme. This chapter hits "pause" at the center of the book and reflects on the fact that only God knows the way to wisdom.

Whatever else one may say about the speech from the whirlwind, it does enable Job to "see the world in the light of God." It does not answer his questions, but it puts them into perspective. It suggests, in fact, that Job would not be able to understand the answers anyway. Although Einstein *could* have explained the theory of general relativity to his beagle, the beagle would not have come away much the wiser.

In Psalm 73 we saw that the psalmist's trip to the temple was followed by a sense of what I described as "wondering chagrin." We see something very similar in Job 42:1-6. Job quotes God's question, "Who is this that hides counsel without knowledge" (see 38:2) and admits that he has "uttered what I did not understand, things too wonderful for me, which I did not know." Then he quotes his own words to God: "Hear, and I will speak; I will question you, and you declare to me." (Cue the wondering chagrin.) Next Job admits that his previous knowledge of God was no more than a rumor, that is, "I had heard of you by the hearing of the ear." Now, however, his eye "sees" God—a statement that is less of a claim to special revelation than it is a summary of the whole reality check that was the whirlwind.

Job's short, humble statement concludes with the famous but difficult words: "Therefore I despise myself and repent in dust and ashes" (42:6). The first thing that must be said is that he is not repenting of some "secret sin" as per the accusations of his friends. If there is any lingering doubt about whether they spoke truly of him, it is dispelled by God's blunt words to Eliphaz in verse 7: "My wrath is kindled against you and against your two friends, for you have not spoken of me what is right, as my servant Job has."

But if Job's "last words" are not repentance for some secret sin, what are they?

As is so often the case, translation is key for interpretation.[20] For one thing, there is no object pronoun for the verb that the NRSV translates as "despise." A better candidate would be the word "recant," which does not require an object. This yields, "I recant" instead of "I despise myself." Similarly, in the next phrase, the word "repent" might be rendered, "reconsider" or "reconsider about." If that is the case, then what is Job reconsidering when he refers to "dust and ashes"?

In Job 30:19, Job says, "He has cast me into the mire, and I have become like dust and ashes." The phrase is also used in Genesis 18:27,

---

[20] This reading of Job 42:6 is, again, courtesy of Ellen Davis. See "Job and Jacob: The Integrity of Faith," in *The Whirlwind: Essays on Job, Hermeneutics, and Theology in Memory of Jane Morse*, ed. Stephen L. Cook, Corrine L. Patton, and James L. Watts (New York: Sheffield Academic Press, 2001), 118.

where it seems to symbolize the human condition: "Abraham answered, 'Let me take it upon myself to speak to the LORD, I who am but dust and ashes." This last example, especially, hints that the phrase may be a kind of metaphor for what it means to be human. Indeed, it echoes what we hear every Ash Wednesday: "Remember that you are dust, and to dust you shall return." Is it possible that when Job says, "I reconsider about dust and ashes" he means that he is *reconsidering what it means to be human*? It is impossible to say for sure, of course, but hearing his words in this vein would fit well with the book's theme, namely, the limits of human wisdom. This was, after all, the overwhelming lesson from the whirlwind. It would appear, then, that Job has learned this lesson well.

Many have wished over the years that the book of Job ended here. The book's prose epilogue (42:7-17) is often judged as a disappointing sell-out to deuteronomic theology. According to this disparaging view, the restoration of Job's wealth and family undercuts the point of the previous forty-one chapters.

A closer look at the content of the epilogue yields a view that is both more appreciative and more profound. Far from being a reprise of the friends' simplistic theme song, the end of Job's story proves beyond a shadow of a doubt that Job *is* willing to serve God, even if there is nothing in it for him. Here is how.

It helps to remember the exact words of the accuser's question from the prologue. In 1:9-11, he asks:

> Does Job fear God for nothing? Have you not put a fence around him and his house and all that he has, on every side? You have blessed the work of his hands, and his possessions have increased in the land. But stretch out your hand now, and touch all that he has, and he will curse you to your face.

Yes the LORD blesses "the latter days of Job more than the beginning" (42:12). Yes Job has twice as much livestock. Yes he even has more children.[21] But has God re-erected that protective fence around his life and his loved ones?

If Job has learned nothing else from his ordeal, he has learned that there are no guarantees. Life is exquisitely precious and terrifyingly fragile. One assumes that he and his wife still carry the deep and abiding

---

[21] Upon reading the end of Job's story in her children's Bible, my young daughter, Ellen, asked this pointed question on behalf of herself and her brother: "If Andy and I died, and you and Dad got new kids, would that make it okay?"

grief for the loss of their first family, so it is no small thing for them to risk being vulnerable to loss on such a scale again. Job knows now that not even a scrupulously righteous life can protect him and those he loves from disaster. It can all be taken away in an instant.

There is a poem by Yehuda HaLevi in the Jewish funeral service that captures what Job now knows only too well:

> 'Tis a fearful thing to love
> what death can touch.
> A fearful thing to love,
> hope, dream: to be—
> to be, and oh! To lose.
> A thing for fools this, and
> a holy thing,
> a holy thing to love.
> For
> your life has lived in me,
> your laugh once lifted me,
> your word was gift to me.
> To remember this brings a painful joy.
> 'Tis a human thing, love,
> a holy thing,
> to love
> what death has touched.

The fact that Job is willing to live and love again even with no guarantees is the most remarkable moment in his story. The fact that he is willing to trust God again defies all logic and expectation. Far from being the weakest part of Job's story, the epilogue is its crowning glory.

One of the most telling exercises one can attempt at this point in the story is to compare and contrast the Job of the prologue with the Job of the epilogue. The character study reveals an early Job whose faith is relatively fragile. His superogatory sacrifices on behalf of his children (just in case they had inadvertently cursed God in their hearts at one of their progressive dinner parties), seems almost neurotic by comparison with the happy-go-lucky parenting style of the epilogue. There, after giving his new daughters wonderfully frivolous names (Dove, Cinnamon, and Eyeshadow), he completely defies social convention by giving them their own inheritances. Although these details may seem small, they are significant—revealing a Job who is not so tightly wound as the one we met at the beginning of the story.

It is also significant that he prays for God to accept the sacrifices of his friends (42:7-9).[22] What must it have cost him to pray for the very people who made his life such a misery? And yet, without Job's prayers, God will deal with them "according to their folly" (v. 8). Without Job's grace, they cannot receive God's grace.

What was it that enabled Job to pray for his "frenemies"? Perhaps his own bitter experience of marginalization enabled him to muster sufficient empathy for the act. Or maybe it had more to do with his experience with the whirlwind. God's words were stern, certainly. But they were also strangely gracious. God forbore to respond to him, after all, so why not respond with forbearance to his friends? Finally, if the voice from the whirlwind taught him anything, it must have taught him that, "This is an interesting planet. It deserves all the attention you can give it."[23] Who wants to waste time holding a grudge when there is a whole world out there at which to marvel?

At the end of Job's story, the narrator takes over and finishes the story for him. The words of Job really are ended (see Job 31:40b). Yet, if Job did speak at this point, we can imagine him saying words like those in Psalm 73:21-26:

> When my soul was embittered, when I was pricked in heart,
> I was stupid and ignorant; I was like a brute beast toward you.
> Nevertheless I am continually with you; you hold my right hand.
> You guide me with your counsel, and afterward you will receive me with honor.
> Whom have I in heaven but you?
> And there is nothing on earth that I desire other than you.
> My flesh and my heart may fail,
> But God is the strength of my heart and my portion forever.

Conclusion

Central to the transformation of both Job and the author of Psalm 73 is an intense experience of God's electrifying presence. For the psalmist, this takes place in the temple; for Job, it takes place in the whirlwind. Neither are the same afterward. Whatever it was that they

---

[22] It is interesting to note that this act of grace opens the floodgates for his own restoration (v. 10).

[23] These are the words of Marilynne Robinson's character, John Ames, in the novel *Gilead* (New York: Farrar, Straus, and Giroux, 2004), 28.

experienced, it gave them a new perspective. This change in perspective gave them a new lease on both life and theology. To return to our quote from Abraham Heschel, they really did "see the world in the light of God."

For those of us who appreciate their initial questions and the courage with which they asked them, this may seem somewhat disappointing. I for one would still like to know why bad things happen to good people and, conversely, why good things happen to bad people. I think, however, that we can take comfort in the fact that God does not belittle our questions. They are good questions. It is only that we must wait for whatever answers God sees fit to give. If we are to believe what God says to the prophet Habakkuk, the answer will someday be so plain that "a runner may read it" (Hab. 2:4). In the meantime, the voice from the whirlwind reminds us that human understanding is limited. To paraphrase Shakespeare, there is way more going on here than is dreamt of in our theology.

Should we not rail against what we perceive as God's injustice? If anything, Psalm 73 and the book of Job give us permission to pray with shocking candor. Railing against God is a time-honored tradition in Scripture, and, if anything, this suggests that we have rather more latitude in this regard than most of us ever take advantage of. While we are at it, we might even try railing at each other—though the book of Job would suggest that this might better be done with more humility than Job's friends employed. Forgiveness and grace at the end of the day are lessons we also might want to learn from Job.

There is a story of a little girl who ran sobbing through the aisles of a grocery store saying, "My mommy is lost!" Her pain was real, but her perspective was limited. There is a sense in which this is the message of both Psalm 73 and the book of Job. It is a message that testifies to the need for a radical shift in perspective. And the only place to get it is in the electrifying presence of God. Thus, disillusioned,

> We come to understand that God does not conform to our expectations. We glimpse our own relative size in the universe and see that no human being can say who God should be or how God should act. We review our requirements of God and recognize them as our own fictions, our own frail shelters against the vast night sky. Disillusioned, we find out what is not true and are set free to seek what is—if we dare.[24]

[24] Barbara Brown Taylor, *The Preaching Life*, 8.

We began with Abraham Heschel's insight, "Worship is a way of seeing the world in the light of God." I hope that Psalm 73 and the book of Job have helped us to appreciate some ways in which that is true. To be honest, however, I do not think I will ever really be done with that quote. Just when I think I understand it, some new experience makes me glimpse new vistas. It is a bit like Alexander Pope's poem, "A Little Learning," which concludes like this:

> So pleased at first the towering Alps we try,
> Mount o'er the vales, and seem to tread the sky;
> The eternal snows appear already past,
> And the first clouds and mountains seem the last.
> But those attained, we tremble to survey
> The growing labours of the lengthened way;
> The increasing prospect tires our wandering eyes,
> Hills peep o'er hills, and Alps on Alps arise!

CHAPTER 9

Navigating the Changing Landscape of World Christianity

Wesley Granberg-Michaelson

When Gregg Mast was elected president of the General Synod of the Reformed Church in America is 1999 and I was serving as general secretary, I called Gregg and asked, "Have you ever heard of Kigali? I would like you to go there." An ecumenical dialogue between the World Alliance of Reformed Churches and the Organization of African Instituted Churches was to be held in Kigali, Rwanda, and I wanted Gregg to be a representative there. He agreed, and it became one of many outstanding ecumenical contributions Gregg has made to the world church. While known primarily as a pastor, historian, authority on worship, and theological educator, Gregg's ecumenical role has been substantial. This essay, in his honor, focuses on the current ecumenical challenges facing world Christianity.

Christian witness, ministry, mission, and evangelism today take place within the radically changing landscape of world Christianity. The changing landscape, in my view, should change our paradigm, theological perspective, and partners, as well as how we share power, as we all seek today to join in God's ongoing mission in the world.

The framework I will share in this essay identifies six specific ways in which the landscape of world Christianity is changing and then suggests possible responses. These changes in our global landscape are geographical, spiritual, theological, economic, migratory, and ecumenical.

The geographical landscape

When we talk about the changing landscape of world Christianity, what immediately comes to mind is the dramatic geographical relocation of the majority of Christians around the globe. The breadth and speed of these changes is without historic precedent; this has been well studied and documented. A review of a few facts brings these changes into focus:

- For one thousand years, Christianity's center of gravity—meaning the point at which an equal number of Christians around the globe were found to the north, south, east, and west—remained in Europe. Then from 1910 to 2010, the center of gravity moved from Spain to a point near Timbuktu, Africa—the most rapid geographical shift in all of Christian history.
- By 1980 more Christians were living in the global South than the global North for the first time in one thousand years.
- In 1910 just 2 percent of Africa's population was Christian. Today one out of four Christians in the world is an African.
- The continents of Latin America and Africa now hold one billion of the world's Christian community, with trends that continue to grow.
- By the year 2025, Asia's present 350 million Christians is projected to grow to 460 million.
- In the last decade, Islam grew in Asia by 1.7 percent, while Christianity grew by 2.4 percent.
- In 1910 fully 80 percent of the world's Christians were found in Europe and North America. A century later, that had dropped to 40 percent.
- For evangelicals, the shift is even more dramatic: 90 percent were found in the United States and Europe a century ago, whereas today, 75 percent of evangelicals are in the global South.
- On any given Sunday, it is estimated that more people attend worship in congregations in China than in the United States.[1]

---

[1] Wesley Granberg-Michaelson, *From Times Square to Timbuktu: The Post-Christian West Meets the Non-Western Church* (Grand Rapids, MI: Eerdmans, 2013), 7-8. The best

These trends are relatively clear. As Christianity continues to grow in Africa, Asia, and Latin America, by the end of this century, in 2100, Christians living in the global South and East will number 2.8 billion—about three times greater than the 775 million Christians projected to be found in the global North.

In many ways, we are witnessing a return of Christianity to the non-Western cultures of Asia and Africa, reflecting more the environment which first gave rise to the church. But now Christianity is embedded in hundreds of cultures and languages demonstrating an incredible diversity of peoples and places which have received its incarnational presence.

Therefore, we can no longer think of Christianity as having a geographical and cultural "center," which for centuries was being rooted in the "West." Of course, for parts of the Christian tradition, such as the Orthodox, this was never true. But now, universally, this is no longer true.

This includes, I would argue, the Catholic Church, accounting for about one-half of all Christians. While Rome may remain its administrative and affectional center, the spiritual vitality and prophetic resonance so admired in Pope Francis has resulted because, for the first time in more than twelve hundred years, the Pope is from the global South. He echoes the voice of two-thirds of all Catholics who today are found in Asia, Africa, and Latin America.

When academics use the term "world Christianity," they refer to the new reality of its multifaceted, highly diverse presence throughout the globe. This means, as never before, that mission today is polycentric and multidirectional. It flows from a multitude of places to a myriad of destinations and then returns.

Further, if there is no center, then how can we speak of "margins"? Perhaps one of the implications of the dramatic geographical shift in world Christianity's landscape is that the Spirit is radically transforming these assumptions. If mission now arises from any number of unexpected places and moves toward unanticipated destinations, then even reversing the definition of who is at the center and who is at the margin does not fully capture the new realities that we are encountering.

But this much is clear. The animating forces, ministries, and movements which will shape the future of world Christianity are emerging largely from the global South. Christians in Africa, Latin

source for all of these statistics is *Atlas of Global Christianity, 1910-2010*, ed. Todd M. Johnson and Kenneth R. Ross (Edinburgh: Edinburgh University Press, 2009).

America, and Asia will now be the primary authors of its vision and direction of its mission.

A key question is whether the established churches in the United States will understand and internalize this new reality. Following the mindset of our nation, with its unmatched global economic and military power, our default assumption is that Christian witness and mission finds its center with us and flows out to the world. But all that has changed. If we do not recognize this, we will be blinded to the movement of God's Spirit in the world today.

The spiritual landscape

Changes in the landscape of world Christianity have to do with far more than just geography. Christianity has now emerged as a non-Western religion. As its dominant expressions are growing today outside the familiar home of Western culture, we are witnessing the spiritual resurgence of non-Western Christianity. With this comes expressions of Christian worship and practice that are focused more on experience and on all the senses, rather than on those forms that are more rationalistic. This cuts across denominational traditions.

The most dramatic evidence of this movement is the rapid, even astonishing rise of Pentecostalism. Modern Pentecostal history is usually dated to the Azusa Street revival in Los Angeles a little more than a century ago. The explosive growth of Pentecostalism around the world in the last century, along with the religious transformation of the African continent, are the two most compelling narratives of Christian history in the twentieth century, and each continues today.

In 1970 about 5 percent of Christians identified themselves as Pentecostal. But today, one out of every four Christians in the world is Pentecostal or charismatic. ("Charismatic" simply refers to those who exhibit Pentecostal gifts and practices but belong to non-Pentecostal denominations.) Approximately 80 percent of Christian conversions in Asia are due to Pentecostal forms of Christianity, and about 25 percent of all Pentecostals are found on that continent. Researchers estimate that there are over eight hundred thousand Chinese charismatic congregations throughout Asia. Meanwhile, Africa is home to almost one out of three of the world's Pentecostals. In Latin America, Pentecostalism is growing at three times the rate of Catholicism.

Globally, Pentecostalism is growing at four times the overall rate of Christianity's growth. Or you can think of it this way: one out of every twelve people alive today is Pentecostal. For a movement generally regarded as only about a century old, this is an astonishing religious development.

What northern liberal and evangelical Christians often fail to recognize is that Pentecostalism has arisen in the global South without the history and baggage of colonialism. Churches in the Pentecostal tradition and style, with their emphasis on immediate spiritual experiences, detached Christianity from its white missionary control and empowered indigenous expressions of Christian faith within many parts of the world.

The Atlas of Global Christianity, the most comprehensive resource describing the changes in world Christianity over the past one hundred years, puts it this way: "Pentecostalism... became the main contributor to the reshaping of Christianity from a predominantly Western to a predominantly non-Western phenomenon in the twentieth century."[2]

Of course, "Pentecostal" is an elastic term, and other newer forms of spiritually expressive Christianity have also taken root in the soil of world Christianity. African Instituted Churches, begun in Africa by Africans, rather than as part of the Western missionary enterprise, continue to grow, along with other forms of Christianity highly contextualized to various non-Western cultures. The overall picture is a spiritual landscape of world Christianity that has been rapidly changed by all these new movements.

Many in the ecumenical community view these trends with alarm. They worry that growing forms of Pentecostal expressions of faith around the world forsake the biblical call to social justice for all and the call to protect the gift of God's creation, in favor of an individualistic piety that retreats from the world. Surely this is an honest and probing concern rooted in a clear ecumenical understanding of witness and mission.

Yet the ecumenical principles of dialogue and mutual understanding need to be applied here. We should listen and learn carefully from the actual lived experience of Pentecostal communities and from their own testimonies. Further, we should give attention to researchers who have studied these communities. Scholars like Donald E. Miller and Tetsunao Yamamori point to the widespread participation of those on the margins of society in Pentecostal communities and the resulting sense of social empowerment.[3]

---

[2] *Atlas of Global Christianity*, 100.
[3] Donald E. Miller and Tetsunao Yamamori, *Global Pentecostalism: The New Face of Christian Social Engagement* (Berkeley: University of California Press, 2007).

When I attended the Pentecostal World Conference in Kuala Lumpur in late 2013 as an ecumenical guest, I was impressed by a presentation from Ivan Satyavrata who heads an Assemblies of God ministry in Kolkata (Calcutta) India. Titled "Power to the Poor: The Pentecostal Tradition of Social Engagement," he argued persuasively how empowerment of the marginalized in society has been a key feature of Pentecostal ministry in many parts of the world, as well as a reason for its growth.

Of course, just like other expressions of Christianity, Pentecostalism includes widely diverse voices and examples of social witness—or the lack thereof. But it is the case that although liberation theology rightly proclaims the option for the poor, the poor themselves have opted largely for Pentecostalism. It is crucial for the broader church community to ask why this is so.

Further, observers of the changing landscape of world Christianity will conclude that Pentecostalism has empowered the most effective missionary movement in terms of the growth of Christianity in the last half century. Numbering now around six hundred million people, the Pentecostal community now totals more than the five hundred million believers who constitute the membership of all the churches belonging to the World Council of Churches.

The theological landscape

As world Christianity relocates itself geographically and displays new forms of spirituality, its foundational theological framework is also shifting. Andrew Walls, one of the pioneers in tracing the pilgrimage of world Christianity, expresses it this way:

> The most striking feature of Christianity at the beginning of the third millennium is that it is predominantly a non-Western religion. . . . We have long been used to a Christian theology that was shaped by the interaction of Christian faith with Greek philosophy and Roman law. . . . These forms have become so familiar and established that we have come to think of them as the normal and characteristic forms of Christianity. In the coming century, we can expect an accelerated process of new development arising from Christian interaction with the ancient cultures of Africa and Asia, an interaction now in progress but with much further to go.[4]

---

[4] Andrew F. Walls, "Eusebius Tries Again: The Task of Reconceiving and Re-visioning the Study of Christian History," in *Enlarging the Story: Perspectives on Writing World Christian History*, ed. Wilbert R. Shenk (Maryknoll, NY: Orbis Books, 2002), 1.

We can think further about the changing theological landscape in the following way. As Christianity has now become a predominantly non-Western religion, it has moved out of the framework of Western culture and the Enlightenment which has served as its theological home for about four hundred years. As world Christianity makes this transition, we can identify, as broad generalizations, three key movements:

The individual and community

Enlightenment thought focused on the primacy of the individual in understanding the political, social, and economic order. Non-Western cultures often begin with the primacy of the community, stressing the values of belonging and mutual relationships.

Rational and supernatural approaches to knowledge

Western Enlightenment culture placed a priority on the mind's ability to know truth through rational thought and inquiry. Non-Western cultures often assume supernatural forces, both good and evil, as means that unlock knowledge of reality and truth.

The material and the spiritual world

Enlightenment thought reinforced a clear boundary between the material and the spiritual, usually circumscribing the latter to a narrow, personalized domain. Cultures in the non-Western world typically assume a far more fluid and interconnected relationship between the material and the spiritual, regarding them as mutually interdependent.

These summaries are, of course, simplistic. Further, for some strains of Christian tradition—thinking here again of the Orthodox, for instance—this does not describe their historical or theological journey. The point, however, is this: for most of world Christianity, the movement out of the enduring, comfortable cradle of Western culture to the non-Western world entails a fundamental reorientation of how culture and faith interact in the process of theology around crucial issues involving how we understand truth and experience reality.

African theologian and author Akintunde E. Akinade describes the development of non-Western Christianity in this way:

> Christianity has blossomed in societies outside the Western hemisphere and has become more powerful and nuanced in the

process. The antistructural character of the non-Western phase of world Christianity plays itself out in characteristics such as charismatic renewal, grassroots revival, massive exorcism, vibrant house churches, robust indigenization efforts, and effective lay leadership. Churches from the Third World are vigorously defining Christianity on their own terms. The new day that dawns will permanently alter the place and nature of Christianity in the twenty-first century.[5]

Therefore, a changing theological landscape, only briefly described here, presents a fresh framework and a new set of questions as we discern the future practice of Christian ministry and mission.

The economic landscape

My purpose here is to address the growing imbalance of economic resources, as well as the resources of social, organizational, and theological capital which divide world Christianity, primarily between the churches of the global North and the global South. Of course, this merely reflects the realities of the overall globalized economy. Continued analysis of how the global economy functions, creating winners and losers, with persisting economic inequalities is being carried out today in many circles, both within the ecumenical community and among secular academic scholars.

But what is the changing economic landscape of world Christianity? While massive growth in the Christian family has occurred in the global South, financial resources and material power remain concentrated in the global North and West. With this comes the continuing, quiet assumption that northern centers of power in the church are still in control and are to shape the destiny of world Christianity. Increasingly, that assumption, although true in some material ways, is becoming more and more a spiritual and even a practical illusion.

The clearest way to understand the division of economic resources within world Christianity is this: at least 60 percent of all Christians are now in the global South, with numbers that continue to increase. Yet they control only 17 percent of income from economic resources, while the other 40 percent of Christians in the North and West control 83 percent of the estimated income within world Christianity.

---

[5] Akintunde E. Akinade, ed., *A New Day: Essays on World Christianity in Honor of Lamin Sanneh* (New York: Peter Lang, 2010), 5.

This in turn affects the amount of available resources that can be allocated to theological education, training, healthcare, and mission outreach. A major survey of theological educators around the world conducted by the WCC underscored these realities. The global North now has too many institutions of theological education which often struggle to enroll enough students, and the global South has too few. One can make the argument that the single most important investment to strengthen the future mission of the global church is to increase the capacity for programs of theological education, ministerial formation, and leadership training at all levels in the churches of the global South.

This same imbalance is reflected in the geographical placement of the organizational headquarters for world Christianity's global institutions and ecumenical bodies. For instance, the World Council of Churches, the Lutheran World Federation, and other ecumenical bodies cling to their comfortable location in Geneva, Switzerland. Geneva is the fifth most expensive city for expatriates in the entire world. The World Communion of Reformed Churches recently moved out of Geneva, but instead of relocating to the global South, where most of its members are, it moved to Hanover, Germany. The Baptist World Alliance is located outside of Washington, DC, and the World Methodist Council has its center in Lake Junaluska, North Carolina. The Anglican Communion, of course, is centered in London. World Vision International has its headquarters in California. This list can go on.

Our theology is influenced by what we see when we wake up in the morning. Context makes a difference. Continuing to place the centers of major global organizations and ecumenical bodies in the global North, regardless of various advantages, underscores in symbolic but powerful ways the imbalance of economic resources and institutional power in world Christianity.

Regarding the imbalance of capacity for theological education and ministerial training, would it be possible or effective to propose a simple tithe on all the income received by seminaries and theological institutions in the global North? Most of these have very professional and well-developed fundraising operations. Imagine if a way were found to direct just 10 percent of these funds to strengthen the capacity for theological education and training in the global South. It is time to have an honest dialogue concerning the economic inequalities among global Christian communities, especially around ministerial formation.

Finally, regarding the geographical location of major organizations and ecumenical bodies, we know that for some, like the WCC and the World Communion of Reformed Churches, this matter has been considered and is now settled, at least for the foreseeable future. But for others, the issue may still be open. Here is the challenge: to search courageously for meaningful ways that shift not only economic resources but also institutional power, organizational culture, and theological capital to those locations in the global South and East that are now destined to shape the future direction of world Christianity.

The migratory landscape

The landscape of migration in the life of world Christianity has been changing in ways we may not have noticed. This has deep implications for our discernment to renew the vision and practice of ministry, mission, and evangelism.

Today an estimated 214 million people are migrants, moving from one country to another for many compelling reasons. This means "people on the move" are equivalent in number to the fifth largest country in the world, and of this number, 105 million are Christian. Therefore, although they make up only a third of the world's population, Christians are overrepresented among migrants, accounting for nearly half of all those who have moved from one country to another. This group alone is equivalent to the twelfth largest country in the world, greater than the populations of Germany, Ethiopia, Egypt, France, and numerous other countries.

The chief destinations of immigrants are North America, Europe, Australia, and the Arab States of the Persian Gulf. Yet immigrants cross borders among countless countries. For instance, 810,000 people in 2012 emigrated from Ghana (while 1.8 million immigrated to Ghana). Of those who emigrated out of Ghana, two-thirds were Christians. And in total, 120,000 immigrated to the United States and 80,000 to the United Kingdom, but 190,000 immigrated to Nigeria. The Philippines had 4.63 million who emigrated, and 76 percent were Christian: 1.8 million immigrated to the United States; 530,000 immigrated to Saudi Arabia, and another 270,000 to Malaysia.

Immigrants are moving largely from nations of the global South, often from countries where the Christian faith is strong and growing. And Christian migrants often take their churches with them. The Redeemed Christian Church of God, founded in Nigeria in 1952 and representative of an African Instituted Church, now has an estimated five million members in 147 countries, including 720 congregations in the United States. At its United States headquarters, north of Dallas,

Texas, it has built a worship pavilion at the cost of $15 million, which seats ten thousand who come for revival meetings and other services. Its US director, Pastor James Fadele, says "We want to plant churches like Starbucks."

In Europe we find similar developments. On any Sunday in London, an estimated 58 percent of those attending church services are nonwhite. Similar situations are found in other major cities. Hamburg Germany, for instance, has sixty African congregations and an African Christian Council, and 30 percent of the members of Spain's Federation of Evangelical Religious Entities are from groups of immigrants originating in Asia and Africa.

Beyond this pattern, Christian migrants also move within and among the continents of Asia, Africa, and Latin America. It is urgent that we assess the missional significance of this global movement of migrant Christians. Jehu Hanciles, a native of Sierra Leone, puts it in this simple but clarifying way: "Every Christian migrant is a potential missionary."[6]

In the church's work with migrants and refugees, we have moved helpfully from seeing migrants as the object of our compassion to our becoming the subject of their destiny. Such empowerment and advocacy is a continuing, urgent need as the number of refugees tragically grows in many parts of the world, including in the United States. As church bodies relate to the more than one hundred million Christian migrants in the world, we must come to understand that many of them, in fact, are the agents of God's mission.

It is worth remembering that in the book of Acts, after the Spirit was poured out at Pentecost, many of those preaching the good news were persecuted and fled Jerusalem. Their faith was carried across cultural, ethnic, and racial boundaries. Philip was sent to Samaria, normally hostile territory, and then toward Gaza, encountering and then baptizing the Ethiopian eunuch. Then, when these early followers ended up as migrants in Antioch, the church that emerged was led by a multicultural group which included Niger, a black African, and Manaen, a former member of Herod's court who had been converted. The church in Antioch became the center of God's mission to the world.

The connection between migration and mission runs deep, functioning in a variety of ways, usually unplanned and unanticipated

---

[6] Jehu Hanciles, *Beyond Christendom: Globalization, African Migration, and the Transformation of the West* (Maryknoll, NY: Orbis Books, 2008), 6.

at the time, in the history of the church. In the changing landscape of world Christianity today, we must once again make this connection between patterns of global migration and God's mission in the world.

The modern missionary movement has put most of its effort into raising resources and providing support for those who are sent to cross boundaries to share in word and deed the transforming love of God known in Jesus Christ. Traditionally, that is what most mission agencies have tried to do. And even as world Christianity makes its decisive shift to the global South, much of the church still works within this paradigm for carrying out programs of mission.

But what if, in fact, migration is a primary means through which the Spirit is moving, unfolding the ongoing work of God's mission in the world? Can we imagine how this could be the case? Can we see this as at least part of the emerging landscape of world Christianity? And if so, how would that challenge and change the practices which have characterized our attempts to participate in God's mission?

These global realities come home, touching the ministry of US congregations. Of the forty-three million people in United States who were born in another country, 74 percent are Christian, 5 percent Muslim, 4 percent Buddhist, and 3 percent Hindu.[7] Immigration into the United States has had its greatest impact on the Christian community. The changing realities, resources, and gifts of world Christianity are being brought to our doorstep. The question is whether we can receive this and see it as a mark of God's mission reaching out to us.

The words of Jehu Hanciles may provide the best perspective on how migration should impact our future understanding of mission:

> First [that] attentiveness to the nature and composition of human migration is crucial for understanding the possibilities and the potential of Christian missionary endeavor; second that in much the same way that the Western missionary movement proved decisive for the current shape of global Christianity, the future of global Christianity is now intricately bound up with the emerging non-Western missionary.[8]

The ecumenical landscape

I conclude this essay by focusing directly on the ecumenical landscape of world Christianity. How it is changing and what that

---

[7] Granberg-Michaelson, *From Times Square to Timbuktu*, 82.
[8] Ibid., 129.

suggests for our mission and ministry. Although much could be said, I want to focus on two realities.

First, the ecumenical landscape is becoming increasingly fractured into endless denominations. Personally, I am grateful for the heritage of the Reformed tradition, which courageously demonstrated, at its beginning, that an understanding of God's truth and his intentions for the church could require, in extreme circumstances, breaking away from established dogma and institutional authority. But in the nearly five hundred years which have followed, it is worth reflecting on where this precedent has brought us.

The idea that any group with a slightly different understanding of Christian truth can separate itself from others in the Body of Christ and establish its own denominational structure has become so commonplace and so prolific that we barely give it a second theological or biblical thought. As we look at global Christianity's landscape, we cannot help but notice how what we confess as "the one holy catholic and apostolic Church" has, in fact, become endlessly and ceaselessly divided. Protestants call these divisions "denominations."

Gordon Conwell Seminary's Center for Global Christianity, located near Boston, keeps the best track of this. And here is our present shameful state of affairs: today there are an estimated 43,800 denominations in the world. This staggering proliferation of divided institutionalized churches never could have been imagined in the first fifteen hundred years of Christian history. Our only proper response is one of repentance.

We are faced, therefore, with the growing complexity, enormous diversity, and proliferating disunity of world Christianity. Further, the trend is going in the wrong direction. In terms of separate denominations, we are becoming more, rather than less, divided. All this is happening despite the enormous progress made by modern ecumenical movement in the past sixty years.

A second feature of this ecumenical landscape is the relative institutional isolation of world Christianity's major streams or traditions. Let me illustrate. In 2013, when I attended the 23rd World Pentecostal World Conference in Kuala Lumpur, Malaysia, 3,710 Pentecostal leaders and participants from seventy-three countries gathered together, as they do every three years. Dynamic preaching, high octane worship, and numerous workshops filled our time at Calvary Church, a Pentecostal megachurch, whose pastor, Prince Guneratnum, serves as the current president of Pentecostal World Fellowship. But the

Pentecostal world lives mostly within its own bubble, and those outside of it—both from other Christian communities and the media—remain largely insulated from a deeper knowledge and understanding of its dynamics.

Less than three months later, I joined with about three thousand official participants and many more Korean visitors at the World Council of Churches' Tenth Assembly in Busan. This gathering was more ecumenically expansive, representing the churches that make up the fellowship of the ecumenical movement as well as other visitors.

Yet what struck me was how the gatherings in Kuala Lumpur and Busan represented two very separate worlds. It is as if these two Christian environments have been hermetically sealed off from one another, almost in a state of ecclesiological apartheid. I am sure that there are not even fifty people in the world who attended both the Pentecostal World Conference and the WCC Assembly. But for the sake of God's mission in the world, the Pentecostal and ecumenical worlds need one another in the journey of Christian unity and mission.

Thus the ecumenical landscape of world Christianity faces divisions which are not simply of doctrine and historical tradition. Rather, these divisions within the worldwide body of Christ are continually reinforced, daily, through institutional power at the local, national, regional, and global levels, which keeps the vast majority of Christians, congregations, denominations, and organizations functioning within their separate worlds, isolated from the other major streams of world Christianity.

Fortunately, there are some places of hope. One way to bridge the major denominational and institutional divides permeating world Christianity is to establish a safe space which gathers those representing the full breadth of the global Christian community. We see that in the emergence of Christian Churches Together in USA. For the first time, official representatives of mainline Protestant denominations, Orthodox churches, some historic Black churches, Evangelical and Pentecostal churches, and the Roman Catholic Church have gathered together in a place of fellowship and witness.

On a worldwide level, this same vision has been the calling and purpose of the Global Christian Forum. Begun as an initiative emerging out of the World Council of Churches at its Eighth Assembly in Harare, in 1998, and then becoming autonomous, the Global Christian Forum has become a fresh and credible movement which offers a way forward that transcends these divisions.

The Pentecostal World Fellowship, the World Council of Churches, the World Evangelical Alliance, and the Pontifical Council for Promoting Christian Unity at the Vatican are the four key organizations now jointly supporting the Global Christian Forum. Nearly all the Christian World Communions—the Lutheran World Federation, the Mennonite World Conference, the World Communion of Reformed Churches, the Organization of African Instituted Churches, and several others—support this initiative in tangible ways as well.

Two global gatherings have been held—in Limuru, Kenya, in 2007 and Manado, Indonesia, in 2011—along with several regional meetings and other consultations. At all of its gatherings, half of the participants are Pentecostals and evangelicals who have not taken part previously in such ecumenical events. As its starting point, the Global Christian Forum always invites each participant to share the story of his or her personal journey of faith, a process which breaks down existing stereotypes and establishes a climate of trust.

The Global Christian Forum is a very modest and fragile initiative. It has only one staff person and an annual budget of little more than $200,000. In the face of the overwhelming complexity and diversity of world Christianity, it seems like a mustard seed. But one hopes it will grow and flourish.

And there are other signs of hope as well on the horizon of the ecumenical landscape of world Christianity. Most notable is Pope Francis. The words he shares and the actions that he symbolizes are creating a climate for ecumenical relations between the Catholic and non-Catholic parts of Christ's body which has not been seen since Vatican II. Despite all the theological discussion and controversy around how we understand the role of the Bishop of Rome, no one can deny the "convening" potential of this office, especially as it is being exercised by Pope Francis. Thus we may hope and also act in expectation of new avenues which can transcend one of world Christianity's most fundamental divisions.

In conclusion, the changing landscape of world Christianity is creating a new "playing field" as the Spirit continues his work of forming and transforming the church. The fundamental challenges, as described in this essay, are geographical, spiritual, theological, economic, migratory, and ecumenical. Navigating each of these challenges requires foundational changes in the ministry and mission of the global church. Fresh forms of deep global division in Christ's body must be confronted if we are to participate anew in God's mission in the world and embody the unity of church.

In the midst of this changing landscape, our invitation is simply to walk together, with old and new partners, on a common pilgrimage. In the post-Resurrection period, we remember the two disciples walking together to Emmaus. Like them, we can share with each other "all that is happening" in our mutual attempts to follow Jesus. When we have accompanied one another faithfully and honestly and come to the table to eat together, then, in unexpected grace-filled moments, we will suddenly know the very real presence of Christ in our communion with one another, and we will race to tell others.

CHAPTER 10

Reformed Christians in Challenging Times: A Reflection from an African Perspective

Setri Nyomi

Introduction

The world has found itself in a place of challenging times. Any Christian leader who is blind to this cannot be effective in a ministry that makes a difference in the world. As an African Reformed Christian, I have chosen this reality to reflect upon in this volume, a festschrift to honor a friend and respected colleague who has given so much of himself and his tremendous gifts to making a difference in challenging times. I met Dr. Gregg Mast for the first time when, as a Reformed leader, he was participating in a meeting in Africa in which Reformed church representatives were in dialogue with representatives of African-instituted churches. His input then, and the contributions he has made as a pastor and theological educator, have shown that he is a person who recognizes challenging times, steps in, and by the grace of God becomes God's instrument, making a difference in our world.

This chapter seeks to respond to some of the world's challenges from an African perspective relying on inspiration from the book of Esther.

Signs of the times

Throughout the world, in many nations, and on all continents, threats to life, peace, health, productive working environments, spiritual well being, and other areas of meaningful life abound. The signs of our times include difficult economic circumstances, health challenges, terrorism, the challenge of living with people who are different from us, the increase of violence in our communities, the use of religion for selfish gain or even to promote hatred, environmental degradation, oppression on the base of gender—the list is endless. Conflicts are escalating, while the economy, environmental disintegration, and disease pose major challenges. Human actions have often been responsible for ushering in a rather dangerous world order.

In 2004 the then World Alliance of Reformed Churches held the Twenty-Fourth General Council, with the theme "That all may have life in fullness." This theme challenged Reformed churches to take a fresh look at the many threats to life at that time and raised questions about God's call into missions, covenant, and prayer around these threats. The theme also led to a lifting up of the plight of any people group who is excluded from fullness of life in any form. This meant, at that time, among other things, taking a serious look at the ways in which globalization and its market forces excluded Africans and others in the Southern Hemisphere. More than a decade after that General Council, the threats of those times persist in the world today.

In addition to the current global threats, we in Africa are still trying to deal with legacies of all kinds, including slavery and colonialism. In addition, the continent of Africa is bleeding because of economic difficulties, conflicts, wars, and HIV/AIDS. This is not to claim that there is no good thing coming out of Africa. Indeed, there are many good things happening in Africa, including the contributions of Africans to the rest of the world. These things, however, do not capture the headlines.

Outlining the signs of our times in this manner can sometimes give the impression that there is a call to lament and decry the kind of terrible world in which we live. This is not how Reformed Christians respond to God. For Reformed Christians, challenging circumstances do not elicit lamenting and giving in to despair. They bring out critical questions such as why we are here, what God is calling us to do, and how we can make a difference in a world such as this. Reformed Christians dig through the Scriptures and our theological resources as we seek answers to these questions and commit ourselves to action.

A time such as this

A study of the book of Esther offers inspiration and challenge for the circumstances in which we live in the twenty-first century. We are challenged by the courage of one person (Mordecai), who refused to let the planned systematic violence against his people proceed. We are challenged by the courage of the young woman (Esther), who took on the role of risking her life and devising a great strategy to save her people. A brief recap of the story will suffice. The third and fourth chapters of the book of Esther confront readers with a life-threatening systematic violence which required action. Haman, a person who was well connected in high places, hatched a plot to annihilate the people of Judah, who were already marginalized because they were strangers in Persia—present-day Iraq. If one looks at the way the system and the culture existed, then it would seem impossible to try to challenge this evil.

Mordecai, however, could not let this go by without action. Earlier, his cousin, Esther, whom he had brought up as a daughter, had become queen. The system was such that even the queen did not have easy access to the king. The cultural and political system in place was difficult to break through, let alone to create an opportunity for being an instrument for change. It is in this setting that Mordecai made clear to Queen Esther that her only viable choice was to take the risk of acting in the interest of life. He concluded this challenge with the pointed statement "Who knows? God may have appointed you to royalty for such a time like this."

In these challenging times, as the world faces all kinds of difficult issues and powerful systems, which often mete out exclusion and death, who knows why God has placed us where we are today, for such a time as this.

The words of Mordecai to Esther still ring in the ears of Christian churches today, no matter which part of the world we find ourselves in. No one should think that, based on our location, we will escape the devastating news that we see happening in other parts of the world. It may be easy for some to think they are safe because they are so far away from places being terrorized by Boko Haram, Al Qaeda, or ISIS; from those African communities devastated by conflicts and wars or diseases such HIV/AIDS and malaria; or from those African countries where difficult economic realities have led to millions of people living below the poverty line, with many battling hunger, ill health, and poor educational facilities. This is also relevant for African Christians, because the temptation is to think that, because the statistics show growth in numbers of Christians, they are safe from the challenges that face Christians in other parts of the world in their quest to share the good news in their secular communities.

Jose Chipenda, the Angola Reformed ecumenist, has often made the statement "We are called to include one another in the struggle for life." In other words, our struggles belong together. The words of Mordecai to Esther, "Who knows, you may have been called to royalty for such a time like this," was an invitation to Esther to be a partner in the struggle for life, no matter her position in life. Esther, as Queen, was called upon to struggle with her people for life. God's people are called to join one another in the struggle for life. Whether we live in Africa, the United States, or in any other part of the world, our struggles belong together. This is the *Ubuntu* spirit that African cultures contribute to the people of faith globally.

Applying this sense of calling to our times

The scope of this reflection gives space for applying this to just two circumstances, which, however, are not the only ones. As one can see in this chapter, there is a long list of circumstances. This author, however, has chosen to focus only on these two areas for reflection to provide examples for similar work on all the other important circumstances. One of these areas is inherent to the life of the church, and the other reflects what the church is called upon to do to make a difference in the world. The two circumstances chosen are:

1. Presenting the good news, the gospel of our Lord Jesus Christ, to people in our communities today, making and sustaining disciples, and seeing the result in church growth.
2. Addressing economic injustice and all its accompanying ills.

These realities are addressed in reverse order.

Economic injustice

Africa has been described as a very rich continent, yet experiencing so much poverty. My country, Ghana, serves as a good example. The colonizing powers found so much gold in that land that they named it the Gold Coast. English was not the indigenous language, so such a label could come only from the colonial powers. In imposing such a name, they were also acknowledging the rich environment they came to discover. Yet, since gaining independence in 1957, Ghanaians have been asking where all the gold has gone, and why they were struggling as a nation.

Situations of this kind have led many to believe that not only has Africa been robbed of her human resources (through slavery) but also that the continent has also been robbed of her mineral resources. In addition, the aftermath of colonialism left a world order in which Africans depended on their former colonial powers for trade and other necessities. To add to these complexities, many African leaders chose to mismanage the economies they were expected to be good stewards of and to focus more on protecting their own power, rather than to seek the welfare of the people they were called to lead. Many such leaders did so with the full knowledge and connivance of powerful governments and financial institutions in more powerful nations.

By the end of the twentieth century, an economic world order came into existence that was unjust to large numbers of people, including many Africans. To address these situations, powerful global financial institutions, purporting to be helpful to Africa, often dictate harsh structural adjustment programs on African countries, programs that are not incentives for economic growth. African peoples are getting poorer and poorer, while the nation's resources are used for servicing debt. To eradicate poverty in Africa, our analysis needs to go deeper than the popular versions we read in the news and see on television. Such popular analyses paint Africa as having so much poverty because those people cannot really get their act together; their poverty is a result of the rampant corruption and other evils they bring on themselves. It is true that there is a level of corruption that African churches need to combat in African nations. The analysis, however, should go far deeper than simply that focus. The economic systems of the world are skewed to exclude people in the global South, and Africa has experienced that exclusion the most. In the emphasis on the market economy, Africa seems dispensable to people with economic power. This is in part the effect of globalization.

While globalization has brought many good things to the world and has made communication and travel much easier, with possibilities that could not have been dreamed of just two generations ago, it also has brought some ills. The extent to which globalization, even with its positive developments, is excluding large sections of people and sacrificing them on the altar of mammon must be addressed.

Meeting in Kitwe, Zambia, in 1996, African Reformed Christians drew attention to this and called on the then World Alliance of

Reformed Churches (WARC) to act decisively on economic injustice and the exclusion experienced through globalization, to act as decisively as people of faith did about racism and apartheid in South Africa. The then WARC took a stand of faith, which led to the excommunication of any church which justified racism and apartheid theologically in 1982.

This call and other processes led to the development of the Accra Confession, which came into being at the Twenty-Fourth General Council. Under the theme noted above, "That all may have life in fullness," delegates at that council felt like the biblical Esther did—their only choice was to act for life. This statement of faith called on churches to reject death-producing evil in an unjust economy and to not be silent at the injustice but rather to remember that God may have called us to such a time as this, so that our actions will be consistent with our faith.

The world's economic systems are literally strangling many. They have affected food security, health care systems, and education systems. The question remains whether there are any Esthers who will hear God's call to risk their lives and speak out to the right ears with the right strategies. Are we going to remain silent, or will we see our struggles as belonging together?

Presenting the good news to people of African descent today, making and sustaining disciples, and seeing the result in church growth

The challenge of our times is the great need for the good news of Christianity to be heard more clearly. Otherwise, the powerful forces of evil will take over—sometimes even using religious language to bring new levels of devastation to the world. Powerful leaders in many powerful countries often resort to religious language to hide their agenda for power and division. Leaders in both predominantly Christian and predominantly Moslem countries have been doing this for decades. So, unless a clear, faithful Christian voice is heard bringing the gospel, people will experience bad news, not the good news of Christ. Thus, Christians are also called for such a time as this, when the good news is often expressed with such a marked lack of clarity, and the church is often unsure of its identity and afraid to stand for the Lord Jesus and speak out. The world needs to hear the Gospel of the Lord Jesus Christ, which will result in transformed lives with new purpose and meaning, lives ready to be instruments of transformation in their own communities.

How many modern-day Christians are ready to be instruments of God, called for such a time as this for the task of transformation? How do we pass on faith in our Lord Jesus Christ to our children? Have we developed effective strategies for evangelism in the secularized societies of our world today? If we say the churches are growing, at least in numbers in Africa, how can Africans maintain that growth and move beyond the triumphalist feeling of elation to being truly committed to disciple making? Are there gifts that Christians in different parts of the world can bring to one another in these struggles?

We as Christians need to rededicate ourselves to sharing our faith unashamedly. This can be done without a sense of arrogance that looks down on non-Christians. Indeed, the notion of excluding people of other faiths from our communities should be foreign to any Christian community. Christians are called to love others and to reflect the life of our Lord Jesus Christ, who so loved us that He came to die for us when we did not deserve it. We too ought to love those of other faiths, whether Muslim, Buddhist, Hindu, or any other background.

Our faith as Christians needs to bring attention to both the spiritual and the social needs of our neighborhoods. Our worship is not in isolation from our struggle for life. Indeed, it is our faith that sustains and supports us when no other system does. And this is what has helped many people of faith survive major struggles which could have crushed other people. Christians often rejoice while going through life's challenges because we know God's action can take us beyond our current circumstances.

The joyful worship that is experienced in many African congregations is not an "opium for the masses"; it is a defiance of the forces of evil. As African Christians respond to the meaning that God brings into their lives, people in our communities can experience what it means to belong to a community of faith and to see the relevance of our churches in their midst. This in turn can lead to church growth in many ways, including people coming to know the freedom that living in Christ brings and discovering how Christians are engaged as instruments of change and transformation in their communities. As Christians touch others, God touches our lives. Our lives become more meaningful. Our joyful worship becomes truly meaningful as, in God, we defy the forces of evil. This dynamic of joyful worship and action that defies the forces of evil leads to growth.

Who knows? This may be why God has called us to be alive today and to be where we are at such a time as this in our communities and as individuals. How willing are Christians today to respond to this calling?

Concluding remarks

Why are we here today? Why has God preserved our lives for such a time as this? The systems that perpetrate evil will not simply yield. We can, however, experience inner growth and see evidence of the power of God over evil in the growth of our churches and as we respond to God by courageously and prophetically moving forward—together—to overcome the forces of death and destruction in our communities.

Rev. Dr. Gregg Mast has shown by his life and commitment that his calling to leadership has been an opportunity to be faithful to God in responding to that call for a time such as this, in each of the places he has served. We thank God for his faithfulness and the impact he and Vicki have made as leaders in the church and in theological education. This chapter challenges Christians to look for opportunities to respond to God's call, even in unusual places and even when such responses are as risky as that which Mordecai and Esther faced. Who knows? God may have called you to your station in life for such a time as this.

CHAPTER 11

Considering the Relationship between the Concept of Gospel and Law in Reformed Theological Discourse

Rodney S. Tshaka

I am quite delighted to have been asked to contribute a chapter to celebrate the life of Dr. Gregg Mast as Reformed theologian and president of New Brunswick Theological Seminary in New Brunswick, New Jersey. I was privileged to be associated with the NBTS, albeit for a brief period. During that time, I had come to know Gregg as someone with a sincere love for the Reformed ecclesial tradition. Through him I also came to appreciate the long-standing relationship that NBTS has had with the then Dutch Reformed Church in Africa. On several occasions we reflected on the processes started by Reformed congregations in the United States to divest from the then apartheid republic because of its obstinate adherence to apartheid as a policy that characterized life in South Africa at that time. My family, especially my wife, Precious, became frequent visitors in Dr. Mast's home, and we are indeed privileged to consider them our friends.

The subject of the agility of the Reformed faith as able to transform itself from being a theology of the oppressor to a theology of the struggle against apartheid is a subject that Dr. Mast believed in. It was for this reason that he was eager to speak to me about the intentional alignment with the struggle against apartheid. Many ministers of the then Dutch Reformed Church in Africa were supported to further their studies at the NBTS. I trust that the matter of Gospel and Law, which could easily be interpreted to suggest a sacrosanct division between the issues of the soul and the body, as a subject respected in Reformed theological discourse, continues to be a matter that determines our engagement as Christians in the world today. This contribution is made at a time when the United States finds itself in a rather precarious position. Precarious, in the sense that it seems to want to forget its very creation, while appearing to support policies that frown on aliens.

Introduction

The confessing church in Germany, which was essentially called into existence by the theological quandary that the church found itself in under the Hitler regime, has played a significant role in dealing with the church's responsibility in the world today. This act, however, was not without its own challenges in terms of how the church should deal with this responsibility. These challenges were precipitated by the many theological interpretations that were united with the aim of ensuring the independence of the church under the regime in question. One significant theological interpretation centered on the concepts of Gospel and Law. The different interpretations of these concepts has resulted in the different views of how the church can and must be involved in the affairs of society.

This chapter will attempt to probe the interpretation of the concepts in question by some of the major theological traditions that were aligned with the confessing church. By doing this, it will illustrate the reason(s) why Karl Barth became increasingly unpopular within the confessing movement. It will also be shown that an interpretation that sought the relationship between Gospel and Law as intrinsic, facilitated the church's response to the Jewish question. In the end, a few comments are made about the Barmen Theological Declaration, which sees no dichotomy between Gospel and Law.

Squabbles within a confessing church

Numerous students of the theology of Karl Barth have suggested that there are sufficient grounds to surmise that the political-economic situation in which his theology was practiced is fundamental to a better comprehension of his theology.[1] Some of those who were uncomfortable

---

[1] F. Marquardt, "Socialism in the theology of Karl Barth," in *Karl Barth and Radical Politics*, ed. G. Hunsinger (Philadelphia: Westminster Press, 1976), 44-77.

with such a reading of Barth have ventured to dismiss such claims and have therefore deliberately ignored Barth's frequent caution to the significance of having the newspaper in sight while attending to the matters of Scripture. This ethical component which is always implied in Barth's theology is also evident in the Barmen declaration,[2] which can also be construed as a summary of his theology, as well as the Belhar Confession,[3] which partly came into being through the inspiration of the theology of Karl Barth.

The question of which one of these two items (the Bible or the newspaper) takes precedence is displayed in Barth's stern emphasis on the Word of God as the point of departure in theological reflection. Although the Word is preferred above other items, it would be unfair to insinuate that the secondary item (in this case the newspaper) did not influence the outcome of a particular theological reflection which concerned him. It is particularly important that we deal with the political situation which necessitated Barth's theological position on the question of the Jews (Judefrage) and the consequent tension, which ensued between him and the Confessing Church.

[2] The word "declaration" is used because of the view that Lutheranism has with regard to the understanding of a confession. Since this article was written by a Reformed Christian, the word "confession" will sometimes be used because this is a notion that is understood differently within the said theological tradition. It is indeed interesting to use the notion of confession more in relation to the Barmen declaration because it was this declaration which, more than other local declarations, influenced the Belhar Confession. One can think of many declarations made during apartheid, that is, message of the people and so forth, but it was the Barmen declaration that galvanized the South African Reformed confessional tradition into penning its own confession, called the Belhar Confession. The usage of the notion of confessional in relation to the Barmen declaration is therefore deliberate in this article. The full title of the declaration reads: "Declaration concerning the right understanding of the Reformation confessions of faith in the German Evangelical Church of the present." This declaration was the result of the confessional synod of the German Evangelical Church, which convened in Barmen on May 29-31, 1934. The meeting was constituted by members of the Lutheran, Reformed, and United churches, seeking a common message against the attempts of Hitler and the Nazis to co-opt the church and make it subservient to Nazi ideology and its Aryan policies. Cf. R. S. Tshaka, *Confessional Theology? A Critical Analysis of the Theology of Karl Barth and its Significance for the Belhar Confession* (Newcastle: Cambridge Scholars Publishing, 2010), 83.

[3] The Belhar Confession of the Uniting Reformed Church in South Africa, is a confession that is moulded in the structure of the Barmen Theological Declaration of Germany. It was the very Barmen declaration and its theology which question the interference of the German state in the affairs of the church which brought about the Belhar Confession. In a manner similar to Barmen, this confession insists that Jesus Christ is the only Lord and Saviour and that apartheid is a sin and a heresy.

The position of Barth as chief author of the Barmen Theological Declaration, as well as a vocal member of the confessing church, was for a long time seen as being controversial. With reference to Barth, it must be stated from the outset that he was blamed for not having said and done enough to alleviate the plight of the Jews under the Hitler regime. Busch refers to a critique by Scholder leveled against Barth. Scholder interpreted the political situation in Germany in the following way. He believes that in 1933, Barth, with his strong emphasis on the first commandment and the exclusive and binding force of God's Word, made a decision, which, although well intentioned, should have been expressed intolerantly. Scholder charged that the weakness of this was that, in focusing upon the preservation of pure doctrine in the pulpits of the church, it saw no challenge in the Nazi state itself. Thus it had the disadvantage of inevitably glossing over the significance of the so-called Jewish question. Barth is then blamed for the struggling confessing church's hindsight of the crisis of the Jews, simply because he was a chief contributor to a decision which called into disrepute the justification of the Jewish discrimination.[4]

Busch questions the sincerity of those who hesitate to agree that Barth was, on the contrary, not unaware of that which afflicted the Jews. While admitting that Barth personally thought that he had not done enough in this respect, Busch asserts that allegations which implied that Barth remained lethargic toward the Jews is frivolous since, he argues, "It was Barth and not Gogarten, Hirsch, or Althaus who finally articulated a confession of repentance toward the Jews, a very confession which is also interpreted as his admission of the failure of the confessing church in dealing more proactively with the Jewish question."[5] It is Busch's view that, during the time of Barth's direct involvement in the German church struggle, he fought for the principle of the exclusive binding character of God's Word. He cautions, however, that the motive behind this must be understood. Initially it ought to be understood that what was central to him was not his criticism of the "German Christians,"[6] who admittedly were unacceptable to him.

---

[4] E. Busch, "Indissoluble Unity: Barth's Position on the Jews during the Hitler Era," in *For the Sake of the World: Karl Barth and the Future of Ecclesial Theology*, ed. G. Hunsinger (Grand Rapids: Eerdmans, 2004), 54.

[5] Ibid.

[6] With the rise of National Socialism, a further division occurred among the Protestants. The one group was the Confessing Church, led by the Reverend Martin Niemöller, and the other group was the "German Christians" faith movement—the more fanatical Nazis, led by Ludwig Mueller. He was an army chaplain of the East

Considering the Relationship between the Concept of Gospel and Law   149

Instead it was his criticism of the inner church's opposition against the German Christians.

It must then be stated that, as much as the Barmen Theological Declaration was opposed to the German Christians, it was just as much opposed to the confessing church, which was the revised version of the Pastor's Emergency League. It was to this group that theologians such as Karl Heim, Hanns Lilje, Martin Niemöller, and Dietrich Bonhoeffer belonged.[7] The Barmen confession opposed this group because it called for the complete freedom of the church "from all political influence" and in this sense criticized the German Christians. It is perhaps not emphasized enough that this confession was a confession, not of a triumphant church, but of a repentant church. The lack of insisting on this attitude drove Barth to maintain in 1933 that the confessing church was saying secretly the same thing that the German Christians were saying openly.[8]

Busch maintains that while, on the one hand, this group called for the complete freedom of the church "from all political influence"— and in this sense, it criticized the German Christians—on the other hand, they articulated a "joyful Yes to the new state" and wanted to bind the church to an "indissoluble service to the German *volk*."[9] By doing this, this group was advocating an analysis which insinuated that the church and the state were two separate entities which co-existed and therefore mutually recognized each other without intervening in the other's affairs.

Busch charges this group with having misunderstood what "confessing" really meant. He is of the view that this group did not understand confession as a matter concerning God's mercy and righteousness over and against the destructive powers, but instead, they thought by confession the most fundamental thing was the protection of the church and its confessional stance over and against

---

Prussian Military district and a devoted follower of Hitler. This movement ardently supported the Nazi doctrines of race and the leadership principle and wanted them applied to the Reich Church which would bring all Protestants into one all-embracing body (cf. W Shirer, 1961: 235); the "leader principle" presupposed that the church was to be organized according to the same principle as the state: "one empire, one leader" (cf. M. Lehmann-Habeck, "Confession and Resistance in Hitler-Germany [1933-1945]," *Mission Studies* 2, no. 1 (1985): 34-38.

[7] E. Busch, "The Barmen Declaration: Its Theology, Background, and Reception," in *Studies in Reformed Theology: Faith and Ethnicity*, ed. E. A. J. G. Van der Borght, D. Van Keulen, and M. E. Brinkman (Meinema: Zoetermeer, 2002), 2:67.
[8] Ibid.
[9] Ibid.

interventions into its life from outside.[10] It was this view that allowed this group to declare the unshakable loyalty of the church to the authoritarian nationalistic state. This was the very issue which forced Barth to register his disdain of the conduct displayed by this group. In opposing this conduct, Barth wrote in 1933 that "The assumption that one could be in agreement with the preamble of the 'German Christians' [in their affirmation of the Nazi state] and then later have a pure church in opposition to them . . . will prove to be one of the most deceptive illusions of an era replete with such illusions. Let us leave out the preamble, completely and sincerely, and then we will speak further about that which follows."[11]

The impact that the two-sector doctrine has on theological reflection

There is a stark difference between the theology of the so-called German Christians and the theology of the confessing church. It is perhaps important to be briefly reminded that the confessing church was a combination of various theological traditions. In the case of the confessing church, we see a combination of Reformed, Lutheran, and United theological traditions which, although there are some significant differences, do not differ greatly. While it was clear that in the case of the former, a concoction of Christendom and Nazi ideology dictated the form of the German Christians; in the latter group, one is confronted with a type of two-sector doctrine which was predominant in this church's opposition to the German Christians.

One way of interpreting the two-sector doctrine during the Hitler regime can briefly be explained as Busch did: "Politically one could be a brown-shirt or German nationalist, and therefore ipso facto be supportive of the state's treatment of the Jews, as long as it proceeded 'lawfully.' Ecclesiastically, one wanted to preserve the confessional stance as inviolable, and therefore not separate oneself from the baptized Jews, even though one viewed them as a foreign race."[12] Barth thought that it was entirely pointless to leave the church on account of the latter, as Bonhoeffer once recommended, in order to build a free church on the foundation of such a two-sector doctrine. For Barth it was more important to repudiate that existing misunderstanding of the church and her relation to the world.

---

[10] Ibid.
[11] Bush, "Indissoluble," 56.
[12] Ibid.

It is this frivolous interpretation of the two-kingdom doctrine that forced Barth to respond to Bonhoeffer. Bonhoeffer had maintained that: "The true church of Christ . . . will never meddle in the state's affairs. . . . The church knows that in the world the use of violent force inevitably is joined with the moral injustice of certain actions of the Government. Therefore, on the question of the Jews, the church today is not allowed to interrupt the government immediately and to demand another policy."[13]

It was therefore important, at least for Barth, to spend some time discussing the problem of this two-sector doctrine, which for him, was located at the heart of his engagement with Gospel and Law (the inseparability of dogmatics and ethics). Barth's Christian ethics takes its point of departure in the formula "Gospel and Law," which for him was also the basic substance of his dogmatics.[14] Simply stated, the Gospel speaks about God's will for us, while the Law tells us what God wills from us. Although they are two issues, in both, we encounter the same God who has a relationship with humanity. They are therefore not to be separated, although they are two distinctive issues.

Karl Barth deals extensively with the subject "Gospel and Law" in *Church Dogmatics* II/2, especially in the chapters 36-39. In those chapters, Barth makes it clear that ethics interprets the Law as the form of the Gospel.[15] Barth's usage of ethics in line with Gospel and Law also demonstrates his disdain for the separation of ethics from dogmatics. Having pointed this out, it then goes without saying that ethics remains essential in our deliberations concerning Gospel and its relationship to Law.

As much as the chapters in question remain fundamental to our understanding of how Gospel relates to Law, it is his later work which re-invites us to ponder the significant relationship which exists between Gospel and Law. In *Dogmatics* IV/3.1, it becomes almost immediately clear that the compulsion that he felt for dealing with these subjects stemmed from the criticism which he had received from theologians of the Lutheran traditions, especially from Lutheran theologians, such as W. Elert, P. Althaus, E. Sommerlath, H. Thielicke, and others.[16]

---

[13] Bush, "Barmen," 68.
[14] E. Busch, *The Great Passion: An Introduction to Karl Barth's Theology* (Grand Rapids: Eerdmans, 2004), 152.
[15] Karl Barth, *Church Dogmatics, II/2*, trans., G. W. Bromiley et al. (Edinburgh: T&T Clark, 1957), 509.
[16] Karl Barth, *Church Dogmatics, IV/31*, trans. G. W. Bromiley (Edinburgh: T&T Clark, 1961), 370.

These Lutheran theologians believed that Barth did not comprehend the relationship between these concepts and that his interpretation, which insisted that they ought to be seen as unified, was not convincing. The issues raised by these theologians left Barth to decipher the possibility of whether he had completely misread Luther, or he simply did not know Luther at all, both of which were possibilities that he did not seem to want to entertain. Barth was certainly aware that Luther himself had been a rather controversial person when it came to these issues. He believed that, with the following issues, in which he outlined his confusion with regard to the interpretation of Gospel and Law, one could see more than one Luther.[17] It was for this reason that he felt compelled to raise the following problems concerning an interpretation which insisted on the separateness of Gospel and Law.

Barth argued that the theologians in question did not possess sufficient biblical grounds to dispute his interpretation of these subjects. He therefore tabled the following points, which registered his confusion about the counter thesis that they raised. He wrote: "I do not understand with what biblical or inherent right, on the basis of what conception of God, His work, and His revelation and, above all, in the light of what Christology they can speak, not of one intrinsically true and clear Word of God but of two Words in which He speaks alternately and in different ways to man according to some unknown rule."[18]

He believed that the type of Gospel that they advocated was problematic, since it did not deal with the matters of forgiveness adequately. In light of this view, he raised the following misunderstanding that he had with regard to their critique of his interpretation. He wrote: "I do not understand the meaning of a supposed Gospel the content of which is exhausted by the proclamation of the forgiveness of sins and which is to be received by man in a purely inward and receptive faith; nor of a supposed Law which as an abstract demand can only be an external ordinance on the one side but on the other is ordained to accuse man and therefore to indicate and prepare the way for the Gospel."[19]

Barth continued to raise another misunderstanding, claiming that he found it, "difficult to comprehend how a concept of a supposed Law can be attained or exploited except [as in the sixteenth century and with very serious consequences in the seventeenth, eighteenth,

---

[17] Ibid., 371.
[18] Ibid., 370.
[19] Ibid.

and nineteenth centuries] by appealing to the idea of a natural law and therefore of a general natural revelation or by falling back on a most primitive form of Biblicism; and I am surprised that this dilemma has not been accepted as a warning."[20]

Barth believed that it was the divorce between these issues that in 1933 and 1934 enabled Protestant theologians to affirm the authoritarian and radically nationalist Führer-state. Because Barth believed that Gospel and Law belonged together, he believed that to equate obedience to the Führer with obedience to God was the fruit of an older theological error,[21] the error which was created in the interpretation of the Gospel, independent of the Law, which had allowed the likes of Friedrich Gogarten to declare that the Law of God "encounters the modern generation concretely in the form of the national socialist movement in both state and people," as a "hard," but for this reason, "authentic" law.[22] Busch rightly maintained that this would exclude the "specifically 'Christian' or 'biblical' Law." Instead the church must be the "nurse and guardian" of the law that is given in nationhood. It must also preach the Gospel of forgiveness, though this does not relate to offenses against that external "law."[23]

The Barmen Theological Declaration and the future: a conclusion

From the commentaries that have been written about this confession, it has become clear that this confession was never meant to stand the test of time.[24] By suggesting that the authors, as well as the synod that adopted this confession, did not think about the necessity of this confession to stand the test of time, does not suggest that this confession would become irrelevant in another time and context; instead to deny this confession some kind of timelessness is simply stimulated by the appreciation of the temporal context of this confession.

Remembering that this was a confession which was borrowed in particular by Reformed churches—around the world—implies that many thought and still think that the context which precipitated this confession also applied to other contexts. The authorship of confessions such as the Belhar Confession of South Africa has confirmed this belief.

---

[20] Ibid.
[21] Busch, "Great Passion," 156.
[22] Ibid.
[23] Ibid.
[24] Among the many commentaries, we find the one by E. Busch to be particularly innovative in pointing this view out. See Busch (2002), 64-82.

Despite the fact that the Belhar Confession was influenced by the theology that influenced the Barmen declaration, it has become clear that the socioeconomic, political, and cultural contexts were different than the contexts that necessitated Barmen. Put this way, the Belhar Confession is not a copy of the Barmen declaration, but it engaged in a critical theological and political conversation with the Barmen confession. South African theologians, such as Dirkie Smit, prefer to speak about a conversation between the Barmen declaration and the Belhar Confession, which has been going on for quite some time now.[25]

What cannot be denied of the Barmen declaration is that it has inevitably made an indelible impression on the Reformed history of the twenty-first century. Yet for this confession to retain its vitality, it is imperative that those who draw from its wells understand that occasions will continue to arise in which the church will have to confess its faith in the light of a palpable thread. Furthermore, it would have been very arrogant for both this confession and its adherents to insist on its timelessness. It is most helpful to emphasize the humility of confession, which this confession had hoped to illustrate but has never been stressed more emphatically. In addition to this, it is also imperative that those who ascribe to this confession learn from the mistakes that were committed both by the interpreters of the Barmen confession, as well as the mistakes inherent in the confession. We have tried to point out some of the criticisms leveled against this confession by the chief author of this confession among others. Therefore, a great injustice would be done to this confession if the shortcomings to these confessions were also not referred to when treating the essence of this confession in the current context.

Although the Barmen confession can be considered an event which was necessitated by particular sociopolitical and theological facets, it nonetheless remains a process. It remains a process because it reveals the church as being perpetually involved in an attempt to define its faith to those outside. It is also a process for it must probe continuously the church's faithfulness and obedience to its head Jesus Christ. More than twenty-five years after its draft, it has become time for us to engage both the strengths and weaknesses of the Belhar Confession. It is clear that Barth and others had to be more vocal after Barmen because they thought that the socioeconomic issues related to the Jewish question were not sufficiently highlighted. Perhaps now

---

[25] D. J. Smit, "Barmen and Belhar in Conversation—A South African Perspective," *Nederduitse Gereformeerde Teologiese Tydskryf* 47 nos. 1 and 2 (2006): 291–302.

is the most opportune time for those who subscribe to the Belhar Confession to begin to interrogate the accompanying letter,[26] which intentionally did not point clearly to the question of apartheid, and call to order those who associated with such an ideology. By taking a leaf from the discourse on the Jewish question and the Barmen declaration, we in South Africa will perhaps move a step closer to dealing with the race issue, which seems to have been avoided at all cost in Reformed theological discourse today.

---

[26] In his book, *Confessional Theology*, R. S. Tshaka explains the accompanying letter as an apology to the then apartheid regime. He maintains that the accompanying letter is produced to assure the then regime that the church which produced the Belhar Confession does not intend to become an alternative to the then apartheid regime but recognizes the position of those who are on the margins of society to confess when the Gospel is at stake. R. S. Tshaka, *Confessional Theology? A Critical Analysis of the Theology of Karl Barth and Its Significance for the Belhar Confession* (Newcastle: Cambridge Scholars, 2010), 257. That view has since changed, and the author looks at that statement in a more critical manner in light of his new-found insights of the debates post the Belhar Confession.

CHAPTER 12

The Black Churches as the "Good Enough Mother": An Analysis of African American Churches from a Winnicottian Perspective

Raynard Daniel Smith

The Negro church touches almost every ramification of the life of the Negro. As stated elsewhere, the Negro church, in the absence of other agencies to assume such responsibilities, has had to do more than its duty in taking care of the general interests of the race. A definitive history of the Negro church, therefore, would leave practically no phase of the history of the Negro in America untouched. All efforts of the Negro in things economic, educational, and political have branched out of or connected in some way with the rise and development of the Negro church.[1]

Carter G. Woodson

Introduction

Since 2006 Dr. Gregg Mast has been the president of a white, mainline institution that has served African American churches in the training of their leadership. African American churches[2] have a long-

---

[1] Carter G. Woodson, "The Negro Church, an All-Comprehending Institution," *The Negro History Bulletin* 3, no. 1 (October 1939): 7.
[2] The term "Black Church" tends to be the dominant term used to describe Black Christianity in social scientific and theological literature. It is the sociological and

standing tradition of being what African American historian Carter G. Woodson identified as "all comprehending institutions." In saying this, Woodson was attempting to capture the way in which African American churches functioned in the life of their constituents in attending to their social, political, economic, emotional, and spiritual needs. In their responsiveness to the changing cultural and social realities of the Black community, they have garnered a reputation as being the vanguard for all oppressed African American people.

Their attainment, however, of middle-class status and the affluence in which African American churches have uncritically internalized the values and norms of individualism and capitalism of the dominant society and become insular in their activities, coupled with the economic and social reality of a bifurcated Black community—of Black middle-class and a significant percentage of impoverished lower-class African Americans—calls for African American churches to re-examine their mission and focus within this contemporary context of a new African American reality in what has been characterized as a "post-racial" society.

This essay will examine the ways in which Black Churches have historically accommodated themselves to the needs—social, political, psychological, and spiritual—of the Black community. It will note how the functioning of Black churches in the lives of African Americans appears analogous to what object relations theorist Donald Winnicott theorizes from his clinical practice as the *good enough mother*. It will then assess the current situation of the Black community and offer a critique and a call for Black Churches to step up to the much-needed task at hand of reassuming the role of attentively responding to the needs of the Black community. It will end with a call to African American churches to reclaim their prophetic voice and action, thereby owning their authentic self, in calling upon America to consider the plight of their "least of these."

---

theological referent used to represent the Black Christian churches in America that are part of the Protestant communion that developed in response to racism during the post-emancipation era. In recognition of the critique that there is no monolithic entity called "the Black Church," I shall use the term only when it is used in the literature. Otherwise I choose to speak of the "Black churches" or "African American Churches" recognizing the plurality of denominations but with an understanding that they each are undergirded by a common *Weltanschauung* or worldview known as the Black sacred cosmos which is a social construction of reality influenced by the confluence of evangelical religion, slave religion, and African retentions. Here my thinking is informed by Meredith McGuire in her text, *Religion: The Social Context* (Belmont, CA: Wadsworth Publishing Company, 1997), 257.

The Black church as pathological

In the early social scientific literature, African American churches are frequently described as otherworldly, compensatory, and therefore pathological institutions.[3] In sociologist E. Franklin Frazier's *The Negro Church in America*, a classic work published in 1963, the author credits African American churches for being the most influential institutions within the life of the African American people.[4] In his analysis, Frazier described predominantly African American churches as a "nation within a nation" providing a necessary arena in which African Americans, living under the cruel treatment of slavery and Jim Crow, could sustain themselves during a time of severe social, psychological, economic, and political oppression. With, however, the dissolution of slavery and a vigorous emphasis toward assimilation, Frazier believed that African American churches now function as impediments to African Americans becoming fully integrated within the larger context of American society.[5] He contended:

> As Negro professors are increasingly taken on the faculties of so-called white colleges and universities and Negro students are admitted to such institutions, Negroes are joining the mainstream of American life. When one comes to the Negro church, which is the most important cultural institution created by Negroes, one encounters the most important institutional barrier to integration and the assimilation of Negroes.[6]

Frazier further observed that African American churches were authoritarian and anti-intellectual and concluded that these tendencies would conspire to inhibit African Americans from being assimilated into the dominant culture. He therefore proposed that these churches could now serve African American people only by their ceasing to exist.[7]

---

[3] See Peter J. Paris, *The Social Teachings of the Black Churches* (Philadelphia, PA: Fortress Press, 1986).

[4] E. Franklin Frazier, *The Negro Church in America* (New York, NY: Schocken Books, 1963), 32.

[5] Ibid., 53.

[6] Ibid., 74-75.

[7] A major assumption influencing Frazier's analysis was that the slaves were stripped of their African culture during the middle passage. Thus, he argued that there was no continuity between African religion and the religious life demonstrated in the Black churches. This is an on-going debate in the study of African American religious experience. For a more in-depth explanation of the debate over African retentions see Albert Raboteau, *Slave Religion: The "Invisible Institution" in the Antebellum South* (New York, NY: Oxford University Press, 1978), 52-55.

In support of Frazier's pejorative view of African American churches, journalist Charles Silberman identified "involuntary isolation" as the source and predicament of African American churches.[8] In Silberman's *Crisis in Black and White*, published in 1964, he argued that the evolution and continued presence of African American churches is a visible indication that African Americans have accepted or acceded to their condition of oppression. Silberman believed that the 350 years of oppression—the period of slavery and segregation—had permanently marred the African American psyche to the point that it was beyond repair. Silberman asserted that, in the Black church, African Americans "involuntarily isolated" themselves from the larger American society. He viewed religious expression within the Black church as lower class, otherworldly, and an opiate to escape problems in temporal life. Clearly, according to Silberman, the organization of Christian churches around the concept of race is not in the best interest of African Americans.

A third interpretation that social scientists have generally taken concerning the Black church is the view of African American churches as compensatory institutions.[9] Though this view is held by many social scientists, it owes its origin to Gunnar Myrdal's *An American Dilemma: The Negro Problem and Modern Democracy*, published in 1944. According to Myrdal, African American churches separated to form their own churches because these churches offered opportunities denied to African Americans within American society at large. He said, "It is probable, however, that the church's main attraction is the opportunity it gives for large masses of people to function in an organizing group, to compete for prestige, to be elected to office, to exercise power and control, to win applause and acclaim."[10] Although Myrdal viewed these aspects as significant and positive incentives, his overall assessment of Black culture and Black institutions—inclusive of churches—was that they were pathological because they were developed in direct contrast to the dominant American culture, which he regarded as authentic and the ego-ideal—the only and perfect way to exist. He contended: "In

---

[8] Charles Silberman, *Crisis in Black and White* (New York, NY: Random House, 1964), also see Anthony Orum, "An Reappraisal of the Social and Political Participation of Negroes," *American Journal of Sociology* 72 (July 1966): 33.

[9] Of this school of thought are St. Clair Drake and Horace Cayton, *Black Metropolis: A Study of Negro Life in the North* (New York, NY: Harper and Row, 1962), and Gunnar Myrdal, *An American Dilemma: The Negro Problem and Modern Democracy* (New York, NY: Harper and Row, 1944).

[10] Myrdal, *An American Dilemma*, 343.

practically all its divergences, American Negro culture is not something independent of general American culture. It is distorted development, or a pathological condition, of the general American culture."[11] Accordingly, Myrdal regarded all activities in African American social clubs, civic associations, and churches as merely an inferior substitute for the types of organizational life of the American mainstream.

The analyses of Frazier, Silberman, and Myrdal fail to grasp the profound influence and complex nature that the Black churches have had—and continue to have—on the African American psyche in a context where race is salient and often used to exclude Blacks from full participation in the life of the dominant society. Their analyses beg the question: How can institutions that have given life and the continuity of self to so many African American people seeking to survive and even thrive in a hostile environment be conceived as pathological? Instead of looking at the Black churches as pathological social institutions that delude African American people, I propose another perspective that originates out of my own experience and observation (having grown up in a Black church context) and from my research on the Black churches.[12] To aptly describe how the African American churches have functioned— and continue to function—in the lives of African American people, I propose that we draw upon the work of Donald Winnicott, psychoanalytic object relations theorist, to describe the Black churches as a *good enough mother*, a concept that suggests that Black churches embrace and provide a *holding* for African American people in response to their living conditions of oppression and domination within the dominant society[13]

The metaphor of "mother"

African American Christians frequently use the metaphor of "mother" in reference to their churches. When this is employed, it is to

---

[11] Ibid.
[12] My own view is in agreement with C. Eric Lincoln and Lawrence Mamiya, *The Black Church in the African American Experience* (Durham, NC: Duke University Press, 1990), 11-16, where Black churches are viewed as vacillating between six dialectic poles over historical time: priestly and prophetic, other-worldly versus this-worldly, universalism and particularism, communal and privatistic, charismatic and bureaucratic, and resistance versus accommodation.
[13] Donald Winnicott, *The Maturational Processes and the Facilitating Environment* (Hogarth, NY: International University Press, 1965) and Madeleine David and David Wallbridge, *Boundary and Space: An Introduction to the Work of D. W. Winnicott* (New York, NY: Brunner/Mazel Publishing, 1990).

distinguish the founding church, out of which others Black churches of that denomination are birthed. This birth can be engendered by events either amicable or contentious, such as disagreements over leadership, warring factions within the church, new vision, expansion, or the spawning of a new church development in another locale. Generally, over time, there is healing. Churches that have come out from the original church when identifying themselves usually refer amicably to the church of their origin as the mother church. Or "mother" can be used to identify the first church within a denomination out of which other churches in that denomination either spawned or are affiliated. For example, Mother Bethel AME, founded by Richard Allen in Philadelphia in 1827, is considered the mother church of the AME denomination.

In his clinical work, Donald Winnicott developed the concept of *holding*, which he based on a mother's ability to provide nurturance to a dependent child, to convey an unconscious psychological dynamic at work in the relationship between mother and child. Holding is something that is derived out of the maternal-infant relationship that meets the physical as well as the psychological needs of the dependent infant. It is crucial to our human development that we be held by parents (mother and father) and other significant loved ones. Holding in this sense refers to the natural skill and constancy of care that is derived from the attentiveness provided by the mother or caregiver to the dependent infant. Winnicott called this attunement *good enough mothering* and stated that it seeks to provide support to the evolving sense of self of the infant. *Good enough holding* creates the necessary provisions for an environment that facilitates the psychic maturation of the infant. Through holding, the infant is enabled to experience a sense of empowerment which, according to Winnicott, is essential to a healthy child's ego development.[14] It provides sufficient inner security that allows the maturing infant to tolerate the inevitable struggles of everyday life in later years. Winnicott sums up holding as follows:

> Holding: Protects from physiological insult. Takes account of the infant's skin sensitivity-touch, temperature, auditory sensitivity, visual sensitivity, infant's lack of knowledge of the existence of anything other than the self. It includes the whole routine of care throughout the day and night, and it is not the same with any two infants, because it is part of the infant, and no two infants are

---

[14] Winnicott, *The Maturational Processes*, 49.

alike. Also, it follows the minute day-to-day changes belonging to the infant's growth and development, both physically and psychologically.[15]

Holding is the work that is done by good enough mothering, which according to Winnicott need not be the biological mother or even a female for that matter. A good enough mother can be anyone who has the capacity to empathize with the evolving needs of the infant and responsibly and consistently fulfills those needs both physically and psychologically. Winnicott makes a distinction between the function of the environmental mother and the object mother. The object mother attends to the material needs of the infant—food, clothing, and shelter—while the environmental mother attends to the infant's psychological needs—nurture and belonging. He asserts that through her faithful discharge of her maternal responsibilities, the good enough mother creates an environment that does not impinge on the evolving ego of the child, granting the ego full opportunity to experience itself as omnipotent. This creates within the child the subjective experience of a "moment of illusion." And as the good enough mother gradually withdraws from attending to her all-encompassing task of nurturing, the child comes to experience the objective reality. The stage of merger, absolute dependence, and sense of being all powerful gives way to the infant's capacity to differentiate between subjective and shared reality. This intricately subjective experience leads to the infant's developing a true, self-possessing capacity to play, which is to be imaginative and creative, that is, to be fully alive.[16]

Black churches and the good enough mother

Just like the good enough mother who, through her consistent administration of empathic attunement to the developing infant's needs, creates a provision of holding for the developing and dependent infant, so too have the Black churches functioned as a provision of holding for despised and rejected African American people living in situations of oppression. In fact, social ethicist Peter Paris asserts that Black churches evolved in direct response to the social climate of racism. He states, "The uniqueness of the Black churches is seen in the fact that they are unequivocally 'race institutions' . . . racism and racial self-respect have been the two warring principles that caused the emergence

[15] Ibid.
[16] Ibid., 50.

of the Black churches."[17] Therefore, their raison d'être has been to create and sustain holding environments for African American people whose humanity has been assailed by the brutal force of white racism. They have historically held individuals, families, and communities in various and sundry ways that encompass the functions of the object mother and environmental mother. Holding for the Black churches has encompassed addressing the social, psychological, and physical, as well as the spiritual needs of African Americans. In their ability to create a provision of holding, the African American churches have well served their constituents. Though they have not been perfect institutions, one can surmise that they have been *good enough*. Victor Anderson in his text, *Creative Exchange*, critiques the romanticized notion that African American churches are perfect institutions. He recognizes that Black churches (and the Black family as well) have been places of safety as well as places of insult.[18] While I celebrate their good qualities, I am cognizant that not all actions undertaken within the Black churches have been life giving. I do, however, note that there are sufficient wholesome qualities within the Black churches that outweigh, but do not negate, the bad. In this sense, Black Churches truly embody what Winnicott describes as good enough.

The evolution of the Black churches

During their infancy, the Black churches emerged within the crucible of slavery as "invisible institutions," providing the African slaves with a sanctuary that was imbued with the confluence of revivalist evangelicalism and the African cultural reservoir. This created sacred space in which African Americans could live out their lives and interpret their experiences.[19] From within this sacred canopy of slave religion, trances, dreams, visions, and the ring shout, they could experience God in the "potential space"[20] and thereby gain renewed psychic energy and spiritual sustenance to endure another day of unwarranted dehumanizing treatment at the hands of the slave master and mistress.

[17] Peter Paris, *The Social Teaching of the Black Churches*, 9.
[18] See Victor Anderson, *Creative Exchange: A Constructive Theology of African American Religious Experience* (Minneapolis, MN: Fortress Press, 2008), 151-63.
[19] For the concept of the African American sacred cosmos, see C. Eric Lincoln and Lawrence Mamiya, *The Black Church in the African American Experience* (Durham, NC: Duke University Press, 1990), 2-7.
[20] According to Winnicott, the "potential space" is that part of reality during the infant's early development that is infused with both subjectivity and objectivity. It is at once the interpenetration of both. See Donald Winnicott, *Playing and Reality* (London, UK: Tavistock Publication, 1971).

While under the watchful guise of the master and mistress, the slaves were constantly on guard. On other hand, in the holding, provisions made by the clandestine, sometimes all night, prayer meetings in the ravines and bulrushes, the slaves could suspend their ego boundaries and connect with each other and with an omnipotent God who delivered Daniel from the lion's den and who they believed would surely one day deliver them. This God had never lost a battle. This God was "a mother to the motherless, a father to the fatherless, and a friend to the friendless." It was in this "potential space," the interpenetration of subjective and objective realities, where the slaves encountered God and poured out their sorrows and their joys. As they cried out to the heavens for freedom, they experienced God anew, and they responded to God's presence in the ecstatic shout and the dance. The spirituals which emerged during this time bore the weight of their sorrows as they sang "I've been 'buked and I've been scorned, I've been talked about sho's you' born," and they resolved within themselves, "Ain' gwine lay my 'legion down."

The extent to which these religious meetings were so meaningful to the slaves is evident in the fact that many risked their very lives to attend them, for there they received sustenance emotionally, psychologically, and spiritually, for living amidst the harsh and brutal conditions of the reality of slavery. African American historian Albert Raboteau rightly acknowledges the psychological import that these services had upon the slaves. He contends: "For those facing the brutal conditions of slavery—the daily physical, psychological, emotional attacks against their worth as a person—to experience the acceptance and affirmation of God renewed their sense of value and importance."[21] Therefore these religious meetings frequented by the slaves served a therapeutic function that kept the slaves sane, if not whole.

With the Emancipation and the Reconstruction period, these "invisible institutions" of the South—Baptist[22] and Colored Methodist Episcopal[23]—and the Black churches of the North—African Methodist

---

[21] Albert Raboteau, *Canaan Land: A Religious History of African Americans* (New York, NY: Oxford University Press, 2001), 46.

[22] According to Henry H. Mitchell, the first documented Black Baptist church was formulated in Prince George County, Virginia, in 1756, on the plantation of William Byrd III. See *Black Church Beginnings: The Long-Hidden Realities of the First Years* (Grand Rapids, MI: Eerdmans, 2004), 53-55.

[23] The Southern Methodists in 1866 set apart their Black congregants to establish their own houses of worship. They became established in 1870 as the Colored Methodist Episcopal Church (CME). They would later change their name to the

Episcopal[24] and African Methodist Episcopal Zion[25]—came into visible existence as the independent Black churches movement. It was a chaotic time for the approximately four million freed people whose previous existence and self-understanding had been defined as chattel. Given no provisions to sustain themselves, these freed Americans of African descent were now faced with a more intense form of domination and oppression that threatened their fragile existence. Winnicott asserted that one important quality of the good enough mother is her ability to be highly adaptable to the evolving needs of the infant. For freed people denied access to the basic and fundamental necessities of life, the Black churches created a provision for addressing their physical as well as their spiritual needs. These Black churches would accommodate themselves to serving the particular social, political, economic, and psychological needs of their Black constituents by establishing schools to counteract illiteracy, forming economic cooperative adventures, publishing literature specifically tailored to their Black clientele, and by providing a "badly needed refuge in a hostile world," but the Black churches were also a place for addressing social needs and arenas for the development of leadership aspirations.[26]

The multifarious functions of the Black churches

Due to the effects of slavery, the family unit was left in total disarray, but the Black churches adapted themselves to this challenge by becoming agencies of social control, emphasizing the sanctity of marriage and countering the tide of sexual promiscuity, thus giving stability to the Black family.[27] Amid the hostile racial climate of the

---

Christian Methodist Episcopal Church in 1954. See Sydney E. Alhstrom, *A Religious History of the American People* (New Haven, CT: Yale University Press, 1972), 708. Also see, C. Eric Lincoln and Lawrence Mamiya, *The Black Church in the African American Experience*, 60-65; and Anne Pinn and Anthony Pinn, *Fortress Introduction to Black Church History* (Minneapolis, MN: Fortress Press, 2002), 54-62.

[24] In 1784 the Bethel African Methodist Episcopal Church was founded by Richard Allen when he and a group of Black members walked out of the St. George's Methodist Episcopal Church after being removed from praying in the balcony. This church was later united with other Black churches that held to the similar tenets of faith and formed the AME denomination in 1816. See C. Eric Lincoln and Lawrence Mamiya, *The Black Church in the African American Experience*, 50-56; Pinn and Pinn, *Fortress Introduction to Black Church History*, 31-43.

[25] The African Methodist Episcopal Zion Church was founded in 1848 in New York. See Lincoln and Mamiya, *The Black Church in the African American Experience*, 20-46; Pinn and Pinn, *Fortress Introduction to Black Church History*, 44-54.

[26] Frazier, *The Negro Church in America*, 35-51.

[27] Ibid., 37-40.

Reconstruction period and the institutionalization of Jim Crow, African American people were constantly living in the shadow of death. By establishing mutual aid societies which provided economic and moral support, the Black churches created a container of holding for those African American individuals and families whose lives were disrupted by the trauma of illness and death.[28] This effort was of special importance in that it provided support to individuals and families in crisis.

While White America insisted on the compulsory ignorance of African Americans as a means of perpetuating their second-class status, the Black churches promoted education by encouraging their predominantly illiterate masses to become readers of the Bible, thereby increasing the literacy rate among its constituents.[29] Many of these churches actually served dual functions within the African American community. At night and on Sundays, many of the Black churches were places of worship and Bible study. During the day, however, they were converted into places of disciplined learning. Furthermore, the Black churches established their own primary schools, secondary schools, and colleges as a means of educating their own people.[30] As the first social institutions fully controlled by African Americans, the Black churches created an arena where African Americans could develop their innate gifts and talents whether in the area of public speaking, music, leadership, organizing, or so forth. In creating an arena for self-development and racial pride, the Black churches' functions embodied Winnicott's understanding of the "good enough environment . . . which facilitates the various individual inherited tendencies so that development takes place according to these inherited tendencies."[31]

Most importantly, the Black churches, in their endeavor to serve the needs of African American people, have functioned as havens from the brutal effects of white racism. The psychological impact of white racism on the African American psyche has been traumatic. African Americans who had been told for so long that they were inferior and continually degraded by the social institutions of the dominant society had internalized feelings of inferiority from the external oppressive

---

[28] Ibid., 40-43.
[29] John Hope Franklin and Alfred A. Moss Jr., *From Slavery to Freedom: A History of African Americans*, 7th ed. (New York, NY: McGraw-Hill, 1994), 286.
[30] Frazier, *The Negro Church in America*, 43-47.
[31] Winnicott, *Home is Where We Start From: Essays by a Psychoanalyst* (New York: W.W. Norton & Company, 1990), 22.

environment. The Black churches, functioning as cultural institutions, served as a corrective measure against this action. They "mirrored" African Americans, thus, affirming their humanity. Though poor and devalued by the wider society, African Americans were continuously reminded of their "somebodyness." They were "children of God—children of the Kingdom." In the "holding environment" of African American worship, the Black churches counteracted the disintegrating forces of white racism which had depleted African Americans at the core of their being. The worship experience of the Black churches served as a therapeutic environment for African American people. Through the call and response "performance" of the singing of Spirituals, Gospel songs, the spontaneous prayers, and the preaching, African Americans found a release for the pent-up feelings of frustration and despair which gnawed at their being and threatened their ego constancy. Through this medium, they symbolized their pain, anger, and frustrations in healthy and safe ways. They cared for each other when giving vent to their feelings overwhelmed them. They understood each other's sorrow and grief. In this "potential space," as the spiritual leaders of "communities of memory," Black preachers recasted and recalled the biblical narratives, crafting sermons that conveyed God's love and concern, encouraged spiritual growth, and offered practical advice for daily living to African Americans seeking to survive within an oppressive environment.[32] It was in worship that African Americans were nourished in the empty place of emotional insufficiency and experienced what Winnicott called "feeling real," which is the ability to be spontaneous and free.[33]

Black churches in the period of mass migration

During the Black migration (1914-1950s) to the urban centers of the North and West, the Black churches functioned as provisions for holding by becoming surrogate families for displaced African Americans. In their quest to escape the ravages of white hostility in the rural South, attainment of better jobs, housing, and education for their children, these African American migrants turned to the storefront churches which dotted the urban religious landscape providing them

---

[32] For the content emphasis of sermons within the Black churches, see Michael I. N. Dash and Christine D. Chapman, *The Shape of Zion: Leadership and Life in Black Churches* (Cleveland, OH: Pilgrim Press, 2003), 27-29.

[33] According to Winnicott, the ability of "feeling real" is derived from the true self that is developed and cultivated in response to the continuity of care and acceptance exhibited by the caregiver's attunement to the infant/child's needs.

with new extended families and a sense of community.[34] Their hopes and aspirations for a better life were dashed by the pervasive and pernicious White brutality encountered in the urban centers. Feeling despised and rejected, these people lifted up their voices and sung gospel songs which articulated their struggles and disappointments while offering them a sense of hope that "there is a bright side somewhere, so don't stop until you find it."

Black churches and civil rights movement

With the advent of the Civil Rights Movement that began with the Bus Boycott of Montgomery in 1955 and its precursor, the death and public viewing of Emmett Till in 1954, the Black churches again functioned as a provision of holding. Middle-class Black churches were in the vanguard toward agitating for the civil rights of their constituents, while Black congregations of the lower class, though seemingly acquiescent, quietly lent their support, though not as publicly. This form of resistance was a function they had known before, during the antebellum period, and due to their profound influence, they became the targets of white retaliation.[35] Not only did they offer a place where African Americans congregated in mass rallies for "ego support"—Dexter Avenue Baptist Church, First Baptist Church, and Holt Street Baptist Church in Montgomery; Ebenezer Baptist Church in Atlanta; St. Thomas AME Church in Birmingham; and Clayborn Temple and Mason Temple COGIC in Memphis—they also gave to the movement some of their best leaders, such as Martin Luther King Jr, Wyatt Tee Walker, Fred Shuttlesworth, Andrew Young, and Fannie Lou Hamer. Through prayer vigils, singing of freedom songs, and preaching, African Americans gained spiritual strength and moral stamina in their struggle for freedom, liberation, and justice. Here at another critical juncture in the life of African Americans, the Black churches gave the movement its rhythm and vitality in the form of the freedom songs. "We shall overcome," spoke of their tenacity and determination to gain equality for all African American people. One participant who was

---

[34] The emergence of the independent Baptist, Holiness, and Pentecostal churches, in particular, the Church of God in Christ, played a significant role in the life of African Americans migrating from areas of the rural South to the urban industrial centers of the North. See Lacy Kirk Williams, "Effects of Urbanization on Religious Life," in *African American Religious History: Documentary Witness*, ed. Milton C. Sernett 2nd ed. (Durham, NC: Duke University Press, 1999), 372-75.

[35] In Mississippi, during the summer of 1964, over thirty-four Black churches serving as Freedom Schools were firebombed by white mob violence.

interviewed by a journalist noted the psychological benefit that came with singing freedom songs:

> The fear down here is tremendous. I didn't know whether I'd be shot at, or stoned, or what. But when the singing started, I forgot all that. I felt good within myself. We sang "Oh Freedom" and "We Shall Not Be Moved," and after that you just don't want to sit around any more. You want the world to hear you, to know what you're fighting for![36]

Freedom songs adapted from the Black churches' repertoire contained an uncanny ability to arrest the fears and apprehensions of African Americans. Through their liturgy, the Black churches possessed the profound ability to impel people to action—to "run on and see what the end is gonna be." True to the words of Winnicott's concept of holding, the Black churches in their capacity to empathize responsibly to the changing needs of African American people have given strength and brought healing and reparations to the fragmented ego of African Americans. It is for these reasons that I disagree with the analysis of Frazier, Silberman, and Myrdal.

The Black churches in the post-Civil Rights Era

Today in the post-Civil Rights era of the twenty-first century, and what some are characterizing as the post-racial era, due to America's election of its first Black president, Barak Obama, in urban centers across America, there are numerous and complex problems plaguing African American communities where the majority of Black churches are physically located.[37] African American professor of religion, Eddie Glaude has critiqued the Black churches, asserting that they are essentially losing their grip on the African American psyche. They have seemingly been silent on bringing issues of importance to the Black community before the administration of the United States. According to Glaude:

---

[36] Jon Michael Spencer, *Protest and Praise: Sacred Music of Black Religion* (Minneapolis, MN: Fortress Press, 1990), 91.

[37] It is estimated that 66 percent of African American churches are located in urban areas, and 79 percent of Black Baptist churches, 64 percent of COGIC churches, 63 percent of AME congregations, 49 percent of CME Congregations, 54 percent of AMEZ congregations, 75 percent of Black United Methodists congregations, and 75 percent of Black Presbyterian congregations are located in urban areas. See Stephen Rasor and Michael Dash, *The Mark of Zion: Congregational Life in Black Churches* (Cleveland, OH: Pilgrim Press, 2003), 10-11.

The Black Church, as we have known or imagined it, is dead. Of course, many

> African Americans still go to church. According to the PEW Research Center's Forum on Religion and Public Life, 87 percent of African Americans identify with a religious group and 79 percent say that religion is very important in their lives. But the idea of this venerable institution as central to black life and as a repository for the social and moral conscience of the nation has all but disappeared.[38]

Glaude delineates three reasons that justify what he sees as the near irrelevance of the Black churches within the public sphere. First, Black churches, despite the claim of being progressive institutions, have a history of acquiescing to the status quo. He is correct in his observations that not all leaders of the Black churches agreed with the social protest movement of civil rights, led by the Reverend Dr. Martin Luther King Jr. Hence, out of this conflict, the Progressive Baptist Church Convention was born.[39] Second, Black churches are no longer the sole social institutions within the Black community that are controlled by African Americans. There are other civic and social advocacy agencies that vie for the attention and allegiance of African Americans—the NAACP, the Urban League, and so forth. In addition, there are even other churches that are not Black churches that have attracted a substantial number of African Americans.

Third, the Black churches appear to be resting on their laurels of deeds done in the past. This point appears to be consonant with the critique of Gayraud Wilmore in his text *Black Religion and Black Radicalism*, where he asserts that Black churches, though infused with a strain of social and political activism, have experienced periods where they have retreated to pacifying the religious needs of their constituencies, demonstrating a lure for reward in the afterlife.[40] He contends that the Black churches are presently in a mode of passive quietism, which is counterintuitive to their raison d'être.

Black theologian Raphael Warnock, in his book, *The Divided Mind of the Black Church*, acknowledges that the dual nature, or what he

---

[38] Eddie Glaude, "The Black Church is Dead," *Huffington Post*. http://www.huffingtonpost.com/eddie-glaude-jr-phd/the-black-church-is-dead_b_473815.html (accessed September, 2011).

[39] Lincoln and Mamiya, The *Black Church in the African American Experience*, 36-39.

[40] Gayraud Wilmore, *Black Religion and Black Radicalism: An Interpretation of the Religious History of Afro-American People*, 2nd ed. (Maryknoll, NY: Orbis Books, 1984).

identifies as the "double consciousness," of Black Christiantiy raises critical questions about the Black churches' mission in American society. He contends:

> As an instrument of salvation through Jesus Christ, is the mission of the black church to save souls or to transform the social order? As it would seek to be faithful to the gospel message and mission of Jesus Christ, is it called to be an evangelical church or a liberationist church? Can it truly be an evangelical church without being a liberationist church? Can it be a liberationist church without also being an evangelical church? Put another way, does the gospel mandate insist that the church organize its institutional life so as to address itself primarily to "the slavery of sin" or to "the sin of slavery'?[41]

According to Warnock, the contemporary scenario of many Black churches is that they have tended to gravitate more toward evangelical piety. In doing this, they have viewed the nurturing of the Black self as having greater importance to the neglect of providing a prophetic critique that challenges white American society, especially in its treatment of its Black and Brown citizens.

The critiques that Wilmore and, most currently, Glaude and Warnock, raise are valid charges against the Black churches, which in many respects, seem to parallel the experience of pre-exilic Israel in the biblical narrative who had gone "awhoring" after other gods. The preaching of the prosperity gospel, materialism, consumerism, and accommodation of the culture of narcissism and American individualism have eclipsed the prophetic voice of many Black churches and the psyche of African Americans.[42] The allure of constructing great multimillion-dollar cathedrals in the jungles of impoverished communities where pastors create their fiefdom is an indictment upon the Black churches, indicative of their apathy for the Black community. The insular focus of worshipping God as transcendent Being with the expectation of individual self-gratification, "I got to get my praise on," within the four walls of the churches to the neglect of impacting the surrounding community that lies in spiritual and physical malaise,

---

[41] See Raphael G. Warnock's *The Divided Mind of the Black Church: Theology, Piety & Public Witness* (New York, NY: New York University Press, 2014), 3.

[42] These tendencies are not new or unique to the present situation. See Stephanie Mitchem's *Name It and Claim It: Prosperity Preaching in the Black Church* (Cleveland, OH: Pilgrim Press, 2007).

is an anathema. Where is the prophetic voice that once raged in the tradition of Moses challenging Pharaoh to "Let my people go"?

The current condition of the Black community

The Black churches' apparent loss of focus on the needs of the Black community is happening at a time when the gains of the Civil Rights movement—Affirmative Action, Voters Rights, and so forth—have been slowly whittling away. While today there is a solid Black middle class, many of whom are members of the Black churches, as we survey the terrain of Black America, we encounter alarming statistics. On the healthcare front, there are major disparities in healthcare and healthcare outcomes. The AIDS epidemic that ravaged America in the 1980s continues to greatly impact the Black community. Although Blacks make up only 13.6 percent of the US population, they account for 44 percent of all new diagnosed cases of HIV.[43] In addition, the rate of HIV diagnosis among Black men is six times that of whites, and the rate for Black women is twenty times that of their white counterparts.[44] According to the US Centers for Disease Control Health Disparities and Inequalities Report (Jan. 2011), "Black women and men have much higher coronary heart disease (CHD) death rates in the forty-five to seventy-four age group than women and men of other races."[45] A higher percentage of Black women (37.9 percent) than white women (19.4 percent) died before age seventy-five as a result of CHD, as did Black men (61.5 percent) compared with white men (41.5 percent).[46] And a higher percentage of Black women (39 percent) died of stroke before age seventy-five, compared with white women (17.3 percent) as did Black men (60.7 percent) compared to white men (31.1 percent).[47] Why are there such gross disparities in reference to healthcare? Where is the voice of the Black churches on the issue of healthcare for their constituents?[48] What should be the role of Black churches, especially

---

[43] https://www.cdc.gov/hiv/group/racialethnic/africanamericans/ (accessed January, 2017).
[44] Ibid.
[45] http://atlantapost.com/2011/02/09/8-important-statistics-that-black-america-should-pay-attention-to-now (accessed September, 2011).
[46] Ibid.
[47] Ibid.
[48] While critiquing the silence of the Black churches during the recent debate on healthcare undertaken by President Obama's administration and the democrats, Eddie Glaude acknowledges that only COGIC Presiding Bishop Charles Blake made a public announcement in support of the Obama Administration.

now with President Donald Trump and the Republican administration that is seeking to repeal the Affordable Care Act which secured access to healthcare for millions of low-income, working-class African Americans. How can the Black churches afford to remain silent on this issue when they have been the vanguard of the Black community? In times past, they have been known to speak out on causes that concern their constituents. Their voice is needed here to speak out and bring to the public square the needs of their citizens who may happen to be people of brown and black hue but who are no less American and most importantly people created in the image and likeness of God, thus deserving of equitable access and healthcare treatment.

Furthermore, when we survey the economic front within the Black community, we encounter more disturbing facts. The recent US Census Bureau data reports, "24.7% of all African Americans live in poverty."[49] The Labor Department statistics showed the unemployment rate among Blacks during the recent economic recession was hovering around 16 percent.[50] Although the economy as a whole has shown great improvement, Black unemployment is yet at 9.6 percent as compared to the national average of 5.4 percent.[51] In addition, according to the most recent government figures from the US Centers for Disease Control and Prevention, "72 percent of mothers in the Black community are raising African American children in single-parent households.[52] Many of these women are working class, where they are minimum-wage earners or poor unemployed, completely dependent upon public government assistance. In the current economic climate, where even a two-income household can encounter challenges financially, these single-parent families struggle for their daily subsistence to provide the bare necessities for their families. They are in need of social and political as well as spiritual support. What are the Black churches doing to address their economic and political concerns? Many of these women look to the Black churches for their spiritual support. Can they also find the social network of support they need to raise their children with the hope of having a brighter future? Can they find the prophetic voice that would advocate on their behalf for a living wage? Where is the voice

---

[49] Atlantapost.com/2011/02/09/8.
[50] Ibid.
[51] https://www.bls.gov/.../unemployment-rates-for-african-americans-by-state-in-2015.htm (accessed January, 2016).
[52] Atlantapost.com/2011/02/09/8.

of the Black churches on issues of poverty, jobs, and family life? What should the action of Black churches be in response to these troubling statistics? Why do the Black churches remain silent on these issues? How can the Black churches remain silent on these issues when in times past Black churches created networks of care for their constituents that helped them to secure stability as they migrated to the urban centers of the North?

In reference to education, the Black churches readily understood the importance of education for their constituents as a means of upward social mobility. Today it is still understood that education is the gateway to social and economic opportunities. The US Department of Education reports, however, "Nearly half of the nation's African students attend high schools in low-income areas with dropout rates that hover in the 40-50% range."[53] "Dropout factories" as they are known (i.e., high schools that routinely have senior classes with 60 percent fewer students than their entering freshmen classes) are estimated to produce 73 percent of African Americans.[54] Where is the prophetic voice of the Black churches on the issue of quality education? Why are the Black churches not holding leaders and elected officials accountable for providing quality education for all citizens, especially those in poor urban areas? Black churches in times past recognized the value of education for the uplift of their constituents. Have they so soon forgotten the power of education and the gains that its procurement has meant for their community? A prophetic voice that advocates for the state and federal government providing the necessary resources is needed on this issue.

The dismal report continues, in relationship to mass incarceration, according to the Bureau of Justice Statistics, "The racial composition of the US prison and jail population as of 2008 was 60.21% African American, mostly male."[55] Michelle Alexander in her book, *The New Jim Crow*, contends that mass incarceration of people of color—Black and Brown people—is responsible for creating what starkly resembles a caste system in American that rivals and even exceeds that of the Jim Crow era.[56] White society's stance on getting tough on drug-related

---

[53] Ibid.
[54] Ibid.
[55] Ibid.
[56] Michelle Alexander, *The New Jim Crow: Mass Incarceration in the Age of Colorblindness* (New York, NY: The New Press, 2010).

crimes has devastated the Black community and contributed to the destabilization of the Black family. The proliferation of access to guns in defense of the Second Amendment has created unprecedented concerns within the Black community, where there is a high rate of violent crimes. It has snuffed out Black innocent lives in its wake. The most recent government statistics indicated that "43% of all murder victims in 2007 were African American, 93.1% of whom were killed by African Americans."[57] But an even greater threat and atrocity has been the loss of Black lives at the hands of law enforcement. Where is the voice of the Black churches on these social justice issues? Why are the Black churches not advocating for a more equitable justice system that believes in the rehabilitation of its citizens instead of discarding them? Why are the Black churches not advocating for stricter gun control laws that would restrict the flow of access to firearms, especially among the criminally minded? What roles are the Black churches taking to ameliorate the hostility and frustration of its constituents? Where is the voice of the Black churches calling law enforcement leaders into account ensuring that they too recognize that "Black Lives Matter."

These statistics are staggering and present a major threat to the survival of the Black community, the Black family, and therefore the Black churches, for the three are inextricably connected. Pastoral theologian Edward Wimberly contends that the present social conditions of African Americans, especially those who are yet locked out of full participation within the dominant society, are a result of a postmodern society that has "disengaged individuals from their communal roots and [made] them relational refugees."[58] This is of significance, since for the Black churches, 81 percent of the total African American population resides in these metropolitan areas. Thus, these are problems which threaten the very survival of African American people and the survival of oncoming generations of African American people. With social scientists predicting the emergence of a "permanent underclass," which is mostly African American, urban, and young, the

---

[57] Atlantapost.com/2011/02/09/8.
[58] Edward Wimberly, *African American Pastoral Care and Counseling: The Politics of Oppression and Empowerment* (Cleveland, OH: Pilgrim Press, 2006). Wimberly borrows and further develops the concept of "relational refugee" from Archie Smith, *The Relational Self: Ethics and Therapy From a Black Church Perspective* (Nashville, TN: Abingdon Press, 1982); also see Edward Wimberly, *Relational Refugees: Alienation and Re-incorporation in African American Churches and Community* (Nashville, TN: Abingdon Press, 2000).

very future of African Americans is being threatened from without as well as from within. This presents a challenge and an opportunity to the Black churches, which in the past have also functioned as vehicles for upward social mobility. Due to this movement, many churches have now become middle-class institutions and in some respects are perceived by the new generation of African American unchurched youth as being totally irrelevant to their existential experience. Cornell West in his book, *Race Matters*, characterizes this segment of Black America as exhibiting a spirit of nihilism, which he identifies as "the lived experience of coping with a life of horrifying, meaninglessness, hopelessness, and (most importantly) lovelessness."[59]

Given the history of the Black churches, how they have functioned as "all comprehending institutions" in the past, can these now middle-class Black churches create a provision of management for this unchurched subculture whose orientation may be so foreign from that of traditional African American church folk? In other words, can the Black churches, in their "middle class institutionalism," create an environment of *holding*, in which hope and meaning, self-respect, and self-love can be ignited and cultivated within this African American subculture, so that they too may experience the love of God that engenders hope and joy—what Winnicott calls "go on being"? As I reflect upon the legacy of the Black churches and their accomplishments of the past amidst the overwhelming circumstances of slavery, segregation, and the Civil Rights struggle, I lift my voice with a resounding Yes! to remind the Black churches that historically they have demonstrated that they can be the *good enough mother* who is attuned to the various needs of her constituents. Black churches share a spiritual function nurturing their constituents in the faith out of which is derived their social activism and social witness grounded in Christianity's concern for the poor and oppressed. Black churches need only to remember their raison d'être and reclaim their mission and once again embody the best of the tradition of the Black Churches' ethos. They have been the "Old Ship of Zion" that has landed many a thousand, instilling in them a sense of hope, identity, and self esteem. It is well within their grasp to be good enough again for African American people/community in this present day of challenge and opportunity. For this present day, Black churches are in need of trained leadership who will be able to continue

---

[59] For a more detailed description of the spirit of nihilism see Cornell West, *Race Matters* (New York: NY: Vintage Books, 1994), 17-31.

in this tradition of being the spiritual and prophetic voice for their constituents. The fact that New Brunswick Theological Seminary has been an institution that has made a deep investment through its Anti-Racism Transformation initiative in educating Black clergy for spiritual and prophetic leadership in the Black Churches will be a lasting tribute to the legacy of President Gregg Mast.

CHAPTER 13

"We Have Not This Subject Among Us": Slavery, the Reformed Dutch Church, and New Brunswick Seminary

John W. Coakley

As president of New Brunswick Theological Seminary, Gregg Mast has led, encouraged, and supported the seminary community in its initiative to become an "antiracist" institution. That initiative has brought with it a commitment to be truthful about the fact of racism in the seminary's history.[1]

In the spirit of that commitment, and in honor of President Mast, I will examine here the role played by the institution of the slavery in the history of the seminary in its formative years, the early nineteenth century. Slavery had a profound effect at that time, not just in the South but in the North as well, in ways both subtle and flagrant; the Reformed Dutch Church (later called the Reformed Church in America), of which the seminary was an organic part, was not immune to those effects.

---

[1] That commitment has been promoted by the Anti-Racism Transformation Team at NBTS, of which I am privileged to have been a member. I thank the other members for encouragement of the research reported here. Recent studies which have served as inspiration include: *Slavery and Justice: Report of the Brown University Steering Committee on Slavery and Justice* (Providence, RI: Brown University, 2006); and Craig S. Wilder, *Ebony and Ivy: Race, Slavery, and the Troubled History of America's Universities* (New York: Bloomsbury Press, 2013).

The picture that will emerge here of the Reformed Dutch Church of the time, and of the seminary as a part of it, is a picture of a Christian community that was not oblivious to the racial injustices of American society. But, although it was deeply implicated in those injustices, it also avoided confronting them directly or even taking, as we might have hoped to find, an unambiguous stand against them.

The fact of slavery

In New York and New Jersey, where most of the Reformed Dutch congregations were located, slavery continued to exist well into the nineteenth century. "Gradual emancipation laws" were enacted in both states—New York's in 1799 and New Jersey's in 1804—each of which stipulated that persons born in slavery after the enactment of the law would become free but only after a stipulated period which brought them into early adulthood; those born before the enactment were to remain in perpetual slavery. But full emancipation in New York came by law in 1827; in New Jersey (even though by 1855 when the Reformed Dutch Church finally debated slavery, there were very few enslaved persons) full emancipation came only with the ratification of the thirteenth amendment to the US Constitution in 1865.[2]

Slaveholding had, at any rate, been a common practice among the Dutch in New York and New Jersey from the early colonial period onward,[3] and many important persons in the seminary's history were implicated in it. John Henry Livingston, the New York pastor whose election to the church's new office of "professor" in 1784 marks the beginning point of the history of the seminary and who initiated the school's operation in New Brunswick in 1810, had grown up in a slaveholding family. He himself owned slaves as late as 1790, according to the census of that year. In the census of 1800, slaves were no longer listed in his household.[4] But he and his wife possessed

---

[2] David N. Gellman, *Emancipating New York: The Politics of Slavery and Freedom 1777-1827* (Baton Rouge, LA: LSU Press, 2006), 153-223; Lawrence A. Greene, "A History of Afro-Americans in New Jersey," *Journal of the Rutgers University Libraries* 56, no. 1 (1994): 4-71; James J. Gigantino II, *The Ragged Road to Abolition: Slavery and Freedom in New Jersey, 1775-1865* (Philadelphia: Univ. of Pennsylvania Press, 2015).

[3] John W. Beardslee III, "The Reformed Church in America and the African-American Community," *Reformed Review* 46 (1992):101-18, esp. 102-5; Gerald De Jong, *The Dutch Reformed Church in the American Colonies* (Grand Rapids: Eerdmans, 1978), 161-69; Andrea C. Mosterman, "Sharing Spaces in a New World Environment: African-Dutch Contributions to North American Culture," diss., Boston University, 2012.

[4] US Bureau of the Census. *Heads of Families at the First Census of the United States Taken in the Year 1790, New York* (Washington: Government Printing Office, 1908), 7:134;

a substantial inheritance from the estate of her father, the merchant Philip Livingston, who had made some of his fortune in the slave trade, and thus the professor continued to benefit from slavery, whether he still owned slaves or not.[5] Similarly the seminary's most famous and generous benefactor in its early years, Elias van Bunschooten, whose gift of $14,640 before his death in 1815 was crucial to the school's early survival, had hereditary wealth from his slaveholding family.[6] The other monetary gifts to endow the seminary came from scores of individuals and congregations throughout the Reformed Dutch Church.[7] It would be difficult to research the place of slaveholding in the lives of all these donors. But among the donors must have been at least some slaveholders, like the Dutch farmers whom the seminary professor David Demarest remembered from his childhood in Bergen County, New Jersey, in the 1820s, "most" of whom "owned one or more slaves."[8]

If the seminary was thus implicated in slavery through the broader Reformed Church, slavery also touched the school's life through the immediate environment in New Brunswick, as we can see especially clearly now as a result of recent work by researchers from the Rutgers University History Department. They have shown, for instance: that "Old Queen's," the building, still standing, which housed both the seminary and Rutgers (originally Queen's) College from 1810 until 1856, was built on land given by the family of James Parker, a slaveholder;[9] that at least one enslaved person was hired out by his owner to help construct the foundation of the building—a man named Will

---

Population Schedules of the Second Census of the United States, 1800, New York, reel 23 (Washington: National Archives Microfilm Publications), 270.

[5] Philip Misevich, "In Pursuit of Human Cargo: Philip Livingston and the Voyage of the Sloop *Rhode Island*," *New York History* 86 (2005): 185-204, esp. 189n11; John W. Coakley, "John Henry Livingston (1746-1825): Interpreter of the Dutch Reformed Tradition in the Early American Republic," in *Transatlantic Pieties: Dutch Clergy in Colonial American*, ed. Leon van den Broeke, Hans Krabbendam, and Dirk Mouw (Grand Rapids, MI: Eerdmans, 2012), 297.

[6] Edward T. Corwin, *Manual of the Reformed Church in America*, 4th ed. (New York: RCA Board of Publication, 1902), 809; Kendra Boyd, Miya Carey, and Christopher Blakley, "Old Money: Rutgers University and the Political Economy of Slavery in New Jersey," in *Scarlet and Black, vol. 1; Slavery and Dispossession in Rutgers History*, ed. Marisa J. Fuentes and Deborah Gray White (New Brunswick: Rutgers University Press, 2016) (hereinafter "*SB*"), 54-55.

[7] Subscription lists for the seminary appear in *Acts and Proceedings of the General Synod of the Reformed Protestant Dutch Church in North America*, 1823 (June), 7-9; 1825 (September), 6-17.

[8] David D. Demarest, "Some Memories Informally Written," typescript, NBTS Archives, 2-3.

[9] Boyd, Carey, and Blakley, "Old Money," 52-53.

who was enslaved to Dr. Jacob Dunham of New Brunswick;[10] that well into the nineteenth century, as newspaper advertisements show, slaves were being offered for sale in the public markets in New Brunswick, and escaped slaves from New Jersey and elsewhere were being captured and imprisoned in the city jail on Bayard Street—all well within a half mile of Old Queen's;[11] and that the local merchant, James Neilson, who donated the greater part of the land on which the seminary campus was built beginning in 1856, was or had been a slaveholder.[12]

Many more examples could be given of the presence of slavery in the immediate social and religious worlds of the seminary. But those given here may suffice to show that connections with slavery were extensive and pervasive.

The meanings of colonization

Given the fact of slavery in the life of the seminary and the Reformed Dutch Church, how did the leaders of these institutions understand and speak about the subject? In fact, there is little evidence that they directly debated the *issue* of American slavery at all, until, as will be seen, on the very eve of the Civil War. Yet something of their prevailing stance toward slavery and abolition can be surmised from the fact of their support of the organization called the American Colonization Society (ACS), launched in 1817 to promote the project of transporting free black persons to Africa to establish the colony of Liberia.[13] In embracing that project, the church and the seminary embraced, by implication, a particular set of views about slavery.

A word here is in order about the ACS and its aims. The organization was by its own lights critical of the institution of slavery, and yet by virtue of its focus on the relocation of freed persons rather than on the means of making them free, it declined to confront the institution itself, and by implication, it thereby reinforced a racist status quo.

An early speech by a New Jersey colonizationist will illustrate the point. This was the address delivered to the first Annual Meeting of the New Jersey Colonization Society (in effect the state chapter of the ACS),

---

[10] Jesse Bayker, Christopher Blakley, and Kendra Boyd, "His Name Was Will: Remembering Enslaved Individuals in Rutgers History," in *SB*, 71-74.
[11] Shaun Armstead, Brennann Sutter, Pamela Walker, and Caitlin Wiesner, "'And I Poor Slave Yet': The Precarity of Black Life in New Brunswick, 1766-1835," in *SB*, 91-107.
[12] Boyd, Carey, and Blakley, "Old Money," 54.
[13] On the historiography of the ACS, see Samantha Seeley, "Beyond the American Colonization Society," *History Compass* 14, no. 3 (March 2016): 93-104, esp. 95-97.

held in July of 1825, by that society's first president, Lucius Q. C. Elmer, then US attorney for the district of New Jersey. Elmer himself was not a member of the Reformed Church, but in speaking for the society, he gave voice to a project that, we know, many Reformed Dutch Church leaders in New Jersey endorsed. Indeed, members of the church were among the distinguished persons named as "Directors, or Honorary Managers" of the society in the report of the meeting, including James S. Cannon, who then held one of the three faculty chairs at the seminary.[14] And a prominent Reformed Church layman, Theodore Frelinghuysen, then the state's attorney general and later a US senator and president of Rutgers College, had addressed a meeting of the nascent society the preceding November.[15] In his speech, Elmer declared that "the first and principal object" of the society was

> to afford an opportunity for the free people of colour among us, to escape that state of degradation to which they are necessarily subject here; a state of degradation apparently beyond the correction of domestic palliatives and internal regulations.

The key word here is "degradation," a word that the ACS literature used frequently to describe the state of African Americans. Elmer explained:

> Our government is based upon the great principle "that all men are created equal." But unfortunately, we have been forced to deny the application of this just maxim to a large class of individuals, distinguished from the rest, only by the colour of their skins.[16]

So "degradation," for Elmer, is a function of the fact that black persons did not, in practice, have the equality that the Declaration of Independence says belongs to all. But Elmer does not proceed then to envision a just multiracial order in America whereby the "degradation" would be removed and equality would reign as it ought. Instead he flatly states that such an order could never be established. For the free black person's

> former origin and the indelible mark of it, conspicuous in his face, impose an impassable barrier to a union with the whites,

---

[14] *Proceedings of the First Annual Meeting of the New Jersey Colonization Society. Held at Princeton, July 1, 1825* (Princeton: Borrenstein [1825]), 39-40.
[15] Theodore Frelinghuysen, *An Oration: Delivered at Princeton, New Jersey, Nov. 16, 1824, before the New-Jersey Colonization Society* (Princeton: Borrenstein, 1824).
[16] *Proceedings of the First Annual Meeting*, 12.

and preclude the possibility of his ever obtaining an equality of rights and privileges as an American citizen.

Thus he considered race, in itself, in America, as an obstruction to equality, an obstruction that *cannot be removed,* and Elmer could imagine "no possible remedy" for the "disabilities" of the black persons' situation other than to enable them to resettle in Africa.[17] He acknowledged, to be sure, the unlikelihood that, even in the best-case scenario, all or even most free blacks would consent to go, but he considered that, even if colonization

> cannot succeed in freeing this country from the living pestilence of a numerous black population, still it may reduce their relative proportion, and improve the character and condition of those that remain. It may open to the rising generation of free blacks, a distant prospect of acquiring reputation and rank and character, and it may stimulate them to exertions to redeem themselves,

by means of the chance to emigrate to Africa.[18]

This conviction of the colonizationists that the "degradation" of African Americans was something irreversible in America but not in Africa reveals a certain paradox or apparent contradiction at the heart of the movement, which, indeed, its opponents, including such black critics as Frederick Douglass and the leaders of the anticolonizationist "convention" movement, would label as rank hypocrisy.[19] For, as Elmer's words illustrate, the colonizationists readily acknowledged that the equality proclaimed by the Declaration of Independence applied to black people. Neither Elmer nor the preponderance of other colonizationists, that is, subscribed to the "scientific racist" view which considered Africans to constitute a separate species, inferior to whites, an early version of which Thomas Jefferson, for instance, had espoused; and they envisioned free blacks' future in Africa in glowing terms of the realization of human potential.[20] But the denial that blacks could

---

[17] Ibid., 13.
[18] Ibid., 16.
[19] See Ousmane K. Greene, "Against Wind and Tide: African Americans' Response to the Colonization Movement and Emigration," diss., University of Massachusetts Amherst, 2007.
[20] "That the Africans are originally an inferior race, and incapable of improvement, has been sometimes urged as an insuperable objection to our plan. But to this intelligent audience, a refutation of this strange notion will hardly be necessary." *Proceedings of the First Annual Meeting*, 13.

ever realize such equality in America—indeed in the place where human equality was most strenuously championed, and even supposing the eventual abolition of slavery in the meantime—stands therefore as the paradox: how can black persons be both equal with whites and yet at the same time incapable ever of being equal with whites?[21]

Yet it was exactly the terms of that paradox which gave colonization rhetoric its appeal to whites, especially white Christians, such as those in the Reformed Dutch Church in New Jersey and New York. For on the one hand, colonization's promoters presented it as a benevolent project for the welfare of others, which appealed to Christian values and their sense of obligation toward blacks as victims of an injustice in which whites could not but acknowledge their own complicity.[22] In addition, it was, as Elmer made sure to mention, an opportunity to promote the spread of the Gospel to the world abroad and thus contribute to the great evangelical world mission movement which was then on the rise. But on the other hand, in its evocation of the "degradation" of African Americans as something *irreversible*, the colonization rhetoric also spoke to a deep racial prejudice among whites or, at the very least, to the extent that the colonizationists accepted the fact of their own guilt in the matter of slavery, a determination to atone only in the way that suited themselves, on the assumption of their superiority to their victims as "degraded" persons. Likewise in its envisioning of the removal of black persons from American soil, that rhetoric spoke also to whites' fear of violence from a growing free black population.[23] And by its envisioning only the *eventual* rather than the *immediate* end of slavery, it reinforced the status quo of "gradual abolition" in New York and especially in New Jersey where, as we have seen, slavery would continue to exist for decades.

Such were the aims of the colonization movement, and there is ample evidence that it had the support of the seminary, as well as the Reformed Dutch Church. In addition to Professor James Cannon, whose name I have mentioned, who was on the list of directors of the

---

[21] On the contradictions of colonization ideas—the "vertiginous absence of logic or argument"—see Nicholas Guyatt, "The Outskirts of Our Happiness: Race and the Lure of Colonization in the Early Republic," *Journal of American History* 95, no. 4 (March 2009): 986-1011, esp. 990.

[22] E.g., Elmer: "Of all this evil [of slavery] we have been, if not the authors, at least the abettors." Ibid.

[23] Matthew Spooner, "'I Know This Scheme Is from God:' Toward a Reconsideration of the Origins of the American Colonization Society," *Slavery & Abolition* 35, no. 4 (December 2014): 566-68.

New Jersey Colonization Society in 1825, the name of John Henry Livingston himself had appeared on a similar list in the minutes of the society's inaugural meeting in 1824, the year before his death.[24] And the name of Philip Milledoler appeared on it in 1826, after his appointment to succeed the deceased Livingston on the faculty.[25] There is a long gap in the surviving series of annual reports of the society after the report of 1827, and when these appear again for the years from 1856 to 1858, there are no seminary faculty members listed among the leaders, although in 1856, the Reformed Church pastor Samuel How of New Brunswick (of whom, more below) is listed as a manager.[26] But miscellaneous manuscript records of the local New Brunswick Colonization Society, founded in 1838, have survived, and among these is a list of its members dating from sometime between 1852 and 1857 on which appear the names of all three of the seminary faculty members at that time—John Ludlow, William Campbell and Samuel Van Vranken—as well as Samuel How and Samuel Woodbridge, the latter being a local Reformed minister who would join the faculty at Ludlow's death in 1857.[27]

Colonization had support not only in the seminary but broadly in the Reformed Church as well, as the General Synod minutes of the period make clear. In 1820 the synod officially received that year's annual report of the ACS and passed a resolution declaring its "objects and plans" to be "benevolent in their design, and if properly supported and judiciously executed, calculated to be extensively useful to this country, to Africa, and to the cause of humanity," and commending the ACS to their congregations.[28] In 1824 the Synod again officially commended the ACS and did so once again in 1825, this time with the suggestion that local churches take up a special collection for the organization on July 4.[29] Thereafter such resolutions, usually with the

[24] *Proceedings of a Meeting Held at Princeton, New-Jersey, July 14, 1824, to form a Society in the State of New-Jersey, to Cooperate with the American Colonization Society* (Princeton: Borrenstein, 1824), 40.
[25] *Proceedings of the Second Annual Meeting of the New Jersey Colonization Society. Held at Princeton, July 10, 1826* (Princeton: Borrenstein, 1826), 28.
[26] *Annual Report of the Managers of the New Jersey Colonization Society Presented at the Twenty-Fourth Anniversary at Trenton, Feb. 14, 1856* (Newark: Daily Advertiser, 1856), 8.
[27] Records of the New Brunswick Colonization Society, Rutgers University Archives and Special Collections. The list is undated, but it was in the period from 1852 to 1857 that all three would have been together on the seminary faculty and thus in New Brunswick.
[28] *Acts and Proceedings*, 1820, 17-18.
[29] *Acts and Proceedings*, 1824, 12-13; 1825, 9.

designation of July 4 or the Sunday closest to it, for the collection—with the implication that the colonization project gave expression to American ideals of freedom—appear in the minutes with only a few gaps, until 1868, that is, through and beyond the Civil War years.[30] In most years, the minutes add very little comment, although in 1834, there is the extended comment that the ACS, among other things, is

> meeting the expectations of its friends, in providing an asylum for the emancipated coloured man of our own country—is spreading through the slave-holding portions of these states a healthful feeling on the subject of slavery, which, it is hoped, will lead finally to the entire removal of that curse from our country,

and will bring freedom and the Gospel to "Africa in her wretchedness."[31] From 1849 on, a representative of the New York Colonization society was usually present to address the synod prior to the passing of the usual resolution. And in 1862, apparently anticipating the Emancipation Proclamation which would soon be announced, the synod coupled the customary resolution with a reference to the "prospect of the immediate emancipation of many thousands" and therefore the need for "greater and more extensive Christian efforts" for their "protection," through colonization to Africa.[32]

There is therefore no doubt about the consistent embrace of colonization by the Reformed Dutch Church and its seminary. Yet one curious—but significant—fact about this embrace must be pointed out: that in spite of it, there was little active *discussion* of the matter. The church's newspaper, the *Christian Intelligencer*, did regularly print reports of the meetings of the ACS and its branch societies and occasionally printed defenses of the ACS against radical abolitionists.[33] But only a few Reformed Dutch leaders were on record to articulate, promote or defend, in their own right, the aims of the colonization movement in print; the church seems in general to have been content to *assume* as self-evident the value of the movement and merely encourage its support. One of the few who spoke out was seminary professor Philip Milledoler

---

[30] Edward T. Corwin, *A Digest and Index of Synodical Legislation of the Reformed Church in America* (New York: Board of Publication, 1906), 20.
[31] *Acts and Proceedings*, 1834, 272.
[32] *Acts and Proceedings*, 1862, 212-13.
[33] Examples of defenses of colonization: *Christian Intelligencer*, Nov. 30, 1833, 69; Oct. 10, 1840, 48. The newspaper was launched in 1831. Reports of colonization-society meetings, letters from Liberia, and announcements of ships sailing to Liberia with colonists are frequent through the mid-1840s but sporadic thereafter.

who, in his capacity as president of Rutgers College, had commended the movement to the college's graduates in a portion of his published commencement speech of 1831, stating that the colonization project promised to uphold the constitutional principles of equality in an effort to "dissipate a cloud hanging over us, which cannot be viewed without shuddering"—whether he is referring to slavery itself, or to the prospect of a large free black population, or both is not clear—and he emphasized the project's prospects for the evangelization of Africa.[34] But besides Milledoler's speech, I have found no other faculty publications from the period that address the matter of colonization or indeed any subject directly related to slavery.[35] The minutes of the seminary's board of superintendents, which in passing open many windows on matters that came up in the life of the school, are silent on these matters. Similarly in the minutes of the Society of Inquiry on Missions, the seminary student society that routinely debated issues facing the church, neither colonization nor slavery appear among the topics.[36]

Why this general silence in the Reformed Dutch Church on issues around slavery? That very question came to the fore at the General Synod meetings of 1855, as we shall see. It is, however, worth noting at this point that the colonization rhetoric itself contained a seed of this silence, in that, the logic of the rhetoric of colonization served to allow its adherents to put off confronting the issue of slavery in the present. For as it pushed the prospect of the end of slavery itself into the future as something too disruptive of the status quo to be undertaken at the moment, it simultaneously salved the conscience of its adherents by deploring the institution itself, with no attempt to defend it. This allowed them de facto the moral high ground, at least by their own lights; they could translate a theoretical rejection of slavery itself into a virtuous proposal for Christian mission. Thus the colonization ideas excused, or anyway abetted, the silence about slavery.

A silence broken—and re-established

In 1855 the silence of the Reformed Dutch Church on the issue of slavery was suddenly broken. The occasion was the resolve of the Classis

---

[34] Philip Milledoler, *Address, Delivered to the Graduates of Rutgers College, at Commencement, Held in the Reformed Dutch Church, New Brunswick, N.J., July 20, 1831* (New York: Rutgers Press, 1831), 12-15.

[35] Corwin, *Manual*, 314, lists among the publications of Joseph Frederick Berg, NBTS professor, 1861-71, a piece entitled "The Olive Branch: A Conservative View of Slavery," which has not otherwise come to light.

[36] On the tenor of the Society of Inquiry minutes, see Coakley, *New Brunswick Theological Seminary: An Illustrated History* (Grand Rapids: Eerdmans, 2014), 19.

of North Carolina, part of the German Reformed Church, to leave that church and apply to join the Reformed Dutch Church instead. The classis was dissatisfied with the "Mercersburg theology" movement within the German Reformed Church, which many evangelical Protestants saw as too soft on Roman Catholicism. The Reformed Dutch Church had itself expressed alarm at Mercersburg theology and, given the otherwise close historical relationship and doctrinal commitments of the two denominations, the North Carolinians thought the Dutch Church was a good match for them.[37] But the North Carolina classis included slaveholders, and when the General Synod received the application, intense debate followed over whether the church should hold fellowship with slaveholders. The debate then continued in a special session of the synod in October of that year.

The record of the debate, both on the floor of synod and in pamphlet exchanges which continued the following year, allow us to listen, beneath the church's erstwhile silence, to its thinking about slavery.[38] In fact the silence itself was, in part, at issue, and even though, by the end of the debate, silence had again won the day, the debate reveals considerable anguish about the matter and the variety of strongly held convictions—though for the most part, those convictions stopped short of advocacy for the immediate emancipation of the enslaved.

As the synod began debating the admission of the North Carolinians, in June, two contrasting views of slavery quickly found expression. One of these views was that of Isaac Duryea (a graduate of Andover Seminary), minister of the Second Reformed Church of Schenectady, and a frank abolitionist. He noted that one could oppose the admission of Classis on the ground of "expediency" alone, given the divisiveness of the issue of slavery in other denominations at that time, but that "I am opposed . . . upon higher grounds than mere

---

[37] Gregg A. Mast, "A Decade of Hope and Despair: Mercersburg Theology's Impact on Two Reformed Denominations," in *A Goodly Heritage: Essays in Honor of Elton J. Bruins*, ed. Jacob E. Nyenhuis (Grand Rapids: Eerdmans, 2007), 163–80.

[38] For brief overviews, see Beardslee, "African American Community," 106-7 and Corwin, *Digest*, 467-68. The *Acts and Proceedings*, June 1855, 531, 535; October 1855, 11-14, record only the committee reports, resolutions, and the roll call of certain votes; for the debates themselves, we must rely on newspaper accounts (as below). As for pamphlets: in addition to those of Ganse and How, to be noted below, two others were produced: "Slaveholding Not Sinful: A Reply to the Argument of Rev. Dr. How" (New Brunswick: Fredonian, 1856), written by the New Brunswick lawyer John Van Dyke, who, however, did not write explicitly as a member of the Reformed Church; and a reply to Van Dyke by How's son, Henry K. How, *Slaveholding Not Sinful: An Answer* (New Brunswick: Fredonian, 1856).

expediency." He declared himself "in conscience opposed to the system of Slavery" and said that, if the North Carolina classis were admitted, he and other "good, conscientious men" would object to having fellowship with slaveholders.[39]

The other opposing view was that of Samuel How (a graduate of Princeton Seminary), minister of the First Reformed Church in New Brunswick and a man with many contacts in the South, who chaired the committee that recommended admitting the North Carolinians. How acknowledged that three of the members of their classis were slaveholders but explained the circumstances that, he implied, made slaveholding necessary in those cases (all having to do with ostensible charity toward the slaves), and he explained that the classis was " taking measures to approach the Legislature of North-Carolina to procure the passage of Legislative enactments legalizing the marriage of slaves, to prevent the separation of children under twelve years from their parents, and to enforce the education of slaves," and thus "making efforts to put down Slavery, and they are beginning just at the point where they ought to begin," namely, apparently, by acting benevolently toward their slaves. And How made explicit his own understanding of the issue of slavery, which he later would develop in detail, in a pamphlet: slavery was, he said, a consequence of Adam's fall, "one of the penal effects with which God in his wrath visits the sins of men." To try to simply extirpate it would be not to take human depravity seriously. The right way to approach it was to apply the ameliorative effects of the Gospel. He did envision the eventual end of slavery but only by the gradual effects of sound peaching: "Send them the Gospel and the liberation of all the slaves will be made peaceably. There will be no bloodshed, no civil convulsions, no dissolution of the union, no heart-burnings." He also invoked the specter of violence if immediate emancipation were attempted.[40]

So the discussion of slavery itself had finally opened, and How and Duryea, from their opposing standpoints, were eager to pursue it. "The subject of slavery," said How, "is a dark and threatening cloud; meet it we must; we cannot shun it." On that point, Duryea did not disagree.

But there was still a strong disposition in the synod against discussing the matter at all. It was George W. Bethune, then minister

---

[39] *New York Daily Tribune*, "General Synod of the Protestant Reformed Dutch Church," June 16, 1855, 6.
[40] Ibid.

of the Church on the Heights, Brooklyn, a senior figure and celebrated preacher who gave voice to that disposition. In a long speech, he opposed the admission of the Classis, not, he said, because he wished to deny fellowship to slaveholders (citing here Jesus' admiration for the faith of the slaveholding centurion [Mt. 8:5-13]), but rather because the present *peace* of the church—whereby slavery was not discussed— was too valuable to be disturbed. "We have not this subject among us, and in determining our action, let us go back to precedent," he said; receiving the North Carolina Classis, and therefore introducing the issue of slavery into the church's discussions, would "bring into activity a more bitter spirit . . . than any other spirit that is existing among a Christian people. I do not want to touch it."[41]

As the June debate neared its end, Thornton Butler, the agent of the North Carolina Classis who had brought its request, withdrew that request, seeing that it was "likely to cause some difficulty in your body," and wishing rather to "remain as we are . . . than to throw a brand into your house." The president of the synod, Ransford Wells (NBTS 1830), minister of the Reformed Church of Schoharie, New York, responded with evident relief, observing that most of the speakers had been swayed by "questions . . . merely of expediency," and thus, he implied, most of the members of the Synod were of a mind with Bethune, wishing to avoid "this great question which has had such disastrous influences upon other Ecclesiastical bodies." A committee was appointed to draft a resolution, which expressed the synod's "prayerful sympathy" for the work of Butler's Classis and commended it to the Reformed Dutch churches for their aid but did not mention the matter of the application.

So for a moment, the question may have seemed to be closed. But it was not. After other business had been transacted, a resolution was passed by a "large majority" to reconsider the whole issue in October, asking Butler to allow the synod to keep the application of the classis in the meantime. Apparently there had been continuing informal discussion after the adoption of the resolution, for, in explaining the vote, Hervey D. Ganse (NBTS 1843), minister of the Second Reformed Church of Freehold, spoke on behalf of "many on the floor who, whatever might be the feeling of the Synod with regard to the application," stood against the position that further discussion would be inexpedient (i.e.,

---

[41] Ibid. Bethune recalled approvingly in the same passage that a few years earlier, the synod had admonished the American Board of Commissioners for Foreign Missions against discussing slavery at its annual meetings. See *Acts and Proceedings*, 1849, 508.

against Bethune's stance) and instead wished the subject of slavery to be confronted "fully and frankly." "They would not hide behind the door as if from a bugaboo and cry, 'Do go away.'"[42]

The debate then continued in October. And at first, the same positions were staked out, though now with more voices being raised.

How opened the discussion with a long prepared speech, which he later put into pamphlet form,[43] stating in greater detail the case he had made in June, arguing that slavery was a consequence of the Fall and thus an "evil," but still not a "sin," since it was allowed by biblical precedent and that it was best addressed not through precipitous action but through the influence of the preached Gospel on human hearts. Speaking in agreement with him were several New Brunswick Seminary graduates, including Edward Stimpson (NBTS 1834), who was minister at Castleton, New York; John C. Van Liew (NBTS 1832), minister of Ephratah and Stone Arabia, New York; Abraham Messler (NBTS 1824), minister at Raritan, New Jersey, who "did not say Slavery was not an evil, but there were circumstances under which it was a blessing"; and Nathaniel Conklin (NBTS 1847), minister at Montville, New Jersey, who in endorsing How's speech claimed to speak on behalf of the whole Classis of Passaic.[44]

Explicitly abolitionist views were also expressed, similar to those of Duryea in June. Thus the synod acknowledged a "protest of certain members of the church of Hastings-upon-Hudson, New York"—where the minister was Philip Phelps Jr. (NBTS 1849)—against admitting the North Carolinians, not just for the expediency of peace but also "on the ground of its connection with Slavery," which is "inseparable" from "oppression and cruelty." Both Anthony Elmendorf (NBTS 1839) of the North Church in Brooklyn and Lawrence H. Van Dyck (graduate of Auburn Seminary) spoke in the same vein.[45]

There were also still efforts to deflect the debate altogether. Thus both Bethune and John B. Alliger (NBTS 1840), minister at Jamaica, New York, made early unsuccessful efforts to have the matter dismissed on various procedural grounds, and eventually, as will be seen, Bethune

---

[42] *New York Daily Tribune*, loc. cit.
[43] Samuel B. How, *Slaveholding Not Sinful. An Argument before the General Synod of the Reformed Protestant Dutch Church, October, 1855* (New York: John A. Gray, 1855). In a second edition (New Brunswick: John Terhune, 1856), How added seven appendices developing various themes of his original argument and a response to Ganse.
[44] *Christian Intelligencer*, "General Synod of the Reformed Dutch Church in Extra Session," November 1, 1855, 69.
[45] Ibid.

renewed his old argument to refuse the North Carolinians, if only for the sake of the church's peace.[46]

Though these speakers carried the debate forward essentially on its previous terms, one speaker offered a fresh, nuanced perspective on the matter. This was Hervey Ganse, who had spoken only at the end of the June meeting. Ganse was opposed to slavery and spoke against How. But he also took How's argument seriously and, uniquely among the speakers, dealt with the specifics of How's argument, yielding some points to him, both on the floor of the synod and in a pamphlet he published the following year—so one might see him, at least at first glance, to be arguing a compromise position. Thus Ganse acknowledged that the Old Testament did condone slavery, but in that sense, he argued that, although not all slavery was divinely permitted, *some* slavery *might* be, specifically where there were "as under the old economy [the Abrahamic covenant], or for other reasons, extenuating circumstances."[47] But as he intimated on the floor of the synod and explained at length in his later pamphlet, the New Testament, in contrast to the Old Testament, stood solidly *against* slavery in the clear ethical mandates of the Gospel and that, if the apostles left no record of opposing the *institution* of slavery in Roman society, it was not because they tacitly approved of it but because Roman slavery was so pervasive that "immediate abolition" was not possible without consequent upheavals, which themselves would have violated not only the Gospel but also "common humanity."[48] Certainly Ganse was, in his very opposition to How, supporting a gradualist rather than an immediatist view of abolition, indeed through the influence of the Gospel; although, as he would make clear in his pamphlet, he saw that influence as occurring through laws and by implication political action, rather than the vaguer processes of the Gospel influence in which How trusted.

But it is clear that, whatever the nuances of Ganse's position, he did not see himself as a figure of compromise, rather he insisted on what he thought was the central point at stake in the debate: namely, whether the synod would unambiguously denounce slavery. His insistence on this point became clear toward the end of the debate, after Bethune had once again made his appeal to the peace of the church and after,

---

[46] Ibid.
[47] Ibid.
[48] "The Gospel changes slavery," Ganse declared. Ibid. See also, Hervey D. Ganse, *Bible Slaveholding Not Sinful: A Reply to 'Slaveholding Not Sinful,' by Samuel B. Howe* [sic] *D.D.* (New York: R. & R. Brinkerhoff, 1856), 27.

apparently under sway of Bethune eloquence, the synod voted to table the whole matter, thus presumably to postpone it indefinitely. At that moment, Ganse refused to be silent and spoke to the issue again. He was ruled out of order because of action to table, but on appeal, the ruling was reversed, and he then proposed a resolution: to deny the classis admission, with, however, an added preamble, which asserted that the Synod "regards the system of American Slavery as embodying the most serious injustice and leading to the most serious social evils," though, nonetheless, it would willingly have communion with slaveholders who were such "not by choice but from the necessity of their position and who to their Christian attention to the present temporal and spiritual interests of their slaves, are adding wise Christian efforts for their ultimate enfranchisement," were it not that their admission "threatens a disturbance of our peaceful Church."[49] Ganse was thus cleverly appropriating into his own statement Bethune's concern for expediency and even How's affirmation of fellowship with benevolent slaveholders—but with the stipulation that the Synod establish a clear witness against slavery. To take that stand was, for him, the essential thing. And that stand was what the synod would be voting on. The debate had thus become a contest between the positions of Ganse and Bethune—between denouncing slavery or remaining silent about it— whatever else was said.

Bethune saw where the contest lay, and he played his hand decisively. He offered substitute resolutions for that of Ganse, with a preamble which removed reference to any condition to be placed on slaveholders and simply declared the synod as unable to "cordially agree" on the request for admission. The choice was clear. After debate, the synod passed Bethune's resolutions and preamble, rejecting those of Ganse. The church had re-established its silence on slavery.[50]

The silence would continue unabated, at least as far as the General Synod meetings were concerned, until June of 1864. It was only then that the Synod adopted a resolution passing judgment on slavery, stating that though "in time past," it had "not deemed it necessary to give forth a judgment in regard to the system of America slavery, inasmuch as it existed in regions beyond the bounds of our Church," now it welcomed the "prospect opened for the ultimate and entire removal of that system which embodies so much of moral and social evil."[51] But by that moment, with the Emancipation Proclamation in

---

[49] *Christian Intelligencer*, loc. cit.
[50] Ibid., 70.
[51] *Acts and Proceedings*, 1864, 503-4.

place for a year and a half, and the Thirteenth Amendment working its way through Congress, such a statement hardly stood as an example of prophetic witness.

Conclusion

Clearly in the years before the Civil War, the people of the Reformed Dutch Church and its seminary at New Brunswick were acutely aware of the crisis over slavery in the United States. But it was the argument for "expediency"—the argument against engaging the issue, for the sake of harmony in the church—that carried the day.

We can—and I do—regret that this was so and wish that our forebears had not avoided what seems to us now the Christian duty of prophetic witness. There can of course be no changing of the fact of the institution's silence at a crucial time, and indeed the memory should not be erased. For the question that faces us is this: in the light of this memory, and with a full awareness of the complexity of that earlier time, which may help us be attentive to the complexity of our own time, what are we to do now as an institution and a community? By what words and actions can we work, not to erase the memory of the silence, but to refuse to imitate it as we encounter the continuing racism of our society?

CHAPTER 14

Urban Ministry in the Twenty-First Century: A Postmodern Womanist Reimagining

Lorena Parrish

A womanist way of being disrupts the "epistemological sea of forgetfulness" and admonishes us to "tell our truths, 'anyway,' even when they tell us our truth is a lie . . . tell it 'anyway.'"[1]

Katie Geneva Cannon

No one sews a patch of unshrunk cloth on an old cloak, for the patch pulls away from the cloak, and a worse tear is made. Neither is new wine put into old wineskins; otherwise, the skins burst, and the wine is spilled, and the skins are destroyed. But new wine is put into new wineskins, and so both are preserved.

Matthew 9:16-17 (NRSV)

---

[1] Katie G. Cannon, Womanist Theology, "Revolutionaries in Zion: The Gumption to Challenge Dominated Forms of Knowledge Acquisition and Religious Power." The Sixth Annual C. Shelby Rooks Lecture at the Center for the Study of Black Faith and Life, Chicago Theological Seminary, October 11, 2012.

Introduction

This work is written in honor of Dr. Gregg A. Mast, to whom I am grateful for having been given the opportunity to serve at New Brunswick Theological Seminary. Throughout Dr. Mast's tenure, he has shown an active commitment to confronting racism and oppressive structures of power and privilege within and outside the seminary walls.

Under Mast's watch, the seminary implemented the first Anti-Racism Transformation Team (ARTT) to dismantle institutional racism in all areas of the institution. Other "firsts" during Mast's tenure include hiring the first African American academic dean and dean of students (2012), as well as the first African American director of Sage Library (2016); bestowing an honorary doctorate upon an African American (2016); developing a course on antiracism and making it a requirement for all students; and requiring all new members of the faculty, board, and staff to participate in antiracism training. As the first African American woman to hold the Dirk Romeyn Professor of Metro-Urban Ministry chair and as the first womanist theologian to head up one of the nation's few doctoral programs in urban ministry, I am grateful and humbled to be part of the legacy of one whose heart for ministry, scholarship, and activism I truly admire. My hope is to further this critical work by employing postmodern womanist theology and praxis to equip faith leaders to do ministry that promotes healing, just communities, and ecclesial and social transformation.

Thus this chapter explores the prospect of utilizing what I term postmodern womanist reimagining as a vehicle for creating new wineskins that can hold new visions and provide new possibilities for twenty-first-century urban ministry. By postmodern womanist reimagining, I mean the use of womanist theological thought, theory, and praxis to critically and creatively engage the present and reorient the future for the sake of fostering liberating and just communities of faith. This reimagining involves truth telling, knowing and acting, and thinking and doing for the sake of cultivating faith communities that are loving, just and transforming, and responsive to a complexity of needs. But before I delve further into this topic, I want to say a word about urban ministry in the twenty-first century.

Urban ministry in a twenty-first-century postmodern landscape

The urban ministry landscape of today is distinct; it presents distinct challenges. These distinctions may include a complexity of factors with which populations marked by a rich diversity of races, ethnicities, languages, cultures, and worldviews must contend, factors like migration, immigration, gentrification, zoning laws, urban stratification,[2] lack of affordable housing, poor education systems, inadequate healthcare, unemployment, poverty, violence, over policing, the prison pipeline, and a shortage of fiscal resources, to name a few. Yet, although urban ministry can be distinguished by these and other distinct challenges, it can no longer be defined merely by location or density of population. Indeed, the process of urbanization is one that has permeated much of the United States and the world.

Recent studies by the United Nations Department of Economic and Social Affairs show that over half of the people on the face of the earth live in urban areas, and rural populations are expected to decrease as urban areas of all sizes continue to grow.[3] In the United States, 80.7 percent of the population lives in metropolitan regions.[4] These areas include not only the concrete labyrinth of large inner cities but also less populated municipalities and their surrounding suburban locales, whose residents, like those in large inner-city communities, must grapple with a growing litany of complex issues and competing demands of increasingly diverse groups of people. Thus urban ministry today is ministry that takes place in large metropolises, small urban clusters, and outlying suburban enclaves. It is ministry that must attend to the intersectionalities and complexities of people's lives, wherever those people may be found.

This means that understanding how to engage in urban ministry in transformative and contextualized ways ought to be of great import to ministers and congregants alike. The challenges of living in a twenty-first-century, highly diverse, and mobile world demand that we develop models for urban ministry that help us to engage across lines of difference and foster racial-social-cultural inclusion, just living conditions, and environmental responsibility. Such models must expose the connection between seeking salvation and creating peaceable communities of healing, wholeness, love, and justice. This chapter will

---

[2] David Claerbaut, *Urban Ministry in a New Millennium* (Waynesboro, GA: Authentic Media, 2005), 57ff.

[3] The United Nations Department of Economic and Social Affairs/Population Division, *World Urbanization Prospects: The 2014 Revision* (New York: United Nations, 2015), 1-2.

[4] United States Census Bureau https://www.census.gov/newsroom/releases/archives/2010_census/cb12-50.html, "Growth in Urban Population Outpaces Rest of Nation, Census Bureau Reports."

present one such model, namely, a postmodern womanist approach to urban ministry.

Postmodernists agree that the age of modernity has declined and, with it, many of the Western assumptions, convictions, and suppositions that were not only the norm and nonnegotiable but also left in their wake harmful notions. Acknowledging that economic, scientific, and technological advances have in large part changed how most of humanity understands the world, postmodernists decenter modernity's metanarratives that sustain and support cultural hierarchies, western imperialism, and patriarchal ethnocentric understandings. Instead they allow for a variety of repressed voices and histories, ignored within the modernity framework, to share and take center stage. This allowance shatters the notion that one voice can speak for all and unveils the discourse of modernity that privilege White, Eurocentric, sociocultural constructions of progress, universality, superiority, and truth. In other words, postmodernism embraces an openness to meaning and authority from unexpected and even formerly undervalued places and persons—from advancements in science and technology to the contextual wisdom and lived experiences of the disenfranchised.

Like postmodernists, postmodern womanist scholars and practitioners of religion also reference and lend authority to a wide range of sources. They begin with the lived experiences, languages, moral wisdom, and values of Black[5] women and use these to address the oppressive living conditions experienced by Black women and all marginalized people. Postmodern womanists have at heart the task of liberation, and they undertake such a task by mining the ways in which theologies, norms, and ecclesial practices either nourish or diminish the lives of the oppressed and disenfranchised. When ecclesial practices and theologies suggest biblical interpretations and norms that ignore the lived experiences of Black women and other oppressed people, a postmodern womanist approach takes seriously the need to disrupt and dismantle such oppressive pattern of religious observance for the sake of fostering communities focused on liberation and salvation for all.

A postmodern womanist approach to urban ministry does not ignore or hide from oppressive patterns but rather equips people to navigate the multiple identities and intersectionality of their lives, such as race, gender, class, culture, ethnicity, sexuality, and able-bodiedness. It focuses on spreading the Gospel for people's salvation,

---

[5] Please see the addendum at the end of this essay titled "Capitalizing the B in Black."

while empowering those same people to take part in social action that provides care for their own and other's spiritual, physical, psychosocial, political, and emotional needs. It dares us to deal with the continuing challenge of institutionalized racism and sexism, living in a world that is at once more mobile and more economically stratified than ever before. It encourages practicing contextualization, border crossing, and bridge building. That is, a postmodern womanist approach calls for building bridges that enable all to experience hope and healing, peace and reconciliation, deep connections and loving relationships, and more equitable and just ways of being with each other. It is focused on enhancing the quality of life for all, especially the oppressed, marginalized, and disenfranchised. And it endeavors to do so by building the kingdom of God here on earth, or as Dr. King termed it, "the beloved community."

My approach to urban ministry is profoundly informed by my experience as a Black woman raised in New York City and by my work as a womanist scholar-practitioner and member of the clergy. I have always had a heart for the city—its people, its pace, and its complexities—and the chance it affords us to address head-on the suffering, needs, concerns, and struggles of the marginalized, while engaging in God's vision for the world—a vision that centers on the pursuit of communal living, spiritual well-being, health, wholeness, and justice for all people.

My many years of attending and serving in a variety of urban church settings, including African American, Caribbean, multiethnic, multicultural, and multilingual congregations, has given me a deep appreciation for the richness of God's revelation through community building and border crossing, allowing for new avenues of reform and new possibilities for communal living. Thus my postmodern womanist way of thinking about urban ministry embodies reformation, that is, attending to, with the grace of God, the many complex issues and practices of our individual and communal life, to envision and bring about communities that exude justice, inclusion, love, and human flourishing.

While there are those who believe that resources from the Black religious experience have relevance only to persons of African or African American descent, I want to suggest that the Black religious experience not only provides shape and substance to urban ministry for Black people but also shares in and can inform the plurality of all ethnic and cultural experiences that form the urban reality. Thus I approach urban ministry through the prism of Black experience in America in general and Black women's experience in particular as a model of urban ministry praxis that has theological relevance to all urban contexts and cultures and from which insights concerning our God-to-human and human-to-human relationships can be learned.

Postmodern womanist theology: its genesis and growth

In order to fully grasp a postmodern womanist approach, it is important to note the genesis and growth of the womanist theological enterprise. Womanist theology arose out of the need for a theology that would take seriously the experiences of Black women as a resource for theological reflection. It is part of the contextual/liberation theologies camp which focused on the theme of liberation and on God as not just the Transcendent One, that is, the "power of the future," to be found in the final consummation of history. God was also the Immanent One, the Almighty Liberator, and the power of liberation in the circumstances of life. God, they argued, cannot be the God of the future unless God is also the "Liberating One," active in the present. The earliest expressions of liberation or contextual theologies in the United States came from James Cone, with his publications of *Black Theology and Black Power* (1968) and *Black Theology of Liberation* (1969). Although others would also contribute significantly to the development of Black liberation theology, Cone pioneered the revolutionary turn in the United States toward seeing sociohistorical context as a significant source for theological constructions.

The emergence of the womanist theological enterprise must also be understood in the context of the twentieth-century women's movements in Europe and North America, organized along racial and ethnic lines and which reached their zenith during the 1960s and 1970s, in terms of both social activism and academic feminist theorizing.[6]

[6] Here I would dare to make the argument that the second wave of feminism in the United States was actually the emergence of "feminisms." There were distinct feminist movements that included the feminist activities of Black women and other women of color. White feminist activism and academic theorizing was not the only feminist movement that played a part in the emergence of womanist theology. Black feminism, with its critique of interlocking oppressions, the Black (male) liberation movement, and the race and class unconsciousness of White women's liberation groups, was not a later "deviant model" of White women's activism. It was a distinct movement that began roughly when White feminist organizing did, albeit on a smaller scale, and it set the stage for the type of multidimensional critical analysis with which womanist theologians would later engage. The absence of Black feminism from the chronicles of history is primarily because Black feminists did not join "mainstream" feminist groups. Nevertheless, their work should be

Here, within theology, biblical criticism, and religious studies, several (White) feminist scholars, such as Mary Daly, Rosemary Ruether, Judith Plaskow, Susan Thistlewaite, Letty Russell, and Elisabeth Schüssler Fiorenza, identified patriarchy and sexism as endemic to the Christian church. In response, they developed theological and philosophical perspectives that spoke to White, middle-class women's struggles for equity and authority in the leadership of the church and the academy.

The theological discourse of both African American men and White feminists had something to contribute to the struggles of African American women, but likewise they both failed to represent the multidimensional issues that typified the life struggles of Black (and other) non-White and poor women. Noting that the paradigms forged by early Black male liberation theologians and feminist theologians were not addressing the gender, racial, and class oppression experienced by Black women, womanist religious scholars began to critique the one-dimensional approaches of feminists who critiqued sexism but not racism and Black male liberation theologians who critiqued racism but failed to address sexism and patriarchy.

Taking a page out of the life text of their abolitionist and women's rights foremother Isabella Baumfree, who claimed the name Sojourner Truth (to speak truth to power on behalf of the liberation of Black women and all Black people), Black women theologians, ethicists, and biblical scholars decided to claim a name for themselves to characterize their approach to constructing a liberating theology. The year was 1985 when they laid claim to the term "womanist" and its four-part definition articulated by awarding-winning novelist Alice Walker in her work, *In Search of Our Mothers' Gardens: Womanist Prose*

> **WOMANIST** 1. From *womanish*. (Opp. of "girlish," i.e. frivolous, irresponsible, not serious.) A black feminist or feminist of color. From the black folk expression of mothers to female children, "you acting womanish," i.e., like a woman. Usually referring to outrageous, audacious, courageous or *willful* behavior. Wanting to know more and in greater depth than is considered "good" for one. Interested in grown up doings. Acting

---

considered as an influence upon the feminist movement as a whole and upon womanist theology in particular. See the Mount Vernon/New Rochelle Women's Group's "Statement on birth control" in *Sisterhood is Powerful*, pp. 360-61 and P. Robinson and "Poor Black Women's Study Papers by Poor Black Women of Mount Vernon, New York," in *The Black Woman: An Anthology*. Also see Giddings 1984; Hill Collins 1990; Hooks 1981, 1984; Omalade 1994; and Smith 1983.

grown up. Being grown up. Interchangeable with another black folk expression: "You trying to be grown." Responsible. In charge. *Serious*.

2. *Also*: A woman who loves other women, sexually and/or nonsexually. Appreciates and prefers women's culture, women's emotional flexibility (values tears as natural counterbalance of laughter), and women's strength. Sometimes loves individual men, sexually and/or non-sexually. Committed to survival and wholeness of entire people, male *and* female. Not a separatist, except periodically, for health. Traditionally a universalist, as in: "Mama, why are we brown, pink, and yellow, and our cousins are white, beige and black?" Ans. "Well, you know the colored race is just like a flower garden, with every color flower represented." Traditionally capable, as in: "Mama, I'm walking to Canada and I'm taking you and a bunch of other slaves with me." Reply: "It wouldn't be the first time."

3. Loves music. Loves dance. Loves the moon. *Loves* the Spirit. Loves love and food and roundness. Loves struggle. *Loves* the Folk. Loves herself. *Regardless*.

4. Womanist is to feminist as purple is to lavender.[7]

Alice Walker's four-part definition became the foundational tenet of a movement among Black female religious scholars who immediately perceived Walker's womanism as not only relevant but also imperative for their work on behalf of US and diasporic women of African descent.

Delores Williams, one of the matriarchs of the womanist theological project, articulates womanist theology as, "a prophetic voice concerned about the well-being of the entire African American community, female and male, adults and children." It is a theology, she states, that "help[s] black women see, affirm, and have confidence in the importance of their experience and faith [in their ability to determine] the character of the Christian religion." It "challenges all oppressive forces impeding black women's struggle for survival and for the development of a positive, productive quality of life." It is, she says, a "theology [that] opposes all oppression based on race, sex, class, sexual preference, physical ability, and caste."[8]

---

[7] Alice Walker, *In Search of Our Mothers' Gardens: Womanist Prose* (San Diego: Harcourt Brace Jovanovich, 1983), xi–xii.

[8] Delores S. Williams, *Sisters in the Wilderness: The Challenge of Womanist God-Talk* (Maryknoll, NY: Orbis Books, 1993), 67.

Like Williams, first generation womanist religious scholars like Katie Cannon, Jacquelyn Grant, Shawn Copeland, Cheryl Townsend Gilkes, Emilie Townes, Renita Weems, Diana Hayes, and Marcia Riggs paid a great deal of attention to defining the relationship between the term womanist and the terms theology, ethics, and biblical scholarship. These intellectual revolutionaries brought Black women's voices from the margins to the center of theological discourse. They named the critical themes, traditions, and methodological strategies that inform the womanist religious enterprise. They validated the religious experiences and wisdom of Black women, and they laid the groundwork for using such experience and wisdom as a resource for God-talk.

Building upon the efforts of the first generation, second generation womanist religious scholars like Kelly Brown Douglas, Linda Thomas, Cheryl Kirk-Duggan, Joan Martin, Barbara Holmes, and Rosetta Ross provided deeper theological reflection based on Black women's lived experiences. They further established normativity within the womanist discourse by taking the initiatives of the first generation and extrapolating from them to create descriptive and constructive works of their own within their respective fields of study. For example, with the publication of her text, *Black Women's Christ, White Women's Jesus*, Jacquelyn Grant was the first womanist theologian to provide a Christological position that focused on the redemptive activity rather than the maleness of Christ. This prompted second-generation womanist theologian Kelly Brown Douglas to provide a more in-depth reflection on Christology in her text, *The Black Christ*, in order to, as she stated, "mov[e] us all closer to appreciating Christ's presence in Black lives, as well as understanding the radical challenge that Christ gives to all Christians."[9] Although this second generation includes many voices and a diversity of perspectives, they have largely focused on providing descriptive and analytical constructs for eradicating black women and Black people's oppression.

A third generation of womanist scholar-practitioners, has begun to broaden the trajectories of womanist God-talk and praxis. Their task, as they see it, is to address the concerns and realities of a pluralistic, technologically saturated, postmodern world where the intersections of Black women's lives with the lives of others are more expansively explored, where disruptions are a part of everyday life, and where interacting with people who are radically different than oneself is normative and constant.

---

[9] Kelly Brown Douglas, *The Black Christ* (Maryknoll, NY: Orbis Books, 1994), 8.

In answering my call to a vocation steeped in justice work, theology, and urban ministry for the twenty-first century, this is where I locate myself. I understand it to be my task to help leaders in the Christian faith tradition to divest of spiritually bankrupt theological understandings and offensive ecclesial practices that promote limiting and shallow notions of diversity, inclusivity, and salvation.

Thus my work focuses on constructing postmodern womanist theological tools and praxis that can help to foster healing, transformation, and reconciliation within a communitarian ethic of care that supports Black women and all those on the margins.

And although I seek to harmonize and coordinate differences so that difference does not become irreconcilable and dissolve into violent destruction, the goal here is not to negate difference by transcending it or imposing upon it the thinking that "We are all just human underneath it all." Instead, my intention is to offer the central organizing principle of womanism, which emanates from a radically subjective place of centering its analysis on Black women's lives and, *owning* that centering, invite others to participate in an equally authentic process.

Such work necessitates not only negotiating the integration of our faith practice with what we preach but also a willingness to be disruptive, to disrupt those beliefs and practices that are life diminishing and that mask injustice through religious legitimation. It champions the freedom, inclusivity, and dignity of all people. It compels us to stretch our minds toward the suffering of others, especially those whose suffering remains largely invisible, and to identify, confront, and alter those ideologies and practices that have historically informed and maintained their oppression. It calls for, what I term, a postmodern womanist reimagining.

The practice of postmodern womanist reimagining

Postmodern womanist reimagining is a ministerial practice that involves not only creatively remembering but also disrupting, reflecting on, and re-envisioning configurations of the past, present, and future in order to challenge the authority of dominant histories and traditions and distance ourselves from a type of "taken-for-grantedness" attitude or inevitability outlook toward the status quo. In other words, it interrogates basing the *what is* and *what is to be* upon the *what was*.

Too often, the reality of the present—*what is*—and the rhetoric of the future—*what is to be*—is uncritically shaped by the authority of the past—*what was*—which is seen as prescriptive and absolute. Rather than cultivating an openness to seeing critically and acting differently, this type of mapping of our lives, with its lack of analysis and critical reflection, offers us few alternatives or options for creating the church and the world we dream of.

But postmodern womanist reimagining provides a way and invites us to *shift*. It calls and equips us to live in the present as a conscientious student of the past, able to discern between those experiences that are destructive and those that inform and help us to transform our present and future.

Postmodern womanist reimagining is a communal practice that entails destabilizing the past in a communal context to emancipate the present and gain agency over the future for the sake of fostering just communities. It does so by employing four steps or processes: (1) creative disruption, (2) case study analysis, (3) redemptive reconstruction, and (4) womanist celebration.

1. First, it employs creative disruption as a theological resource.
2. Second, it uses case study analysis, much like social workers use it to assess symptoms and diagnose problems in order to empower an individual or a given community.
3. Third, it gives birth to new visions and redemptive actions.
4. Last, it celebrates the work of the community, recognizing the presence of the divine and human transcendence in the redemptive work of womanist reimagining.

The first step, using creative disruption as a theological resource, lurches us into a new mode of awareness or "awakeness," a place where growth and shifts can begin to take place. Allowing disruptions that occur in the routine of our daily lives to serve as catalysts for initiating an exploratory process of discerning exploitative systems and identifying oppressive behavior patterns awakens us to what must be altered for justice to occur. Allowing creative disruption to take place in communal settings opens up space for new beginnings in communal living. It does this by encouraging critical self-reflection and calling into question those ideologies and practices that sanction oppression. It problematizes the unquestioned authority given to the past that allows it to hold undue sway over the present and the future. It gives us permission to ask "What just happened? Why did it happen? What was our response? How did our response to this situation serve us as a community of Christ's disciples, committed to solidarity, accountability, liberation, and just living?

These questions lead to the second step, case study analysis. Case study analysis allows for the examination of a unique case, or rather, a disruption in our lives, to help us gain insight into our responses to that disruption and the relevance of such to larger social phenomena. Case studies capture the critical and controversial moments and social contexts in which individuals and whole communities experience socioethical dilemmas that shape their identities and inform their embrace of others.

The third step, redemptive reconstruction, is the process of conceiving a new vision of community and redemptive actions we can take to implement new norms, values, and options. Using idealistic brainstorming and a type of consequentialist thinking, the community expounds upon their options and then takes strategic steps to create for themselves and others the new community they desire.

The first and second steps create cognitive dissonance between what was, what is, and what is to be to make room for new present and future possibilities. The third step, redemptive reconstruction, generates and implements a redemptive and liberating *what's possible now*. The first two steps can be likened to creating new wineskins. The third step constitutes the creation of new wine. All three steps lead to a way of being that disrupts an "epistemological sea of forgetfulness" and admonishes us to "tell our truths, 'anyway.'"

The last step, womanist celebration, involves, acknowledgment, thanksgiving, and commemoration. This is where the community comes together to celebrate and give thanks to the Creator and one another for the work of reimagining, shifting, and transformation. Womanist celebration is praise for the Divine, as well as, as the womanist definition says, appreciation for "The folk, roundness, food, the moon, the whole community, and all of creation, regardless." Womanist celebration is communal and recognizes and honors human transcendence that is present in radical love and just engagement. And it fortifies and emboldens the community to shift again, to continue their work.

A practical application

Sunday service on this warm spring day had started like any other. We were a highly diverse multicultural congregation in an urban neighborhood representing many cultures. The music minister offered several selections as the congregation, representing more than twelve countries, gathered for morning worship. The children and preteens, who had started their Sunday worshipping with the adults in the sanctuary, now exited with their Sunday school teachers to engage in their own worship activities. It was my turn as part of the senior pastoral staff to co-lead the service. Everything went as expected until right after the offering. There was no way we could have known or predicted what was about to happen.

When I had finished presiding over the offering, and we prayed over the gifts, a middle-aged woman of Latina and African American decent, let us call her Ana, quickly approached the front. As I made my way up the steps into the pulpit, she made her way down front to the mic on the floor. Ana did not look visibly distraught or upset. When I turned around and saw her at the microphone, she gave a huge smile and then proceeded to speak. Now I thought that Ana's presence down front was part of the service, that my colleague had asked her to make an announcement. I later found out that my colleague was thinking the same thing with respect to me.

But as Ana began to speak we soon realized that not only was her speech not a planned part of the worship but also that we were listening to a woman suffering from a mental health condition. After stating how much she loved her church, she began to talk about her recent hospitalization and not getting enough attention from her pastors or congregation.

I rushed down from the pulpit to stand by Ana's side to comfort her and gently usher her from the mic. As I did so, my colleague also stood up to join me. And when he reached out to touch Ana, she became distraught. Sobbing, she began to yell, "Don't touch me!" All of this took place in front of a shocked and silent congregation. I was able to escort Ana to the back of the sanctuary, where I and several women spoke and prayed with her. The pastor had directed someone to call the police, and the police arrived right before service ended. They handcuffed a sobbing Ana and took her to the hospital, as she repeatedly said, "All I wanted to do was to say my piece."

I was allowed to accompany Ana to the hospital. Later that day, I found out that our service had ended without a word about Ana. There was no prayer on her behalf and no words about what had happened. No one seemed to know what to say. People left worship silenced, disturbed, and injured. We needed to break the silence and acknowledge that things were not okay. We needed to discern what had happened on that Sunday and to probe whether our actions were aligned with Jesus' ministry and God's transforming power, or whether we had aligned ourselves with status quo attitudes and behaviors that marginalize those suffering from mental illness, particularly Black and Latina women. How did our response hold up and bring into being representations of the good and God's good news, which for postmodern womanists include survival, justice, acceptance, full inclusion, discipleship, recognition, and quality of life? *We needed to engage in postmodern womanist reimagining.*

During our staff meeting the next day, which began and almost ended without a mention of what had transpired, I asked the pastor if we could take some time to reflect on Sunday, to express how each of us felt and what we experienced. My colleague began to talk about the need to create "safe space" for all with regard to the actions taken. I wanted us to probe deeper into our subjective notions of what "safe space" meant and to talk about what some congregants had articulated, namely, that Ana's cry for help and her being handcuffed had left them feeling deeply hurt, unsafe, and unsure of our church's ability to serve as a sanctuary for all. I wanted us to probe our silence around the well-being and mental health disorders of women of color. I wanted us to interrogate how, historically, those whose lives are already impacted by sexism, racism, classism, ethnic bias, and language differences have experienced unique and considerable challenges in dealing with mental illness and having access to treatment and communities that focus on and foster their well-being.

I needed us to engage in postmodern womanist reimagining so that we might begin to critically think and act in ways that opposed human oppression rather than collude with such. I invited us all to think about what drove us to respond as we did, whether there were fears, past experiences, or theological understandings that attributed to the actions we took on that Sunday. What did we think might have happened if we had responded differently? We might view Sunday's disruption as an opportunity, as a chance to creatively challenge and disrupt our ways of being, so that we might further live into being loving, just, and inclusive.

This line of questioning initiated the first step—creative disruption. As we committed to probing our theology, ideologies, and knowledge around mental illness, we began the difficult dialogue of naming our own racial, ethnic, cultural, and socioeconomic backgrounds, as well as the unjust privilege that resulted in silencing and demonizing Ana and, in fact, all those women and men who, on that day, sat in silence as they watched the situation unfold and secretly dealt with their own depression, anxiety, and other life challenges.

Having the gumption to begin this difficult dialogue allowed us to move into the second phase of womanist reimagining, case study analysis, that is, embarking upon an analysis of ourselves.

For the next six weeks, we reimagined new ecclesial possibilities. We named what creating safe space meant to each of us and what creating safe space might look like according to Christ. We reflected on Scripture, particularly the words and ministry of Jesus. We read and spoke about the church's silence around mental disorders. We told stories and talked about our ignorance, shame, assumptions, and desire to know more. I shared statistics, including the fact that one out of four Americans will suffer from some kind of mental illness at some point in their lives.[10] We discussed the factors that have historically conspired to stigmatize Blacks and Latinos in general, and Black and Latino women in particular who live with mental illness and the decision that many make, because of these factors, to delay or avoid seeking help. We learned of the particular challenges our urban context presented and about the caregivers, family members, and friends of those with mental health concerns who bear their own scars and thoughts because they have no safe place to talk about the impact of mental illness, either upon their own lives or the lives of their loved ones. We learned that many of them had sat through church, week after week, suffering in anguish and stigmatized silence. They informed, challenged, and helped to reorient us toward thinking about what it means to be radically inclusive. And this led us to embark upon the third step of womanist reimagining, redemptive reconstruction.

We began by asking ourselves what steps might we take to live into our desire to be a radically inclusive and diverse "come as you are" church family, inclusive of those whose minds are diagnosed with an illness. And we ended by creating a constructive and transformative response that entailed having congregation-wide conversations about mental health; contacting local psychiatrists and other mental health professionals to assist us in designing and facilitating a mental health conference to further the congregation and our larger community; and starting a new support ministry group for members and nonmembers dealing with depression, anxiety, and bipolar disorder, a ministry that Ana was instrumental in helping to form and to lead.

I offer womanist reimagining as a critical ministry tool to assist the urban church in creating spaces of inclusion and becoming a sanctuary for all by recognizing, validating, and being responsive to

[10] http://www.thekimfoundation.org/html/about_mental_ill/statistics.html.

the lived experiences, struggles, and triumphs of all people who live on the underside of history. Postmodern womanist reimagining offers a critique of our ways of being in community that jeopardize the possibility of inclusivity and liberation. It supports fostering a collective vision of communal advancement for the purpose of transforming the lives of those who experience invisibility, marginalization, and oppression. It begins with lived experience of being black and female, but it necessitates a moral commitment to advancing the life, freedom, dignity, and flourishing of all people. It propels us to weave tapestries of possibility and new ways of being that veer us from a familiar malaise toward wholeness.

The task is never easy. And every attempt does not necessarily yield the outcome we desire. But as one of my womanist colleagues, Monica Coleman, states, "As creative transformation leads us into the future, it necessarily challenges the world as we currently experience it."[11]

---

[11] Monica Coleman, *Making a Way Out of No Way: A Womanist Theology* (Minneapolis: Fortress Press, 2008), 89.

Addendum

Capitalizing the "B" in Black

My capitalization of the word "black" throughout this article is intentional. For me, "Black" signifies a group equivalent to African American, Afro Caribbean, and people of the African diaspora, just as Asian, Irish, French, and Italian do for those respective groups. It speaks to and respects the unknown familial and national past disrupted by slavery. Additionally, it speaks to the unique struggle we have had to endure with regard to naming ourselves, and it affirms our right and power to do so. From the beginning of our presence in this country, people of African descent have had to fight for the right to name themselves. We have had to contend with being collectively called Africans without any reference to our different tribes, cultures, and countries. We were subsequently referred to as "negros," "negars," "nigras," and "niggras"—the borrowed Spanish term for black. Then we were labeled by the US Census Bureau (between 1850 and 1920) as "black," "negro," "mulatto," "quadroon" or "octoroon"—all of which depended upon the census taker's visual assessment. By 1930 only one of these categories remained, that of "negro."

In the mid-1920s, W. E. B. Du Bois began a letter-writing campaign, insisting that book and magazine publishers, as well as newspaper editors, capitalize the "N" in Negro when referring to Black people. Although Du Bois himself did not regularly use the word "Negro"—as indicated by one of his most famous works, "The Souls of Black Folk," he recognized it as the official name for the race, and as such, wanted that word to confer respect on the page as well as in daily life.

In 1926 Du Bois' request was denied by the *New York Times* and most other newspapers. In 1929, when the editor for the *Encyclopedia Britannica* informed Du Bois that *Negro* would be lowercased in the article he had submitted for publication, Du Bois quickly responded, calling "the use of a small letter for the name of twelve million Americans and two hundred million human beings a personal insult." The editor yielded to the use of the capital N, as did many other mainstream publications including the *Atlantic Monthly* and, eventually, the *New York Times*.

I stand with DuBois and countless other academic and linguist scholars who have argued the case for years that naming ourselves does matter. It is an act of respect and recognition of our history and our whole selves.

CHAPTER 15

Ancient Hebrew Nouns and the Questions of Today: A Modern-Day Lesson from Qoheleth

Beth Tanner

The best collegial relationships are synergistic. The sharing of ideas with each other creates an environment of enrichment and learning. One such encounter came in the spring of 2016. President Mast stopped by my office with a Hebrew question. He was working on a sermon and asked if הבל (*hebel*) and רוח (*ruach*) could be considered theological opposites. We discussed the possibilities and theological directions, and that conversation and the questions we explored stayed with me. The question would surface occasionally, and I would pick up a book or search for an article to further my own understanding of it. This article is the result of that inquiry.

The ancient Hebrew language is constructed with a significant amount of word play. The language is highly metaphorical, and many words have multiple definitions. This wide range of meanings causes Hebrew students and even seasoned scholars to puzzle over the exact meaning of a word as it is used in a verse. For example, the root ר(ה or ר(ע means "that which is harmful."[1] Every negative person or hap-

---

[1] E. Jenni, *Das Wort 'olām im Alten Testament* (Berlin: Verlag Alfred Topelmann, 1956), 1:659.

pening is assigned this single word without an indication of the degree of harmfulness or evilness. A stubbed toe is "harmful" or "evil," as are the evildoers of prophetic and psalmic fame. Could everything harmful in this ancient culture be considered harmful to the same degree? In the ancient world, did they experience the same confusion we have concerning the degree to which something was evil? Or does this single word indicate the complexity of the meaning of "harmful" or "evil"? Could it indicate that one person might see a high degree of "evil" in a person or event and at the same time others see it as a lesser problem? Is it the context alone that provides the exact definition of this common word? These questions are still debated today. Whatever the cause, this feature of the Hebrew language makes translation difficult. The only thing that is clear is they chose to use a single word for a complex and multilayered concept, such as the word "evil."

Other Hebrew words cause a dilemma when translated into the English language. For example, the root משפט means both "justice" and "judgment" in its original language. The theological thought is profound—God's judgment is not an end to itself but is the same event as the ushering in of God's justice. Judgment and justice are not two different actions or concepts but are one and the same. Yet when English translations are reviewed, the English language forces an interpreter to choose between the two words, and that choice often tells more about the theological leanings of the interpreter than of the original text. It provides a type of bellwether mark of one's theology, because where one will translate the phrase as "God's judgment," another will see this scripture as an example of "God's justice."

All of these examples are part of a distinct set of words called Hebrew abstract nouns. These are nouns that do not identify things but concepts. These concepts in English are represented by a plethora of words, often with shades of meaning in their definitions. In Hebrew, words often have multiple and often even unrelated meanings. Words such as "justice/judgment," "worshiper/servant," and "to give/to place" cause the interpreter great difficulty. The two words President Mast contemplated are also abstract nouns. Their meanings vary depending on the context, and they also can have multiple meanings even within a single verse. They are flexible, and it is that very flexibility that sparks possibilities.

הבל (*Hebel*)

This word appears only fifty-five times in the Hebrew bible. In Genesis, it appears as the name of one of Eve's sons, "Hable," or "Abel."

Scholars have long noted the narrative's double entendre concerning Abel's fate and the name.[2] The word is used sparingly in the prophets: it is used twice in Isaiah, four times in Jeremiah, and once in Zechariah. It is also rare in most of the writings: it is used five times in Job, once in Proverbs 21:16, and in just three psalms.

By far the largest discussion about this word comes from the study of the book of Ecclesiastes. Here it takes a central place, appearing thirty-eight times in twelve chapters. But it is not simply the number of occurrences; its placement also matters. The word is also placed at the beginning, in 1:2, and at the end, in 12:8, forming an *inclusio* for the entire book.[3] Second, it appears throughout the book as a theological refrain. Its meaning and its range are one of the most heavily debated issues in the study of Ecclesiastes "so that its interpretation has become perhaps the most crucial of many challenges involved with Ecclesiastes. Because of its central use in the book, the approach taken to הבל dramatically shapes the way the entire book is understood."[4]

The literal sense of the Hebrew word means "vapor" or "breath." This, however, introduces the first complication. "Vapor" and "breath" do not seem equivalent terms, unless one is speaking of their ethereal character. The Greek word used in the Septuagint maintains the range of the Hebrew understanding of "futility" or "transitoriness." The best known but most problematic translation probably stems from the Latin translation, "vanitas," meaning "futility," as well as "untruthfulness" and "empty pride."[5] The Latin word becomes the English "vanity" in the KJV of 1611 and is still used today in several translations including the NRSV, ESV, and NAB. Language, of course, continues to morph and change, so the *Oxford Dictionary* notes currently the meaning of "vanity" is either "excessive pride in one's appearance or achievements," or "the quality of being worthless."[6] Ogden states some continue to use "vanity" "as a type of 'code word' that is able to embrace the various shades of meaning found in the Hebrew term used in Qoheleth, but this is useful only for scholars who work in the book. However, to almost all readers of an English Bible today, the negative connotations of the term 'vanity' has shifted from the original meaning of 'transitoriness,' and for that

---

[2] Karolien Vermeulen, "Mind the Gap: Ambiguity in the Story of Cain and Abel," *Journal of Biblical Literature* 133 (2014), 29-42.
[3] Roland Murphy, *Ecclesiastes* (Dallas: Word, 1998), 3.
[4] Douglas Miller, "Qohelet's Symbolic Use of הבל," *Journal of Biblical Literature* 117 (1998), 437.
[5] http://www.latin-dictionary.org/vanitas, accessed December 17, 2016.
[6] https://en.oxforddictionaries.com/definition/vanity, accessed December 12, 2016.

reason, we see it as an unfortunate choice."[7] The Tanakh translates it as "futile," and the NIV uses "meaningless." All of these are preferable to "vanity" but still lose some of the ethereal sense of the Hebrew. This problem also serves as a cautionary tale for scholars and preachers; we not only must deal with the issues of the ancient meanings of an abstract noun but must also be aware of how our living language of English continues to morph and change and without study and research can cause the original meaning of the word to be lost in the process.

Scholars are, likewise, divided on the meaning of the word and thus the meaning of the book of Ecclesiastes. Murphy argues for the traditional translation of vanity. "The modern reader may desire a larger view of the situation and may conclude that humankind is not helpless. But this relativization is not Qoheleth's doing. It comes only from placing him in a broader context of biblical thought and theology."[8] Fox agrees with Murphy's evaluation of the book of Ecclesiastes as negative, but for different reasons. Fox states the author of the work changes the definition of the word from the literal sense of a "vapor" and its ephemeral meaning to the meaning of "absurd." "The absurd is a disjunction between two phenomena that are thought to be linked by a bond of harmony or causality, or *should* be so linked. Such bonds are *sine qua non* of rationality, and all deduction and explanation presupposes them. Thus the absurd is irrational, an affront to reason—the human faculty that seeks to discover order in the world around us."[9] To Fox, Qoheleth provides a new definition for the word. To both of these scholars, Qoheleth's view of the world is one of pessimism and futility.

Another group of scholars does not see the message of Qoheleth as either "vanity" or "absurd." Davis notes in the Hebrew language of the Bible, "Metaphorical meanings are not divorced from literal meanings, as a master craftsman of language like [Q]oheleth (12:10) would have surely known."[10] It is not hopeless at all. Davis sees Qoheleth as having the same understanding as the writers of Psalm 39, "The psalmist is not saying, 'Life is a cruel joke!' but rather, 'Life is so short; let me not live it stupidly.'"[11] Likewise, Limburg quotes Luther who understood

---

[7] Graham Ogden, *Qoheleth*, 2nd ed. (Sheffield: Sheffield Press, 2007), 26.
[8] Roland Murphy, *Ecclesiastes* (Dallas: Word, 1998), lix. Leong Seow also uses "vanity," arguing there is no better English translation; *Ecclesiastes* (New Haven: Yale University Press, 1997), 102.
[9] Michael Fox, *A Time to Tear Down and A Time to Build Up: A Rereading of Ecclesiastes* (Grand Rapids: Eerdmans, 1999), 30-31.
[10] Ellen Davis, *Proverbs, Ecclesiastes, and the Song of Songs* (Louisville: Westminster John Knox Press, 2000), 167.
[11] Davis, *Proverbs, Ecclesiastes, and the Song of Songs*, 167.

the meaning as "Let us, therefore, be content with the things that are present and commit ourselves into the hand of God, who alone knows and controls both the past and the future."[12] Ogden sees the word as the philosophical underpinning of the whole book and presents a theological conundrum. "We find Qoheleth here impressing on his young readers the fact we must live with many unanswered questions. It does not mean for one moment that life therefore is 'vanity'; rather, the pain of faith is living with many questions unanswered."[13] Brown combines many of these definitions, "The outcome of the examined life and world is a heightened awareness of life's 'vanity' (hebel): its futility and fragility, its absurdity and obscurity are all rooted in the inscrutably sovereign will of God."[14]

The meaning of the word and thus the meaning of the book is not the musings of one who is overly proud or self-dependent. On the contrary, Qoheleth has every advantage given to a human and finds that even that is not enough to understand life and its purpose. Work—that is, toil—without a greater understanding is futile and worthless. It offers no peace of mind or comfort. It is indeed "hebel." Life is transitory, and Qoheleth provides this book as an attempt to come to grips with the reality of what it means to be a creature, not the Creator and controller of the universe.

רוּחַ (Ruach)

This word appears 378 times in the Old Testament. It occurs sparingly in the Pentateuch. It is common in the so-called historical books—forty-seven times from Joshua to 2 Kings. It is rare in the prophetic books, except in Isaiah (52 times) and Ezekiel (52 times). By far the greatest number of occurrences is in the writings. The word has three meanings: wind, breath, and life force or spirit. Unfortunately, it is not always clear which meaning is meant in a given passage.

The most concrete of the definitions is when the word refers to the natural movement of air or wind. For example, this is the meaning in the Exodus plague narratives where God brings both an east and a west wind (Ex. 10:13, 19; 14:21). The verses where the actual wind is

---

[12] James Limburg, *Encountering Ecclesiastes: A Book for Our Time* (Grand Rapids: Eerdmans, 2006), 21.
[13] Graham Ogden, *Qoheleth* (Sheffield: Sheffield Phoenix Press, 2007), 23. Likewise, Norbert Lohfink sees this as a philosophical work; *Qoheleth*, trans. S. McEvenue (Minneapolis: Fortress Press, 2003), 12.
[14] William Brown, *Ecclesiastes* (Louisville: Westminster John Knox Press, 2000), 14.

clear are the smallest number of occurrences, but as Davis indicated, all of the other metaphorical meanings must be related to the base understanding of wind. The wind is both pleasant and destructive, although there are several other words used when the wind is one of destruction. The wind is real in the moment and temporary and outside the control of humans. The wind in the ancient Near East is understood as an entity controlled by the gods. In the Bible, the wind is usually sent by God as in Genesis 1:2.

The second range of meanings are related and are also more abstract. They probably originate from the idea that the "wind" comes from God. Thus this metaphor was expanded to include breath and then expanded further to include life or life force, commonly called spirit. It is important, however, to understand this "spirit" in the Hebrew Bible is not the same as the dualism of flesh and spirit in the Greek understanding. The Hebrew concept is that a person is one whole, not two entities existing as one. The spirit, or life force, is not divisible from the body until the influences of Persian and Greek philosophy begin to alter the previous understandings in Judaism. The religion and philosophy of these empires speculated on the nature of humans and on questions of the afterlife. This interaction with other cultures prompted Hebrew thinkers to expand their view of humans and death and what came after death. Thus the very late Ecclesiastes text states, "The dust returns to earth, as it was, but the ruach returns to God who gave it" (12:6). This represents one of the few texts in the Hebrew Bible which separates the body and its life force or breath. What is clear throughout the Hebrew Bible is that both the wind and the breath are given by God, and neither are ultimately controlled by humans.

God is the acting agent of ruach, and as a result, the concept becomes personified. The ruach of God acts as a type of intermediary. In other cultures, the word "ruach" means "wind" but never is this an extension of the direct actions of God.[15] It is, however, in the Bible. It provides the way Joseph was able to interpret dreams (Gen 42:38); it rested on Moses and was then "distributed" to the elders of Israel (Num 11:17) and Joshua (Num 27:18). In Judges, Samuel, and to a lesser extent, 2 Samuel and 1 Kings, many texts use the formula "The ruach of the LORD [or God] is upon [fill in the name]." For example, Judges 3:10 reads, "The spirit of the LORD came upon him, and he judged Israel; he went out to war, and the LORD gave King Cushan-rishathaim of Aram into his

---

[15] Lloyd Neve, *The Spirit of God in the Old Testament* (Cleveland, TN: CPT Press, 2011), 1.

hand; and his hand prevailed over Cushan-rishathaim." Neve explains how ruach is understood in the ancient culture, "In the Old Testament literature, ruach is not only used to express God's activity *as he relates himself* to his world, his creation, and his people. It is also Israel's way of describing God, not as he in himself, but as he communicates with the world his power, his life, his anger, his will, and his very presence."[16]

A complication arises when ruach is described as "evil" or "deceitful" and is sent not to aid humans but to mislead them. This occurs in only four texts: Judges 9:23-24; 1 Samuel 16:14-23, 18:10-12, and 19:9-10; 1 Kings 22:19-23; and 2 Kings 19:7. In the Judges text, God sent an evil spirit between Abimelech and the leaders of Shechem to cause dissention among the parties that leads ultimately to Abimelech's death. The Samuel text recounts God's withdrawal of favor from Saul: "But the spirit of the LORD departed from Saul, and an evil spirit from the LORD troubled him" (1 Sam. 16:14). Here we learn there is both an "evil spirit" and God's spirit, and it appears they are both deliverers of God's will. Saul's mental breakdown allows for the rise of David and the founding of Jerusalem. Similarly, in 2 Kings, God sends the "spirit" to the King of Assyria to mislead him so he will return to his land. The spirit's deceit aids Hezekiah and Judah's survival. The final text tells of the prophetic deception of Ahab by his four hundred prophets. The deception is revealed to him by the lone-disagreeing prophet, Michiah, who sees God sitting in the heavenly council asking who will entice Ahab to go to war. The spirit volunteers and states, "I will go out and be a lying spirit in the mouth of all of your prophets" (v. 22). Here the *ruach* is completely independent and speaks up for itself in the heavenly council, much like the Satan—the adversary—of Job. So what are we to make of this ruach? First, despite its independence in 1 Kings 22, the spirit is still sent by the LORD, and in each instance, the narrative sees the person receiving the evil or lying spirit as the one acting against the God's will. The theological and philosophical possibilities are troubling. Is God in control of what is evil and lying and harmful? Did God create this separate entity? Unfortunately, these questions are modern ones. The Hebrew Bible accepts the existence of this spirit[17] but never comments on where either an evil spirit or evil itself originates.

The ancients were content with God sending an evil spirit. Indeed, this concept is common in the Near East. Hamori writes, "Many

---

[16] Ibid., 2.
[17] Ester Hamori notes that spirits in general and evil spirits in particular were known and reflected in the literature of the Near East; "The Spirit of Falsehood," *Catholic Biblical Quarterly* 72 (2010), 16-17.

types of spirits and demons acted as divine agents with both positive and negative functions. The divine agent is generally neutral, sent for the benefit or detriment of the recipient, depending on the will of the god."[18] So does the evil or harmful spirit tell us more about the spirit of the LORD? It appears that it does. The spirit of the LORD may not be as Neve describes at all. If these spirits are equal, then the spirit of the LORD is not God's activity but should be understood in the same way as the messenger of the LORD. It is not a part of God but an agent of God. The texts are not clear on the question we have; are there two spirits or one spirit that brings a message that is either good or harmful? The spirits, like the wind, serve God but are not God. In addition, these spirits do nothing to comfort the theological discomfort they produce. They do not explain their actions.

The final use of ruach means breath. It is used both of animals (Gen. 6:7) and humans (Ps. 135:7). It can indicate life (Ps. 146:4), the internal self (Dan 2:1), or the heart (Gen 45:27). The lack of it is death (Ps. 104:29). It sometimes comes from the winds as an intermediary for God (Ezek. 37:9). Although it does have a range of meanings, all involve the life force of humans and animals. It is the difference between what is alive and what is dead. Occasionally, there are references to God's breath, and it is always in relationship to God's power or justice in creation (Ps. 33:6 and Exod. 15:8) and as recompense for the wicked (Isa. 4:9, 11:4, 30:28, 33:11; Job 4:9). God's breath, therefore, is an anthropological metaphor that functions like God's Spirit above and is the very life force that makes the world exist and again is gifted and removed by the Almighty.

Hebel and ruach

With all of these options for ruach. It is not surprising that it can be difficult to determine which definition applies in a particular verse. The same is also true for the uses of hebel. Is, therefore, the original thesis that they are theological opposites correct? First, it is probably essential to limit the parameters to the book of Ecclesiastes and the philosophical and theological purpose in it. It is the only book where the terms are used together and also the only book in which "hebel" appears often enough for a full understanding of its meaning. From the discussion above, it is clear this is not an easy question to answer. Each word has a range of meanings. They are also not natural opposites; each represents a concept that is intangible and difficult to grasp.

---

[18] Hamori, 17.

I will begin with some of my presuppositions. As a Reformed Christian theologian, my theological underpinnings are grounded in hope. Not hope in humanity and unbridled human progress but hope in the belief that God's purposes are being worked out in the world, in the church, and in my life. Yet this is not a Pollyanna belief. There is tragedy and evil and greed and hurt in this world, and at times the world and its human occupants appear irreparably broken. Like Qoheleth, I understand how one can look around at one's work, one's life, and one's world and wonder about the meaning of it all. I, like the writer, live in a country where we have an abundance of the world's resources. We bend humans and nature to our will, just as the writer declares in the second chapter of Ecclesiastes. Like him, we should be happy and content with all of our stuff. Yet we are not. We are a country of privilege which acts out against others with vitriol. We are broken and sinners. Yet despite this, I believe God's purposes are being worked out, even if I cannot see them. God places God's world into human hands.

As a biblical scholar, I also know the Hebrew Bible has no problem expressing pain and sin and brokenness, yet I do not believe the ones who collected these books selected this one because it offered no hope, no light, no learning. In the Persian and Greek periods, the Jews were struggling to adapt their theology for a world community. They were no longer living in a small area at the terminal end of the Mediterranean Sea. Jewish communities were now in many of the areas that touched the Mediterranean, with large communities in Alexandria and Babylon. They had interacted with these cultures and their understanding of God and humans. Ecclesiastes is but one of the books to address this globalization. Unlike the book of Ezra, which wants to isolate the Jews from those who are not of pure ancestry, Qoheleth is attempting to respond to the cultures where God has now planted the people. New questions require new thinking. Lohfink notes, "The Book of Qoheleth can only be understood as an attempt to profit as much as possible from the Greek understanding of the world, without forcing Israel wisdom to give up its status."[19] Thus, this book and the meaning of these two words are a lesson in doing theology in a period of globalization. Like the problems of translation today, the writer is trying to both preserve the traditions of the past and respond to the global realities around him.

Several texts in Ecclesiastes place these two words together in a repeating phrase, "All is hebel and a chasing after ruach" (1:14, 17; 2:11,

---

[19] Norbert Lohfink, *Qoheleth: A Continental Commentary*, ed. S. McEvenue (Minneapolis: Fortress Press, 2003), 6.

17, 26; 4:4, 16; 6:9). The word "hebel" is discussed above. The NRSV and most English translations state, "All is vanity and a chasing after wind." These translations have also chosen the most concrete definition of ruach as a physical wind. This meaning certainly reinforces the ethereal character of hebel. Put simply, the word choice aids the English-speaking reader to understand its meaning. This translation would appear to demonstrate that the original question asked by Dr. Mast was invalid. Using only these verses, the two nouns are not opposite but synonymous. A check of the commentaries demonstrates a focus in these verses on hebel and an acceptance of the use of "wind" as an adequate translation of ruach.[20] But does it fit in the context? Lohfink does not think so and translates it as "an inspiration of air" instead of a "chasing after wind."[21]

Poetry does not lend itself to a single translation, yet that is what is available in English. The phrase could be "a chasing after wind," but if this is the only option, much of the meaning is lost. In much of the book, the author wants to know the meaning of work, wisdom, pleasure, justice, and life. What is it all about? There are certainly what appear to be contradictions in the book concerning the result of toil and its ability to comfort. Eccl 5:10 states, "The lover of money will not be satisfied with money; nor the lover of wealth with gain. This is also hebel." Then in Eccl 5:19, he states, "Likewise all to whom God gives wealth and possessions, and who he enables to enjoy them, and to accept their lot and find enjoyment in their toil—this is the gift of God." Which is it? Qoheleth's comprehensive understanding of life is that it is fine to accept the life you have and enjoy these gifts, but do not mistake that for something that has eternal value. Humans can only be free when they stop chasing their own value as autonomous beings. It is hebel and a chasing after breath. You can chase it until the day you die, but you will never control your breath or what you gain while it remains in your body.

Turning to the final possibility for hebel, one can also translate the verse as "All is hebel and a chasing after the spirit." One can try to chase immortality, but that too is hebel and will not lead to an extra moment. The same can be said for chasing after the life force. It is noted above that there is a change in how the "spirit" is perceived in this book. Chapter 12 begins the discussion about the life of the spirit

[20] See for example Murphy, Miller, and Ogden.
[21] Lohfink, 43.

beyond death.[22] Lohfink noted this was at least in part because of the introduction to the beliefs of other cultures. Qoheleth is also saying that another's focus on life after death is also hebel. The human has no control over the God-given life force. It cannot be bargained with or bartered for. A human's ultimate fate lies not in her or his hands but in the hands of God. We do not see or know beyond the grave. What happens is all a faith statement, not one based on human merit or actions or wealth. Like every breath we take on earth, the future belongs to the LORD alone.

Qoheleth is not anti-life, thinking everything is futile. Hebel is to misinterpret the control a human has over his life. You can chase wind, or breath, or spirit; it does not matter, for the result will be the same. All will result in a limited and an ultimately false understanding of ruach. These actions are indeed the very opposite of a life lived with a clear understanding of how humans in general and individuals in particular are creatures and not Creator. To realize one's limitations is the message of the book. All that is valued other than God will disappear. Psalm 146 expresses the same understanding, "Do not put your trust in princes, in whom there is no help. When their ruach departs, they return to the earth; on that very day their plans perish" (3-4).

It takes Qoheleth a lot of thought to become wise. When humans forget they are human and not God, their thoughts and efforts are hebel. Here I can agree with Fox's definition of absurd. But that is not the only meaning for Qoheleth that he wants the world to know. He repeats that life is fleeting, and humans have no control over being born or what happens after death. Ruach as a messenger of God is eternal and this "messenger" abides with us for a time before returning to God (Eccl 12:9). To think otherwise is absurd.

We are God made; we are stardust, and our moments are hebel. I find this a comfort. For the decade of Dr. Mast's tenure as president, we have been engaged in the hard work of becoming an antiracist institution. This work can be daunting and painful as we are called to speak truth to power, even when those powers are us and the churches we serve. Sometimes racism and sexism and classism seem as if they have a power and a personality of their own and refuse to go down without an epic battle. According to Qoheleth, these powers are hebel. They are

---

[22] There was an earlier perception that after death, all humans went to Sheol. So there was an understanding of a life after death. What is different here is the focus on the separation of the spirit and the body.

nothing. They will not stand. In a fight for justice, human sin is hebel, and ruach is the life force that encourages us to work for a better world.

Are these two words therefore theological opposites? Yes and no. In the human realm of sin and brokenness, they are. When we forget that ruach is not something in our control, when we care more about our breath or lives than the lives of others, then we have moved away from our intended purpose and become hebel, absurd, an antithesis of life lived in God's kingdom. We fight the very God who loves us. Yet when we are aligned with the values of God's kingdom and understand that our breath is a gift and is to be used for the good of all, then they are not opposites at all. When we understand our place in the world and accept our limitations and even celebrate our temporary moments, we are not chasing wind but accepting God's world.

Theological reflection is not usually about finding a definitive answer. The type of question that tickled the intellect of Dr. Mast sent me on my own exploration of the idea, and at the end of it all, the answer is still not clear cut, for it depends on one's view of life. This is the stuff of theological exploration. It is not a search for an answer as with a math problem. It is an exploration of the self, of the ancient text and its difficulties, and of our world. It changes us and deepens our intellectual and theological knowledge, as well as our faith. These are the characteristics Dr. Mast has displayed as pastor, president, and colleague, and as such, it has been a pleasure to work with him.

Index

7 Kinds of Smart, 50

Accra Confession, 142
ACS. *See* American Colonization Society
Affordable Care Act, 174
Africa and globalization, 141; and theft of resources, 141–42; and the Gospel proclamation, 142–43; joyful worship in, 143; plight of, and World Alliance of Reformed Churches, 142
African American: and civil rights, 169–70; and current Black community, 173–78; and Declaration of Independence, 184; and education, 167; and mass migration, 168–69; and prosperity gospel, 172–73; as compensatory institution, 160–61; as mother, 161–64; as mutual aid society, 167; as pathological, 159–61; as race institution, 163–64; evolution of, 164–66; function of, 166–68; in post-Civil Rights Era, 170–73; involuntary isolation of, 160; irrelevance of, 171–72; and music in Germany, 65–82; social status of, 158
Ahrends, Petra-Angela, 77
Akinade, Akintunde E., 127
Alexander, Michelle, 175
Alliger, John B., 192
Alston, Wallace, 6
Althaus, P., 151
American Colonization Society, 182–88; and evangelism, 187; and Frelinghuysen, Theodore, 183; and Reformed leaders, 183; and the Reformed Church in America, 186–87; New Brunswick Colonization Society and, 186
American Dilemma, An, 160

Anabaptists, 96
Anderson, Victor, 164
Anti-Racism Renewal Team, 6
Anti-Racism Transformation Team, 179
Aristophanes: and different creation story, 57; and same-sex orientation, 56–57
Armed Forces Radio Network, 67
Armstrong, Thomas, 38
Articles of Dort: and education, 11–12
Atlantic Monthly, 213
Atlas of Global Christianity, The, 125

baptism: and rebaptism, 96–97; sermon on, 94–98
Barmen Theological Declaration, 146, 148–49; and the future, 153–55
Barna, George, 39
Bartelworth, Martin, 79, 80
Barth, Karl, 146–48; and Jews in Germany, 148, 151
Baumfree, Isabella (Sojourner Truth), 203
Belgic Confession: and baptism, 96
Belhar Confession, 1, 3, 4, 147, 153–54
Bethune, George Washington, 192–93, 194; and North Carolina Classis, 190–91
Bible, Gender, Sexuality: Reframing the Church's Debate on Same-Sex Relationships, 53
Black, capitalizing the "B" in, 213
Black Christ, The, 205
Black Lives Matter, 176
Black Nativity, 67
Black Religion and Black Radicalism, 171
Black religious experience: relevance of, 201
Black. *See* African American
Black Theology and Black Power, 202
Black Theology of Liberation, 202
Black Women's Christ, 205
Bolks, Seine, 25
Bonhoeffer, Dietrich, 66, 149

Boston Latin School, 12
Bowen, Murray, 41
Bradberry, Travis, 34
Brown, Brené, 32
Bundesrepublik Deutschlands (West Germany), 69
bus boycott of Montgomery, 169
Butler, Thornton: and application of North Carolina Classis, 191

Café of the Gates of Salvation Gospel Choir, 78
Caligula, Gaius: and same-sex relations, 55
Calvin, John, 9
Campbell, William, 186
Cannon, James, 185
Cannon, Katie Geneva, 197, 205
case study analysis, 208, 211
Center for Global Christianity, 133
Center for Global Studies, 6
Central College: origins of, 24–25
Central University of Iowa. *See* Central College
Chipenda, Jose, 140
Choralerna (Gospel choir), 68
Christian Churches Together, 134
Christian Day Schools, 29
Christian Action, Commission on, 2
Christian Unity, Commission on, 85, 86, 87
Christian Worship, Commission on, 86, 87, 90
Church Dogmatics, 151
Church Herald, 5
Classis of Holland, 23, 24
Classis of Wisconsin, 23
Clayborn Temple, Memphis, TN, 169
Cochran, John, 2
COCU. *See* Consultation on Church Union
"Coetus," 17
Coleman, Monica, 212
College of Physicians and Surgeons, NY, 17
colleges in the Reformed Church, 17–26
Collegiate School, NY, 12, 15

Columbia Academy, Bergen County, NJ, 15
Columbia College, NY, 17, 18
Common Lectionary, 85
Common Lectionary: The Lectionary Proposal by the Consultation on Common Texts, 85
Cone, James, 202
"Conferentie," 17
conflict: and Christian ministry, 138-40; and lessons from Esther, 139-40
Conklin, Nathaniel, 192
Consultation on Church Union, 86; Commission on Worship of, 84-85
Consultation on Common Texts, 85, 86
Copeland, Shawn, 205
Cordell Academy, Cordell, OK, 16
Corwin, Edward Tanjore, 29
Council of Constance (1414-18), 65
Creative Exchange, 164
Creative Kirche, 79
Crisis in Black and White, 160
Cuyler, John Cornelius, 20

Dailey, William N. P., 21
Daly, Mary, 203
Davis, Ellen, 107-8
Declaration of Independence and black people, 184
DeGroat, Chuck, 37
Demarest, David, 181
Demarest, William Henry Steele, 20
deomographics: change in Christian, 122
Deutsche Demokratische Republik, 69
Dexter Avenue Baptist Church, Montgomery, AL, 169
Dillard, Anne, 114
Dio Chrysostom and same-sex relations, 57-58
disruption, creative, 207, 210
Divided Mind of the Black Church, The, 171-72
Douglas, Kelly Brown, 205

Du Bois, W. E. B., 213
Duryea, Isaac: and abolition, 189-90
Dutch Reformed Church in Africa, 145

Early, Jay, 37
Ebenezer Baptist Church, Atlanta, GA, 169
Elert, W., 151
Elmer, Lucius Q. C., 183
emancipation: full, in New Jersey, 180; full, in New York, 180
Emancipation Proclamation, 187, 194
emotional health: example of for pastor, 44-45
emotional intelligence, 34; and relationship management, 43-45; and Scripture, 33-34; and self-awareness, 36-37; and self-management, 38-41; and social awareness, 41-43; and the Heidelberg Catechism, 33; as a tool for the pastor, 45; characteristics of, 32-33; development of, 45-51; families of, 34-35; importance of, in ministry, 35-45; ways to develop, 47-48
Emotional Intelligence 2.0, 34, 50
Emotional Intelligence Mastery, 50
Emotionally Healthy Spirituality Course, 50
empathy, in ministry, 42-43, 48
Encyclopedia Britannica, 213
English Language Liturgical Commission, 89
Erasmus Hall, Brooklyn, NY, 10, 14-15
Esther: conflict and lessons from, 139-40
Eucharistic developments, 89-90
Eucharistic Service of the Catholic Apostolic Church and Its Influence on Reformed Liturgical Renewals of the Nineteenth Century, The, 3
Explanatory Articles, and education, 13-14

Federation of Evangelical Religious Entities, Spain, 131
Ferris, Isaac, 22
Fifth Avenue Presbyterian Church, NY, 26
Fiorenza, Elisabeth Schüssler, 203
First Baptist Church, Montgomery, AL, 169
First Church, Albany, NY, 3, 15
First Congregational UCC, River Falls, WI, 75
First Dutch Reformed Church, Schenectady, NY, 20
First Reformed Church, Orange City, IA, 25
First Reformed Church, Pella, IA, 24
First Vatican Council (1870), 65
Fischer, Ulrich, 79
Fisk Jubilee Singers, 66–67
Fisk University, 66
Flatbush Reformed Dutch Church, Brooklyn, NY, 14
Frazier, E. Franklin, 159
Frelinghuysen, Frederick, 19, 22
Frelinghuysen, Theodore, 19; and the ACS, 183
Fresh Expressions (church renewal movement), 79–80
Friedman, Edwin, 41
fullness of life theme at WARC, 138

Gallatin, Albert, 21
Ganse, Hervey D., 191; opposition to slavery, 193–94
Garden Street church, 21
gender, 53
German Gospel choirs. *See under* Gospel choirs
Germany: confessing church in, 146
Gilkes, Cheryl Townsend, 205
Glaude, Eddie, 170–71
Global Christian Forum, 134, 135
Gogarten, Friedrich, 153
Golden Gate Quartet, 67
Goleman, Daniel, 32, 34, 35
Gospel choirs: and the embodiment of joy, 72–82; as spirit-filled community, 80–81; diversity of, 77–78; effect of, 71; German, Scandinavian origins of, 67–69; in contemporary Germany, 70–72: origins in Germany, 69; social body of, 78–81
Gospel music: spatial structure of, 74–76
Grant, Jacquelyn, 205
Greaves, Jean, 34

habit, 49
Hageman, Howard G., 2, 5
HaLevi, Yehuda, 117
Hamer, Fannie Lou, 169
Hamman, Jaco, 39, 48
Hanciles, Jehu, 131, 132
harmony, artificial, 43
Harvard University, Boston, MA, 18
Hastings-on-Hudson (Reformed church), NY, 23
Hawkins, Edwin, 69
Hayes, Diana, 205
Hayford, Jack, 39
hebel, 216–19, 222–26
Hebrew language: nature of, 215–16
Heidelberg Catechism, 48; and emotional intelligence, 33
Heim, Karl, 149
Hertzog, Ann, 19
Heschel, Abraham Joshua, 105, 120
Hidden Wholeness, A, 31
Hoezee, Scott, 33
Holland Academy, 16, 23
Holmes, Barbara, 205
Holt Street Baptist Church, Montgomery, AL, 169
homosexuality. *See* same-sex desire
Hope College, 10, 15; origin of, 23–24; *Remembrancer*, 27
hope: in the Reformed tradition, 223
Hospers, Henry J., 25
How, Samuel, 186; and reopening of slavery discussion, 192; and slavery, 190
Hughes, Langston, 67

injustice: economic, 140–42

In Search of Our Mothers' Gardens: Womanist Prose, 203
Inside Out, 34
"Internal Family Systems," 37, 50
International Committee on English in the Liturgy, 88
International Consultation on English Texts, 88

Jackson, Mahalia, 67
Jefferson, Thomas, 184
Jews: and Barth in Germany, 148–49
Job: examination of, 111–18
Johnson, E. Patrick, 78
Jordan, Clarence, 81
Jordan, Eric, 46
Joybells (Gospel choir), 68

Kefas Gospel Choir, 68
King Jr., Martin Luther, 69, 169, 171
Kirk-Duggan, Cheryl, 205
Koinonia Farms, 81

lectionary: changes and the, 84; purpose of, 86
Lencioni, Patrick, 42
Lilje, Hanns, 149
Lima Eucharistic Liturgy, The, 90
Linn, William, 21
Little Learning, A, 120
liturgical process for approval in the RCA, 90–91
liturgical revision principles, 91
liturgical texts and language, 88–89
liturgy: reform starts with, 65–66
Livingston, John Henry, 13, 15, 18, 186; and slaves, 180–81
Livingston, Philip, 181
Lord's Supper: sermon on, 98–103
Ludlow, John, 186
Lutheran World Federation, 135
Luther, Martin, 152

Mabon, William V. V., 21
Mann, Horace, 14
Martin, Joan, 205
Mason Temple COGIC, Memphis, TN, 169

Mast, Gregg A.: and "Questions of Faith," 5; and social witness and worship, 2–3; and South Africa, 3, 137, 145; as president of NBTS, 5, 145, 157, 179, 198, 215; as synod president, 4–5, 121; in pastoral ministry, 3–4; leadership style of, 31-32, 83, 144, 226; ministry of, 1–8, 93–94; on denominational staff, 5
Matthews, James R., 21, 22
Mennonite World Conference, 135
Mercersburg theology, 189
Messler, Abraham, 192
Methodist Church, Odense, Denmark, 80
Milledoler, Philip, 187
mindfulness, 49–50
ministry: conflict and Christian, 138–40
Mordecai, 139
Morse, Samuel F. B., 21
mother, good enough, 161
Murray, Andrew, 3
musical performance: spatial structure of, 72–73
Myers-Briggs scale, 46
Myrdal, Gunnar, 160

NAACP, 171
Nassau Presbyterian Church, Princeton, NJ, 6
NBTS and the ACS, 185–87
Negro: capitalization of, 213
Negro Church in America, The, 159
Neilson, James, 182
Nero and same-sex relations, 55
New Brunswick Colonization Society, 186
New Brunswick Theological Seminary, 18
New Jim Crow, The, 175
New York Times, The, 213
New York University, 10, 17, 18; origin of, 21–23
Niemöller, Martin, 149
North Carolina, Classis of: applicant to join RCA, 188–91

North Reformed Church, Newark, NJ, 2
Northwestern Classical Academy. See Northwestern College
Northwestern College: origin of, 16, 25-26
Nouwen, Henri, 36

Obama, Barak [Hussein], 170
Oggel, Pieter J., 24
Old Dutch Church, Kingston, NY, 94
Organization of African Instituted Churches, 121, 125, 130, 135
Oslo Gospel Choir, 68
Our Reformed Church, 5

Palmer, Parker J., 31
Paris, Peter, 163
Parker, James, 181
parochial schools and the RCA, 28-29
Pastor's Emergency League, 149
Paul Robeson Choir, 69
Pentecostalism: growth of, 124
Pentecostal World Conference, Kuala Lumpur, 126, 133
Pentecostal World Fellowship, 133, 135
Peter Hertzog Theological Hall, 19
Phelps Jr., Philip, 15, 20, 23, 192
Philip Milledoler, 186
Philo: and same-sex relations, 58
Pioneer School, 16, 23
Plan Calendar, RCA, 85
Plaskow, Judith, 203
Plato: and same-sex orientation, 55-57
Pleasant Prairie Academy, German Valley, IL, 10, 16
Pontifical Council for Promoting Christian Unity, 135
Pope, Alexander, 120
Pope John XIII, 65
postmodernism: nature of, 200; womanist, nature of, 200-201; womanist theology, genesis and growth of, 202-6

Prayers We Have in Common, 88
Praying Together, 89
Prince Guneratnum, 133
professor of theology, 5
Progressive Baptist Church Convention, 171
Protestant Church in Baden, 79
Psalm 73: examination of, 106-11
Pulpit and Table, 3

Queens College, 15, 17, 18-19. See also Rutgers College
Quinn, Robert, 36, 39, 40

Raboteau, Albert, 165
Race Matters, 177
racist: scientific, 184-85
reconstruction: redemptive, 208, 211
Redeemed Christian Church of God, Nigeria, 130
Reformed tradition and critical questions, 138
Rehaag, Angelika, 76
relationship management: components of, 43-44
Revised Common Lectionary, 86
Riggs, Marcia, 205
Risager, Thomas, 80, 81
Roelandsen, Adam, 12
Roman Catholic Church: and influence on mainline Protestant churches, 84-85
Romeyn, Dirck, 20
Ross, Rosetta, 205
ruach, 219-22, 222-26
Ruether, Rosemary, 203
Russell, Letty, 203
Rutger, Henry, 18
Rutgers College, 17; independence of, 19-20. See also Rutgers University
Rutgers Preparatory School, 15
Rutgers University, 6, 10

Sacrament of the Lord's Supper: A New Text—1984, The, 90
safe space: nature of, 210, 211
Sage Library, 6

Index   233

same-sex desire: and Sodom and Gomorrah in Philo, 58; origin of, 59; origin of, in Judaism, 57
same-sex marriages: and Paul, 55; and Nero, 55; and Philo, 58; and Plato, 55-57
Sanctus and Benedictus, 89
Satyavrata, Ivan, 126
Scazzero, Peter, 33, 50
Schenectady Academy, 20
Schieffelin Fund, 28-29
Schieffelin, Henry Hamilton, 26
Schieffelin, Jacob, 26
Schieffelin, Maria Theresa (Bradhurst), 26
Schieffelin, Samuel B., 26; and church-sponsored schools revival, 26-30
Scholte, Hendrik P., 16, 23
schoolmaster, 13; qualifications of, 11
Schwartz, Richard, 37
Second Reformed Church, Irvington, NJ, 3
Second Vatican Council (1962-65), 65, 87; and major changes in liturgy, 83-84
self-awareness: components of, 36; in ministry, 36-37. *See also* emotional intelligence
self-management: components of, 38
Sexuality: Reframing the Church's Debate on Same-Sex Relationships, 53
Shuttlesworth, Fred, 169
Silberman, Charles, 160
Sister Act, 76
slave markets in New Brunswick, 182
slavery: in the Bible, 193; Reformed Christian view of, 185; Reformed Church in America discussion about, 188-95
Smit, Dirkie, 154
social awareness: components of, 41
Society of Inquiry on Missions, 188
Sodom and Gomorrah in Philo, 58

Sojourner Truth, 203
Sommerlath, E., 151
Sound of Music, 113
South Reformed Church, NY, 21
spirit: as life force, 220; evil, 221-22
spirituals and jubilee, 67
Steinke, Peter, 41
Stimpson, Edward, 192
Stockholm Gospel Festival, 76
St. Thomas AME Church, Birmingham, AL, 169
suffering, 111-18
Sunday school movement, 29
Sursum Corda, 89
Swan Lake, 72
symposium and same-sex orientation, 55-57
Synod of Dort, 9
Synod of Dort: and education, 11-12

Taylor, Barbara Brown, 108
Tchaikovsky, Peter Ilyich, 72
Teach Us to Pray, 4
Thielicke, Helmut, 151
Thistlewaite, Susan, 203
Thomas, Linda, 205
Till, Emmett, 169
Townes, Emilie, 205
transgender person: story about a, 94-98
Trump, Donald J., 174

Ubuntu spirit: contribution to Christianity, 140
Underwood, Horace, 6
Union College, Schenectady, NY, 10, 15, 17, 18, 20
Union Theological Seminary, NY, 66
Urban League, 171
urban ministry: defined, 199; in twenty-first-century, 198-202

Van Bunschooten, Elias: and slaves, 181
Van Dyck, Lawrence H., 192
Van Liew, John C., 192
Van Raalte, Albertus C., 16, 23
Van Schaick, Myndert, 22

Van Vleck, John, 16, 24
Van Vranken, Samuel, 186
Voorhees, Elizabeth, 20
Voorhees, Ralph, 20
voorleser. *See* schoolmaster

Walker, Alice, 203–4
Walker, Wyatt Tee, 169
Walls, Andrew, 126
WARC. *See* World Alliance of Reformed Churches
Warnock, Raphael, 171
Warnshuis, A. Livingston, 20
Weems, Renita, 205
Welker, Michael, 101
Wells, Ransford, 191
West, Cornell, 177
Westend Gospel Singers, 75
Western Theological Seminary, Holland, MI, 24
White, George L., 67
White Women's Jesus, 205
Will (a slave), 181–82
Williams, Delores, 204
Wilmore, Gayraud, 171
Wimberly, Edward, 176
Winnicott, Donald, 158; and African American church, 161–64; and good enough holding, 162–63
Wisconsin Memorial Academy, Cedar Grove, WI, 16
wisdom: limits of human, 111–18; of Solomon, and perversion, 59
womanism: nature of, 206
womanist: celebration, 208, 211; Christology, 205; definition of, 203–4;
womanist reimagining: four steps of, 207–8; postmodern, 206–8; practical application of, 208–12

womanist theological project, 204
womanist theology: postmodern, genesis and growth of, 202–6
Woodbridge, Samuel Merrill, 22, 186
Woodson, Carter G., 157, 158
World Alliance of Reformed Churches, 121, 138, 142; and the plight of Africa, 141
World Christianity: and the economic landscape, 128–30; and the ecumenical landscape, 132–35; and the geographical landscape, 122–24; and the migratory landscape, 130–32; and theological education, 129; and the spiritual landscape, 124; and the theological landscape, 126–28
World Communion of Reformed Churches, 135
World Council of Churches, 126, 134, 135
World Evangelical Alliance, 135
worship. *See* Christian Worship, Commission on
worship space: spatial structure of, 73–74
Worship the Lord: The Liturgy of the Reformed Church in America, 91
Wright, N. T.: and same-sex relations, 54, 60–61

Yale University, New Haven, CT, 18
Young, Andrew, 169

Zwemer, James F., 26

Publications in the Historical Series of the Reformed Church in America

The following Historical Series publications may be ordered easily through the Wm. B. Eerdmans web site at www.eerdmans.com/

The home page has a section titled "Categories" at the upper left, under which find "series" and click it. "Sets and Series" will appear. Alphabetically, well down the page under G, click on The Historical Series of the Reformed Church in America. Titles will appear with the option of adding to cart. Books may also be ordered by hard copy or at your local bookstore.

You may also enter the following URL into your browser: http://www.eerdmans.com/Products/CategoryCenter.aspx?CategoryId=SE!HSRCA

1. *Ecumenism in the Reformed Church in America*, by Herman Harmelink III (1968)
2. *The Americanization of a Congregation*, by Elton J. Bruins (1970)
3. *Pioneers in the Arab World*, by Dorothy F. Van Ess (1974)
4. *Piety and Patriotism*, edited by James W. Van Hoeven (1976)
5. *The Dutch Reformed Church in the American Colonies*, by Gerald F. De Jong (1978)
6. *Historical Directory of the Reformed Church in America, 1628-1978*, by Peter N. VandenBerge (1978)
7. *Digest and Index of the Minutes of General Synod, 1958-1977*, by Mildred W. Schuppert (1979)
8. *Digest and Index of the Minutes of General Synod, 1906-1957*, by Mildred W. Schuppert (1982)
9. *From Strength to Strength*, by Gerald F. De Jong (1982)
10. *"B. D."*, by D. Ivan Dykstra (1982)
11. *Sharifa*, by Cornelia Dalenburg (1983)
12. *Vision From the Hill*, edited by John W. Beardslee III (1984)
13. *Two Centuries Plus*, by Howard G. Hageman (1984)
14. *Structures for Mission*, by Marvin D. Hoff (1985)

15. *The Church Speaks*, edited by James I. Cook (1985)
16. *Word and World*, edited by James W. Van Hoeven (1986)
17. *Sources of Secession: The Netherlands Hervormde Kerk on the Eve of the Dutch Immigration to the Midwest*, by Gerrit J. tenZythoff (1987)
18. *Vision for a Christian College*, by Gordon J. Van Wylen (1988)
19. *Servant Gladly*, edited by Jack D. Klunder and Russell L. Gasero (1989)
20. *Grace in the Gulf*, by Jeanette Boersma (1991)
21. *Ecumenical Testimony*, by Arie R. Brouwer (1991)
22. *The Reformed Church in China, 1842-1951*, by Gerald F. De Jong (1992)
23. *Historical Directory of the Reformed Church in America, 1628-1992*, by Russell L. Gasero (1992)
24. *Meeting Each Other in Doctrine, Liturgy, and Government*, by Daniel J. Meeter (1993)
25. *Gathered at Albany*, by Allan J. Janssen (1995)
26. *The Americanization of a Congregation*, 2nd ed., by Elton J. Bruins (1995)
27. *In Remembrance and Hope: The Ministry and Vision of Howard G. Hageman*, by Gregg A. Mast (1998)
28. *Deacons' Accounts, 1652-1674, First Dutch Reformed Church of Beverwyck/Albany*, trans. & edited by Janny Venema (1998)
29. *The Call of Africa*, by Morrill F. Swart (1998)
30. *The Arabian Mission's Story: In Search of Abraham's Other Son*, by Lewis R. Scudder III (1998)
31. *Patterns and Portraits: Women in the History of the Reformed Church in America*, edited by Renée S. House and John W. Coakley (1999)
32. *Family Quarrels in the Dutch Reformed Churches in the Nineteenth Century*, by Elton J. Bruins & Robert P. Swierenga (1999)
33. *Constitutional Theology: Notes on the* Book of Church Order *of the Reformed Church In America*, by Allan J. Janssen (2000)
34. *Raising the Dead: Sermons of Howard G. Hageman*, edited by Gregg A. Mast (2000)
35. *Equipping the Saints: The Synod of New York, 1800-2000*, edited by James Hart Brumm (2000)
36. *Forerunner of the Great Awakening*, edited by Joel R. Beeke (2000)
37. *Historical Directory of the Reformed Church in America, 1628-2000*, by Russell L. Gasero (2001)
38. *From Mission to Church: The Reformed Church in America in India*, by Eugene Heideman (2001)
39. *Our School: Calvin College and the Christian Reformed Church*, by Harry Boonstra (2001)

40. *The Church Speaks, 2*, edited by James I. Cook (2002)
41. *Concord Makes Strength*, edited by John W. Coakley (2002)
42. *Dutch Chicago: A History of the Hollanders in the Windy City*, by Robert P. Swierenga (2002)
43. *Doctors for the Kingdom*, Paul Armerding (2003)
44. *By Grace Alone*, Donald J. Bruggink (2004)
45. *Travels of an American Girl*, June Potter Durkee (2004)
46. *Letters to Hazel*, Mary Kansfield (2004)
47. *Iowa Letters*, Robert P. Swierenga (2004)
48. *Can Hope Endure, A Historical Case Study in Christian Higher Education*, James C. Kennedy and Caroline J. Simon (2005)
49. *Elim*, Robert P. Swierenga (2005)
50. *Taking the Jesus Road*, LeRoy Koopman (2005)
51. *The Netherlands Reformed Church, 1571-2005*, Karel Blei (2005)
52. *Son of Secession: Douwe J. Vander Werp*, Janet Sjaarda Sheeres (2006)
53. *Kingdom, Office, and Church: A Study of A. A. van Ruler's Doctrine of Ecclesiastical Office*, Allan J. Janssen (2006)
54. *Divided by a Common Heritage: The Christian Reformed Church and the Reformed Church in America at the Beginning of the New Millenium*, Corwin Smidt, Donald Luidens, James Penning, and Roger Nemeth (2006)
55. *Henry J. Kuiper: Shaping the Christian Reformed Church, 1907-1962*, James A. De Jong (2007)
56. *A Goodly Heritage, Essays in Honor of the Reverend Dr. Elton J. Bruins at Eighty*, Jacob E. Nyenhuis (2007)
57. *Liturgy among the Thorns: Essays on Worship in the Reformed Church in America*, James Hart Brumm (2007)
58. *Old Wing Mission*, Robert P. Swierenga (2008)
59. *Herman J. Ridder: Contextual Preacher and President*, edited by George Brown, Jr. (2009)

60. *Tools for Understanding*, edited by James Hart Brumm (2009) 404 pp. ISBN: 978-0-8028-6483-3

"Beginning with Donald Bruggink's own notion that 'history is a tool for understanding,' the dozen essays in this volume are tools for understanding four areas of his life and his fifty-five years of ministry. While all the contributors to this volume have benefited from Bruggink's friendship, teaching, and ministry, the first and last essays are by the contributors he has known longest, who had a formative role in his life"

— Eugene Heideman and I. John Hesselink.

61. *Chinese Theological Education*, edited by Marvin D. Hoff (2009) 470 pp. ISBN: 978-0-8028-6480-2

This book offers insight into the emergence of the Christian church after Mao's Cultural Revolution. While reports of Communist oppression have dominated American perceptions of church and state in China, this is an increasingly dangerous view as China changes. Dr. Marvin D. Hoff, as executive director for the Foundation for Theological Education in Southeast Asia, traveled at least annually to China for the period covered by this book. The original reports of his encounters with Chinese Christians, especially those involved in theological education, are a historic record of the church's growth—and growing freedom. Interspersed with Hoff's accounts are reports of essays by Chinese and other Asian Christians. Introductory essays are provided by Charles W. Forman of Yale Divinity School, Daniel B. Hays of Calvin College, and Donald J. Bruggink of Western Theological Seminary.

62. *Liber A*, edited by Frank Sypher (2009) 442 pp. ISBN: 978-0-8028-6509-0

Liber A of the Collegiate Church archives contains detailed seventeenth-century records of the Reformed Dutch Church of the City of New York, including correspondence, texts of legal documents, and lists of names of consistory members. Especially significant are records pertaining to the granting in 1696 of the royal charter of incorporation of the Church, and records relating to donations for, and construction of the church building on Garden Street. The full Dutch texts have never before been published.

63. *Aunt Tena, Called to Serve: Journals and Letters of Tena A. Huizenga, Missionary Nurse to Nigeria*, edited by Jacob A. Nyenhuis, Robert P. Swierenga, and Lauren M. Berka (2009) 980 pp. ISBN: 978-0-8028-6515-1

When Tena Huizenga felt the call to serve as a missionary nurse to Africa, she followed that call and served seventeen years at Lupwe, Nigeria, during a pivotal era in world missions. As she ministered to the natives, she recorded her thoughts and feelings in a diary and in countless letters to family and friends--over 350 in her first year alone. Through her eyes, we see the Lupwe mission, Tena's colleagues, and the many native helpers. Aunt Tena (Nigerians called all female missionaries

"Aunt") tells this profoundly human story. Interesting in its own right, the book will also prove invaluable to historians, sociologists, and genealogists as they mine this rich resource.

The extensive letters from Tena's brother Pete offer marvelous insights into the Dutch Reformed subculture of Chicago's West Side. Because his scavenger company later evolved into Waste Management Inc., those letters are especially valuable. Pete's winsome descriptions and witty dialogue with his sister add a Chicago flavor to this book.

64. *The Practice of Piety: The Theology of the Midwestern Reformed Church in America, 1866-1966*, by Eugene P. Heideman (2009) 286 pp. ISBN: 978-0-8028-6551-9

"With the instincts of a historian and the affection of a child of the RCA, Gene Heideman has accessed both Dutch and English sources in order to introduce us to the unique theology and piety of the Midwestern section of our denomination from 1866 to 1966. Through the words of pastors, professors, and parishioners, he has fleshed out the Dutch pilgrims of the 19th century who found their roots in the Netherlands but their fruit in America. Accessing the Dutch language newspaper *De Hope*, and the writings and lectures of a century of Western Seminary professors, the history of the RCA in the Midwest has come alive. This book is a gracious and winsome invitation to its readers and other scholars to dig deeper and understand more fully the theological and ethnic heritage of those who have helped ground our past and thus form our future."

— Gregg A. Mast, president, New Brunswick Theological Seminary

65. *Freedom on the Horizon: Dutch Immigration to America, 1840 to 1940*, by Hans Krabbendam (2009) 432 pp. ISBN: 978-0-8028-6545-8

"It's been eighty years since the last comprehensive study of the Dutch immigrant experience by a Netherlands scholar—Jacob Van Hinte's magisterial *Netherlanders in America* (1928, English translation 1985). It was worth the wait! Krabbendam has a firmer grasp of American history and culture than his predecessor, who spent only seven weeks on a whirlwind tour of a half-dozen Dutch 'colonies' in 1921. Krabbendam earned an M.A. degree in the USA, is widely traveled, versed in American religious culture, and has written the definitive biography of Edward W. Box (2001). *Freedom on the Horizon* focuses on the ultimate meaning of immigration—the process by which one's inherited culture is reshaped into a new Dutch-American identity. 'Only the steeple was retained,'

Krabbendam notes in his tale of a congregation that tore down its historic church edifice in favor of a modern new one. This is a metaphor of the Dutch immigrant experience writ large, as told here in a masterful way."

— Robert D. Swierenga, Kent State University

66. *A Collegial Bishop? Classis and Presbytery at Issue*, edited by Allan Janssen and Leon Vanden Broek (2010) 176 pp. ISBN: 978-0-8028-6585-4

In *A Collegial Bishop?* classis and presbytery are considered from a cross-cultural, indeed cross-national, perspective of the inheritors of Geneva and Edinburgh in their contemporary contexts in the Netherlands, South Africa, and the United States.

"Dutch theologian A. A. van Ruler compares church order to the rafters of a church building. Church order sustains the space within which the church is met by God, where it engages in its plan with God (liturgy), and where it is used by God in its mission in and to God's world. Presbyterian church order intends to be faithful to its root in God's Word, as it is shaped around the office of elder and governed through a series of councils of the church."

Alan Janssen
— Pastor, Community Church of Glen Rock, NJ

67. *The Church Under the Cross*, by Wendell Karssen (2010) 454 pp. ISBN: 978-0-8028-6614-1

The Church Under the Cross: Mission in Asia in Times of Turmoil is the illustrated two-volume account of Wendell Paul Karsen's more than three decades of cross-cultural missionary work in East Asia.

In one sense a missionary memoir of Karsen's life and ministry in Taiwan, Hong Kong, China, and Indonesia, the work also chronicles the inspiring story of the Christian communities Karsen served—churches which struggled to grow and witness under adverse circumstances throughout years of political turbulence and social upheaval.

68. *Supporting Asian Christianity's Transition from Mission to Church: A History of the Foundation for Theological Education in Southeast Asia*, edited by Samuel C. Pearson (2010) 464 pp. ISBN: 978-0-8028-6622-6

"This volume, telling the story of how one North American ecumenical foundation learned to move from a 'missions' stance to one of 'partnership,' is at once informative, intriguing, and instructive for anyone curious about or interested in the development of contextual theological education and scholarship in China and Southeast Asia. It traces the efforts of Protestant churches and educational institutions emerging from World War II, revolution, and colonization to train an indigenous leadership and to nurture theological scholars for the political, cultural, and religious realities in which these ecclesial bodies find themselves."

— Greer Anne Wenh-In Ng, Professor Emerita, Victoria University in the University of Toronto

69. *The American Diary of Jacob Van Hinte*, edited by Peter Ester, Nella Kennedy, Earl Wm. Kennedy (2010) 210 pp. ISBN: 978-0-8028-6661-5

"This is a charming translation, scrupulously annotated, of the long-lost travel diary of Jacob Van Hinte (1889-1948), author of the monumental Netherlanders in America. Van Hinte's energetic five-week sprint in the summer of 1921 from "Dutch" Hoboken up the river by dayliner to Albany and on to the Dutch-settled towns and cities in the Midwest convinced him that the "migration to America had been a blessing" to the Dutch. But in his brief sojourn among the descendants of the immigrant generation, he also became aware of the "tales of misery" and the "noble struggles" of the settlers that will put readers of all ethnic backgrounds to wondering about their own poignant histories."

— Firth Fabend, author of Zion on the Hudson: Dutch new York and the New Jersey in the Age of Revivals

70. *A New Way of Belonging: Covenant Theology, China and the Christian Reformed Church, 1921-1951*, by Kurt Selles (2011) 288 pp. ISBN: 978-0-8028-6662-2

"As someone who spent much of my childhood on the mission field described in this book, I anticipated having my early memories refreshed by reading it. I did indeed find the book to be an accurate and thorough account of the work of the CRC China Mission as I remember it, but—more surprising—I also learned a good deal of new information. Kurt Selles has performed an important service for the history of missions by uncovering so much new information and doing such impressive research under difficult circumstances. Although the events took place more than a half-century ago, Selles has been able to retrieve a vast amount of detail. His analysis of the cross-cultural dynamics of this work is insightful. Anyone interested in the successes and failures of Christian mission should find this study interesting and informative."

— J. William Smit, professor of sociology, Calvin College, child of CRC China missionary Albert Smit

71. *Envisioning Hope College: Letters Written by Albertus C. Van Raalte to Philip Phelps, Jr., 1857-1875,* edited by Elton J. Bruins and Karen G. Schakel (2011) 556 pp. ISBN: 978-0-8028-6688-2

These letters between the colony's leader and the first president of Hope College in Holland, Michigan, are sequentially placed in historical context and richly footnoted. They offer an intimate view of Van Raalte as he seeks funding for his college from the Dutch Reformed Church in the east, as well as insights into his pioneer community in the midst of conflagration and war.

72. *Ministry Among the Maya,* by Dorothy Dickens Meyerink (Dec. 2011) 434 pp. ISBN: 978-0-8028-6744-5

Dorothy Meyerink entered her ministry among the Maya of Chiapas, Mexico, in 1956, and spent her entire service there. *Ministry Among the Maya* is an exciting account of persecution and success, relating the story of how, through the faithful witness of the laity and the early ordination of Mayan ministers, a strong, large, indigenous church was established and continues to flourish. Meyerink interweaves her personal experiences and the history of the church with reflections on the effective application of church growth principles.

73. *The Church Under the Cross, Vol. 2,* by Wendell Karsen (Dec. 2011) 802 pp. ISBN: 978-0-8028-6760-5

See volume 67.

74. *Sing to the Lord a New Song: Choirs in the Worship and Culture of the Dutch Reformed Church in America, 1785-1860,* by David M. Tripold (2012) 304 pp. ISBN: 978-0-8028-6874-9

As their privileged status evaporated in America's melting pot, the Dutch Reformed Church was forced to compete with a host of rising Protestant denominations in the New World. Survival became linked to assimilating within a new American way of life, with its own distinct language, culture, and religious practices. Gradually, organs, hymns and institutional church choirs were added to the traditional singing of the Psalter—innovations that altered the very fabric of Dutch Reformed religious life in America.

Sing to the Lord a New Song examines how choirs in particular revolutionized the Dutch Reformed Church in the nineteenth century, transforming the church's very nature in terms of worship, ecclesiastical life, institutional structures, and even social, fiscal, and moral practices. Moreover, the book examines how choirs helped break social barriers, particularly those regarding the status and role of women in the church.

Includes audio CD.

75. *Pioneers to Partners, The Reformed Church in America and Christian Mission to the Japanese,* by Gordon Laman (2012) ISBN: 978-0-8028-6965-4

Beginning with Japan's early exposure to Christianity by the very successful Roman Catholic mission to Japan in the sixteenth and seventeenth centuries, and the resultant persecution and prohibition of Christianity, Laman lays the groundwork for understanding the experience of nineteenth-century Protestant missionaries, among whom those of the Reformed Church in America were in the forefront. The early efforts of the Browns, Verbecks, Ballaghs, and Stouts, their failures and successes, are recounted within the cultural and political context of the anti-Western, anti-Christian Japan of the time.

Verbeck's service to the government helped bring about gradual change. The first Protestant church was organized with a vision for ecumenical mission, and during several promising years, churches and mission schools were organized. Reformed Church missionaries encouraged and trained Japanese leaders from the beginning, the first Japanese ministers were ordained in 1877, and the Japanese church soon exhibited a spirit of independence, ushering in an era of growing missionary/Japanese partnership.

The rise of the Japanese empire, a reinvigorated nationalism, and its progression to militarist ultranationalism brought on a renewed anti-Western, anti-Christian reaction and new challenges to both mission and church. With the outbreak of World War II, the Japanese government consolidated all Protestant churches into the Kyodan to facilitate control.

Laman continues the account of Reformed Church partners in mission in Japan in the midst of post-war devastation and subsequent social and political tensions. The ecumenical involvement and continued clarification of mutual mission finds the Reformed Church a full participant with a mature Japanese church.

76. *Transatlantic Pieties*, ed by Hans Krabbendam, Leon van den Broeke, and Dirk Mouw (2012) 359 pp. ISBN: 978-0-8028-6972-2

Transatlantic Pieties: Dutch Clergy in Colonial America explores the ways in which the lives and careers of fourteen Dutch Reformed ministers illuminate important aspects of European and American colonial society of their times. Based on primary sources, this collection reexamines some of the movers and shakers over the course of 250 years. The essays shed light on the high and low tides, the promises and disappointments, and the factors within and beyond the control of a new society in the making. The portraits humanize and contextualize the lives of these men who served not only as religious leaders and cultural mediators in colonial communities, but also as important connective tissue in the Dutch Atlantic world.

77. *Loyalty and Loss, the Reformed Church in America, 1945-1994*, by Lynn Japinga (2013) ISBN: 978-0-8028-7068-1

Offering a meticulously researched yet also deeply personal history of the Reformed Church in America throughout much of the twentieth century, Lynn Japinga's *Loyalty and Loss* will be of intense interest to the members of the RCA, reminding them of where they have come from, of the bonds that have held them together, and of the many conflicts and challenges that they have together faced and ultimately surmounted.

For those outside the RCA the questions of identity raised by this book will often sound very familiar, especially, perhaps, in its account of the church's struggle throughout recent decades to reconcile the persistently ecumenical spirit of many of its members with the desire of others within the denomination to preserve a real or imagined conservative exclusivity. Others may find the conflicts within the RCA reflective of their own experiences, especially as they relate to such issues as denominational mergers, abortion, the Viet Nam war, and women's ordination.

78. *Oepke Noordmans: Theologian of the Holy Spirit*, Karel Blei (tran. By Allan Janssen) (2013) ISBN: 978-0-8028-7085-8

Oepke Noordmans was one of the major Dutch theologians of

the twentieth century, whose recovery of a vital doctrine of the Holy Spirit placed him at the center of thought on the nature of the church and its ministry.

In this volume Karel Blei, himself a theological voice of note, has provided a lucid introduction to and summary of Noordmans's thought and contextual impact. The book also includes substantial excerpts of Noordmans's writing in translation, offering a compact representation of his work to an English-speaking audience.

79. *The Not-So-Promised Land, The Dutch in Amelia County, Virginia, 1868-1880*, by Janet Sjaarda Sheeres (2013) 248 pp. ISBN: 978-0-8028-7156-5

The sad story of a little-known, short-lived Dutch immigrant settlement.

After establishing a successful Dutch colony in Holland, Michigan, in 1847, Albertus Van Raalte turned his attention to the warmer climes of Amelia County, Virginia, where he attempted to establish a second colony. This volume by Janet Sheeres presents a carefully researched account of that colonization attempt with a thorough analysis of why it failed. Providing insights into the risks of new settlements that books on successful colonies overlook, this is the first major study of the Amelia settlement.

A well-told tale of high hopes but eventual failure, *The Not-So-Promised Land* concludes with a 73-page genealogy of everyone involved in the settlement, including their origins, marriages, births, deaths, denominations, occupations, and post-Amelia destinations.

80. *Holland Michigan, From Dutch Colony to Dynamic City* (3 volumes), by Robert P. Swierenga (2013) ISBN: 978-0-8028-7137-4

Holland Michigan: From Dutch Colony to Dynamic City is a fresh and comprehensive history of the city of Holland from its beginnings to the increasingly diverse community it is today.

The three volumes that comprise this monumental work discuss such topics as the coming of the Dutch, the Americans who chose to live among them, schools, grassroots politics, the effects of the world wars and the Great Depression, city institutions, downtown renewal, and social and cultural life in Holland. Robert Swierenga also draws attention to founder Albertus Van Raalte's particular role in forming the city—everything from planning streets to establishing churches and schools, nurturing industry, and encouraging entrepreneurs.

Lavishly illustrated with nine hundred photographs and based on meticulous research, this book offers the most detailed history of Holland, Michigan, in print.

The volume received the Historical Society of Michigan 2014 State History Award in the Books, University and Commercial Press category

81. *The Enduring Legacy of Albertus C. Van Raalte as Leader and Liaison*, edited by Jacob E. Nyenhuis and George Harinck (2013) 560 pp. ISBN: 978-0-8028-7215-9

The celebration of the bicentennial of the birth of Albertus C. Van Raalte in October 2011 provided a distinct opportunity to evaluate the enduring legacy of one of the best-known Dutch immigrants of the nineteenth century. This book of essays demonstrates his unique role not only in the narrative of the migration to America but also in the foundation of theological education for Seceders (Afgescheidenen) prior to his emigration. These essays were all presented at an international conference held in Holland, Michigan, and Ommen, Overijssel, the Netherlands, with the conference theme of "Albertus C. Van Raalte: Leader and Liaison." Three broad categories serve as the organizing principle for this book: biographical essays, thematic essays, and reception studies.

Van Raalte began to emerge as a leader within the Seceder Church (Christelijk Afgescheidene Gereformeerde Kerk) in the Netherlands, but his leadership abilities were both tested and strengthened through leading a group of Dutch citizens to the United States in 1846. In his role as leader, moreover, he served as liaison to the Reformed Protestant Dutch Church in America in the eastern United States (renamed the Reformed Church in America in 1867) to the Seceder Church in the Netherlands, and to the civil authorities in the United States, as well as between business and their employees.

These fifteen essays illuminate the many facets of this energetic, multi-talented founder of the Holland kolonie. This collection further enhances and strengthens our knowledge of both Van Raalte and his Separatist compatriots.

82. *Minutes of the Christian Reformed Church, Classical Assembly, 1857-1870, General Assembly, 1867-79, and Synodical Assembly, 1880*, edited and annotated by Janet Sjaarda Sheeres (2014) 668 pp. ISBN: 978-0-8028-7253-1

"Janet Sheeres, noted scholar of the Dutch in North America, here turns her skill to the early years of the Christian Reformed Church in North America. She has painstakingly researched all the individuals who attended denominational leadership gatherings and the issues discussed and debated at these meetings. Her extensive annotations to a new translation of the minutes provides unprecedented and cogent insight into the early years of the denomination and the larger Dutch trans-Appalachian immigration of the nineteenth century. The annotations reflect Sheeres's characteristically detailed research in both Dutch and English. Scholars of immigration, religion, Dutch-American immigrants, and the Christian Reformed Church will benefit from data in this book, and the appendix of biographical data will be invaluable to those interested in family research."

— Richard Harms, archivist of the Christian Reformed Church

83 *New Brunswick Theological Seminary: an Illustrated History, 1784-2014.* John W. Coakley (2014) ISBN: 978-0-8028-7296-8

This volume marks the 230th anniversary of New Brunswick Theological Seminary and the reconfiguring of its campus by retelling the school's history in text and pictures. John Coakley, teacher of church history at the seminary for thirty years, examines how the mission of the school has evolved over the course of the seminary's history, focusing on its changing relationship to the community of faith it has served in preparing men and women for ministry.

In four chapters representing four significant eras in the seminary's history, Coakley traces the relationship between the seminary in New Brunswick and the Reformed Church in America, showing that both the seminary and the RCA have changed dramatically over the years but have never lost each other along the way.

84. *Hendrik P. Scholte: His Legacy in the Netherlands and in America.* Eugene P. Heideman (2015) 314 pp. ISBN: 978-0-8028-7352-1

This book offers a careful contextual theological analysis of a nineteenth-century schismatic with twenty-first-century ecumenical intent.

Hendrik P. Scholte (1803-1868) was the intellectual leader and catalyst of a separation from the Nederlandse Hervormde Kerk. Leaving the state church meant being separated from its deacon's funds, conflict with the laws of the state, and social ostracism. Due to poverty, Scholte emigrated with a group that settled Pella, Iowa. Schismatic tendencies continued in this and other nineteenth-century Dutch settlements with the most notable division being between those who joined the

Reformed Church in America and those who became the Christian Reformed Church in North America.

As Heideman says: "Although this book concentrates on what happened in the past, it is written with the hope that knowledge of the past will contribute to the faithfulness and unity of the church in the future."

85. *Liber A:1628-1700 of the Collegiate Churches of New York, Part 2*, translated, annotated, and edited by Frank J. Sypher, Jr. (2015) 911 pp. ISBN: 978-0-8028-7341-5

See volume 62.

86. *KEMP: The Story of John R. and Mabel Kempers, Founders of the Reformed Church in America Mission in Chiapas, Mexico*, by Pablo A. Deiros. 558 pp. ISBN 978-0-8028-7354-5

"This faithful story reveals God's power to transform thousands of people's lives through a couple committed to spreading God's message of love and devotion. The Kempers' commitment to their slogan "Chiapas para Cristo" was evidenced in all that they did. They were our surrogate parents, mission colleagues, and mentors."
— Sam and Helen Hofman, career RCA missionaries in Chiapas, Mexico.

"Employing a creative narrative style, Pablo Deiros has fashioned a fully documented biography into a compelling story of the lives and witness of John and Mabel Kempers. *Kemp* is a must read for those who are interested in the intersection of the Christian Church and the social revolution in Mexico during the twentieth century, the struggles of Maya cultures in Chiapas, and the transformative impact of the gospel of Jesus Christ among the people of Chiapas. *Kemp* is an inspiring and engaging history."
— Dennis N. Voskuil, Director, Van Raalte Institute

87. *Yes! Well...Exploring the Past, Present, and Future of the Church: Essays in Honor of John W. Coakley*, edited by James Hart Brumm. 324pp. ISBN: 978-0-8028-7479-5

In this volume, authors from around the world present essays in honor of John W. Coakley, L. Russell Feakes Memorial Professor

Emeritus of Church History at New Brunswick Theological Seminary in New Jersey. Following the pattern of Coakley's teaching, the contributors push readers to think about aspects of the church in new ways.

Contributors include: Thomas A. Boogart, James Hart Brumm, Kathleen Hart Brumm, Jaeseung Cha, James F. Coakley, Sarah Coakley. Matthew Gasero, Russell Gasero, Allan Janssen, Lynn Japinga, Mary L. Kansfield, Norman J. Kansfield, James Jinhong Kim, Gregg A. Mast, Dirk Mouw, Ondrea Murphy, Mark V. C. Taylor, and David W. Waanders

88. *Elephant Baseball: A Missionary Kids Tale*, by Paul Heusinkveld. 282 pp. ISBN: 978-0-8028-7550-1

This fascinating book recounts the up-and-down experiences of a missionary kid growing up overseas away from home in the 1960s. A sensitive autobiographical exploration of the universal trials of adolescence, Paul Heusinkveld's *Elephant Baseball* luxuriates in narrative fluidity—truly a riveting read.

89. *Growing Pains: How Racial Struggles Changed a Church and a School*, by Christopher H. Meehan. 206 pp.